Teach Yourself
▶GW-BASIC®◀

Teach Yourself
▶GW-BASIC®◀

Bob Albrecht

Osborne McGraw-Hill
Berkeley New York St. Louis San Francisco
Auckland Bogotá Hamburg London Madrid
Mexico City Milan Montreal New Delhi Panama City
Paris São Paulo Singapore Sydney
Tokyo Toronto

Osborne **McGraw-Hill**
2600 Tenth Street
Berkeley, California 94710
U.S.A.

Osborne **McGraw-Hill** offers software for sale. For information on software, translations, or book distributors outside of the U.S.A., please write to Osborne **McGraw-Hill** at the above address.

This book is printed on recycled paper.

Teach Yourself GW-BASIC®

234567890 DOC 99876543210

ISBN 0-07-881678-5

▶Contents◀
At a Glance

►Contents◄

2 Do It Now: Direct Statements

37

3 GW-BASIC Programs

77

►Introduction◄

On May 1, 1964, at 4:00 A.M., Professor John Kemeny and one of his students simultaneously entered and ran separate BASIC programs on the Dartmouth College Time-Sharing System. Thus was born BASIC, the first computer language designed to be learned and used by just about anyone. On that day, BASIC's creators, John G. Kemeny and Thomas E. Kurtz, realized their dream of providing easy computer access for all Dartmouth students and faculty. BASIC was destined to become the "People's Computer Language," used by more people than any other programming language.

If you have a computer, you probably have BASIC. BASIC is bundled with or built into tens of millions of personal computers. Most versions of BASIC in use today are some form of Microsoft BASIC.

This is a beginner's book about the most widely used version of BASIC, Microsoft's GW-BASIC. GW-BASIC is virtually identical to BASICA, the version distributed by IBM. GW-BASIC will run on any IBM-compatible computer.

The most personal way to use a computer is to learn a general-purpose programming language, apply it to interesting problems, and produce useful solutions—**your** solutions. With a little help from this book, you can learn how to read and understand programs written in BASIC, and you can learn to express yourself in BASIC. You will be able to write your own BASIC programs to tell the computer what to do and how to do it—programs that produce results.

If you are a beginner, learning GW-BASIC (or BASICA) is a great way to start programming. With this book, you will learn how to write programs in good style that people can read and understand. You will be able to use GW-BASIC to write the best software for you.

I learned about BASIC soon after its creation, and immediately switched from FORTRAN to BASIC as the best language for teaching children how to program. I printed cards and buttons with the message SHAFT (Society to Help Abolish FORTRAN Teaching) and traveled around the country, spreading the word about BASIC to teachers and students in elementary and secondary schools.

I have been using BASIC since 1964, the year BASIC was created by Kemeny and Kurtz at Dartmouth College. BASIC gave me a quick way to explore or solve a problem. As I became older, BASIC became better, and BASIC continues to improve as it evolves to meet the needs of its users. I currently edit a magazine called *The BASIC Teacher,* for any of you who might enjoy reading further about personal programming. I hope you find the camaraderie and satisfaction that I enjoy in personal programming, personal problem-solving, and personal BASIC.

If you enjoy programming, consider moving up to the greatest BASIC ever, Microsoft's QuickBASIC. QuickBASIC is fine for beginners or for those who know a little GW-BASIC; QuickBASIC is excellent for people who want to write professional-level software. You can transfer everything you learn in this book to your use of QuickBASIC. In fact, the programming style used in this book is designed to help you move easily to QuickBASIC and versions of BASIC yet to come.

HOW THIS BOOK IS ORGANIZED

Teach Yourself GW-BASIC is for people who have no previous programming experience. The tutorials in this book are designed to teach you GW-BASIC while you solve problems and perform tasks such as number crunching, text manipulation, and graphics and sound creation.

This book has nine chapters and four appendixes. Each chapter (except Chapter 1) begins with a Skills Check, so you can review what you learned in the previous chapter. The chapters are divided into sections that include interesting examples and exercises. There is a Mastery Skills Check at the end of each chapter that allows you to evaluate whether you are ready to move on to more difficult material or need additional practice and review.

This book contains 265 exercises, with answers to 258. To optimize your learning experience, do the exercises, then compare your answers to those listed in Appendix D. Remember, your answers might be different from the ones shown, yet still be correct.

Appendix A samples elements of GW-BASIC not covered in the chapters and suggests ways for you to continue learning about GW-BASIC.

Appendix B is a list of GW-BASIC's *keywords* (vocabulary). Appendix C contains ASCII codes and characters. Appendix D provides answers to 258 exercises.

One more thing. As you use this book and your computer, remember:

YOU CAN DO NOTHING WRONG!

You can't harm the computer by typing stuff into it. You may make mistakes, but that is a natural part of exploring and learning. Risk it! Try it and find out what happens. You can learn more from your own patient exploration than from this or any book.

CONVENTIONS USED IN THIS BOOK

To make this book easier to use, the following conventions have been followed:

- Information for you to type appears in **boldface** text.

- Keys for you to press are shown in keycaps, as in (ENTER). If you should press two keys at the same time, the keycaps will be joined with a hyphen, as in (ALT)-(C).

- GW-BASIC keywords are shown in capital letters.

- Comments to help you understand an instruction or program line appear in *italic* type and are enclosed in parentheses.

LEARN MORE ABOUT GW-BASIC

GW-BASIC is a rich and powerful computer language. This book helps you get started learning how to read, understand, and express yourself in GW-BASIC. Here are two other Osborne/McGraw-Hill books that will help you build your skills and learn more about GW-BASIC:

The GW-BASIC Reference, by Don Inman and Bob Albrecht, is a comprehensive reference guide covering all elements of the language. It is an excellent companion book to *Teach Yourself GW-BASIC.*

GW-BASIC Made Easy, by Bob Albrecht and Don Inman, is an introduction to GW-BASIC for people with no previous programming experience. It is faster-paced than *Teach Yourself GW-BASIC* and covers more of the language, including sequential and random-access files, as well as a different approach to graphics.

The author has also prepared supplementary materials that you can use to expedite learning GW-BASIC. A *Teach Yourself GW-BASIC Convenience Disk* contains more than 100 programs that appear in the book. You can use it to enter programs instead of typing them from the keyboard. A workbook called *Math and Science WorkBook #1* is also available. It contains additional examples, tutorials, questions, answers, exercises, and solutions. Information on how to order the disk and workbook follows this introduction.

As you learn GW-BASIC, you may become curious about even more powerful forms of BASIC. The author suggests QuickBASIC as the best language beyond GW-BASIC. You can easily transfer your GW-BASIC skills to QuickBASIC. In fact, *Teach Yourself GW-BASIC* is written using examples and a programming style designed to speed your transition to QuickBASIC. When you are ready to move up to QuickBASIC, consider the following Osborne/McGraw-Hill books:

QuickBASIC Made Easy by Bob Albrecht, Wenden Wiegand, and Dean Brown
Using QuickBASIC by Don Inman and Bob Albrecht
QuickBASIC: The Complete Reference by Steven Nameroff

Double Your Pleasure . . . and Eliminate Drudgery

The new Convenience Disk for
TEACH YOURSELF GW-BASIC

You've made a wise choice, I honestly believe, in buying and using the new "Teach Yourself GW-Basic." The title says it all: It's the best way to teach yourself GW-BASIC programming. To help you teach yourself even better — and more enjoyably — I've created a special Convenience Disk.

Now you can save yourself from typing any and all named programs of ten or more lines, beginning with Chapter 5 and running to the end of the book; it's all done for you on the Disk. And the Disk has a bunch of programs not shown in the book. All together, there are over 100 files.

The Disk is annotated to make it easier to understand; there are helpful remarks on many of the programs and I illustrate the use of key words, many of which are not in the book.

There are ASCII files with very useful information. And choice Zappy Artist programs. And a lot more.

So that's why I say you'll double (maybe even triple) your pleasure while you eliminate drudgery. As the author, I really want you to enjoy and learn from this book. That's why this Convenience Disk was created . . . and why the price is only $7.50.

Sincerely,

Bob Albrecht

To order:

The Convenience Disk is available in 3 1/2" or 5 1/4" disk format; make sure you indicate the size. Please enclose a check or money order for $7.50 plus applicable sales tax* for each Convenience Disk. That's all; there are no shipping or handling charges. And please indicate clearly your name and complete mailing address.

Mail your orders to: **THE MAIL ORDER EMPORIUM**
530 HILMAR ST.
SANTA CLARA, CA 95050

You may combine your order for the Convenience Disk with an order for Math and Science WorkBook #1, as featured on the reverse side of this page.

Please allow four weeks for delivery.

*California residents should add 7% tax, or 53¢, for each disk.

Now you can apply GW-BASIC to math and science . . . with

The GW-BASIC Math and Science WorkBook #1

This 64-page work book — a big 64 pages (8 1/2" x 11") — isn't for everybody who's learning GW-BASIC; not everybody's into math and science. Darned shame, too: Math and science, especially when applied to current problems like the environment and energy matters, are hot, to put it bluntly.

You're interested in learning GW-BASIC; that's why you're reading "Teach Yourself GW-BASIC." If you're also interested in math and science, then this work book is for you.

My colleague and co-author on several books, Don Inman, has created a fascinating work book. Don is really qualified; I consider him one of the best writers and teachers of math and science. He's ambitious, too; he's planning on a series of work books. That's why we're calling it "WorkBook #1."

WorkBook #1, first in a series, concerns itself mostly with number crunching. The WorkBook will show you how to create programs that will handle math. It's designed for students at the ninth grade level and above.

I said that this work book isn't just for everybody. But if you think it's for you, we've made it easy. It's just $5.00. And that includes shipping and handling.

Sincerely,

Bob Albrecht

To order:

Please enclose a check or money order for $5.00 plus applicable sales tax* for each Math and Science WorkBook #1. That's all; there are no shipping or handling charges. And please indicate clearly your name and complete mailing address.

Mail your orders to:　　**THE MAIL ORDER EMPORIUM**
　　　　　　　　　　　　530 HILMAR ST.
　　　　　　　　　　　　SANTA CLARA, CA 95050

You may combine this order with an order for the Convenience Disk offered on the reverse side of this page.

Please allow four weeks for delivery.

*California residents should add 7% tax, or 35¢, for each WorkBook.

·Why·

This Book Is for You

If you want to learn quickly how to read and understand programs written in GW-BASIC or BASICA, this book is for you. Acting as your personal tutor, this book guides you at your own pace through the BASIC language. You will soon learn how to work effectively with numbers, graphics, sound, and text.

Teach Yourself GW-BASIC uses the Mastery Learning Technique. This approach first establishes topics that can be covered in one session, thoroughly discusses each topic, and then gives you examples and exercises you can work with, as well as supplying the correct answers for these exercises at the end of the book. This method ensures that you will be able to move at your own pace, confident at every step in your knowledge and understanding.

With the expert guidance of the master of BASIC, Bob Albrecht, you will soon be writing programs of your own that do exactly what you want them to do.

Getting Started

▶1◀

CHAPTER OBJECTIVES ✓

You can learn to read and understand BASIC. You can learn to express yourself in BASIC, and use it to make the computer do what **you** want it to do, the way **you** want it done. With this book, you can learn to read, understand, and write BASIC programs.

This chapter gets you started. It introduces the versions of Microsoft BASIC called GW-BASIC and BASICA. You will learn how to load BASIC into your computer, and how to use some simple commands to "customize" your BASIC work and play environment. You will then enter and run a small BASIC program.

LEARN A BIT ABOUT BASIC

1.1

BASIC is a computer language—a language you use to communicate with your computer. Compared to human languages like English, Spanish, or Japanese, a computer language is very simple. BASIC has a small *vocabulary* (list of words that it knows), and a simple *syntax* (rules of grammar that it follows).

A program is simply a set of instructions—a plan for doing something. You may have already used or created a program. For example:

A recipe for baking cookies

Instructions for opening a combination lock

Directions on how to get to someone's house

Those mind-boggling instructions for assembling toys, tricycles, playpens, and furniture

A BASIC program is a set of instructions that tells the computer what to do and how to do it, in the language the computer understands: BASIC. A set of instructions to make the computer do what **you** want it to do, following the rules of BASIC, is called a *program*—**your** program.

BASIC was created in 1964 by Dartmouth professors John G. Kemeny and Thomas E. Kurtz. The original Dartmouth BASIC was limited, with a vocabulary of only 16 words. As the years passed, BASIC became better and better, answering the needs of people who wanted a powerful, yet easy-to-use computer language. Today's versions of BASIC are rich and powerful languages, but they remain easy to learn and use.

Microsoft BASIC is the worldwide de facto standard for BASIC. Some form of Microsoft BASIC is built into, or bundled with, most computers used in today's homes, schools, and businesses. The version of Microsoft BASIC covered in this book is the one used on computers compatible with the IBM PC. It is known by various names, including the following:

- **GW-BASIC** is the generic form of Microsoft BASIC. If you have an IBM PC "clone," you probably have this version.

- **BASICA** is virtually the same as GW-BASIC, licensed to and distributed by IBM.

In this book, the term GW-BASIC is used to mean any of the aforementioned versions of Microsoft BASIC. All GW-BASIC programs in this book will also run in Microsoft QuickBASIC, a state-of-the-art structured BASIC for both beginners and professional users. You can begin with GW-BASIC, and then transfer your skills to QuickBASIC. The programming style used in this book is designed to make it easy for you to move on to QuickBASIC.

Exercises

1. What is BASIC? GW-BASIC? BASICA?

2. BASIC has a small vocabulary and a simple syntax. What does syntax mean?

3. What is a BASIC program?

1.2 | KNOW A DOLLOP OF DOS

The author assumes that you have some knowledge of MS-DOS (Microsoft Disk Operating System), or of PC-DOS, the version of MS-DOS licensed to IBM. Hereafter, the term DOS will be used for MS-DOS, PC-DOS, and any other compatible disk operating system.

In particular, it is assumed that you know how to use the following DOS commands:

DIR   The DIRectory command. Use it to list the names of all files on a disk.

DISKCOPY   Copies everything on a disk to another disk.

FORMAT   Formats a disk. A brand-new disk must be formatted before it can be used. You can format a previously used disk, but do so with caution; formatting erases previously stored information from the disk.

COPY   Copies named files, or groups of named files.

For an excellent and inexpensive introduction to DOS, try *Easy DOS It* by Ron Bauer, from EASY WAY Press, Inc., P.O. Box 906, Rochester, Michigan 48308-0906. Phone: (313) 651-9405. For a thorough introduction to DOS, try *Teach Yourself DOS* by Herbert Schildt, an Osborne/McGraw-Hill book.

The author also assumes that you are using DOS and GW-BASIC from disk drive A. Therefore, when you load DOS into your computer, you will see the famous DOS *A prompt* (A>) and blinking *cursor* (_), as shown here:

A>_

In this case, drive A is your *default disk drive*. Information is read from or written to drive A (the default drive) unless you designate another disk drive.

If your system has a hard disk drive, however, you are probably using DOS from your hard disk. You see a *C prompt* (C>) and blinking cursor. In this case, your hard disk is the default drive. Information is read from or written to the hard disk (the default drive) unless you designate another drive.

GW-BASIC may reside on a floppy disk or on the hard disk. Use the DOS DIR command to locate the GW-BASIC file. You are likely to see one of the filenames listed next in the display or printout of the directory.

GWBASIC.EXE

BASICA.EXE

BASIC.EXE

In this book, the filename GWBASIC.EXE is assumed. If the filename on your disk is different, substitute it for GWBASIC.EXE as you read through this book.

Exercises

1. What is DOS?
2. Suppose the default drive is drive A. What do the disk drive designation, DOS prompt, and cursor look like on the screen?
3. Suppose you are using DOS from your hard disk, which makes the hard disk the default drive. What do the disk drive designation, DOS prompt, and cursor look like on your computer's screen?

1.3 | LOAD DOS INTO YOUR COMPUTER

Begin by loading DOS into your computer. If your computer does not have a hardware clock and calendar, set the date and time when you load DOS. In this book, it is assumed you will use drive A. If you use a hard disk system, change all disk drive references throughout this book accordingly. After you load DOS, you will see the DOS opening screen with information similar to the following:

```
Microsoft MS-DOS 3.20
(C)Copyright Microsoft Corp 1981, 1986
Current date is Tue  1-01-1980
Enter new date (mm-dd-yy): 4-1-91
Current time is  0:01:33.27
Enter new time: 13:30

A>_
```

This information is for a computer that does not have a built-in clock and calendar. Therefore, the date and time were entered by the user. Note the disk drive designation (A), the DOS prompt (>), and the blinking cursor (_), as shown here:

A>_

This is the DOS *command line*. At the DOS command line, you can type a valid DOS command and press the (ENTER) key. The computer will immediately execute your command. In the next section, you will enter a DOS command to load GW-BASIC into the computer's memory.

Exercises

1. Suppose drive A is the default drive. What does the DOS command line look like on the screen?

2. If your system has a hard disk, suppose it is the default drive. What does the DOS command line look like on your screen?

LOAD GW-BASIC INTO YOUR COMPUTER 1.4

In this section, it is assumed that you will load GW-BASIC from a disk in drive A. If you want to load GW-BASIC from your hard disk, usually drive C, make appropriate substitutions in the following discussion.

You have loaded the DOS COMMAND.COM file into your computer's memory. You can see the cursor blinking on the DOS command line, as shown here:

A>_

Before you load GW-BASIC, make sure that a disk containing GW-BASIC is in drive A. This disk may contain the GW-BASIC file under the name GWBASIC.EXE (no hyphen), BASICA.EXE, or BASIC.EXE. In this book, the filename GWBASIC.EXE is assumed. If the filename on your disk is different, make the appropriate substitution for GWBASIC in the discussion that follows.

Now let's load GW-BASIC.

Type **GWBASIC**
and press the (ENTER) key

Note that you do not have to type the file extension (.EXE) in order to load GW-BASIC (or BASICA or BASIC). When you press (ENTER), DOS looks for the GWBASIC.EXE file on the disk in drive A and reads it into the computer's memory. If it can't find the desired file, you will see the following message:

```
A>GWBASIC
Bad command or file name

A>_
```

If this happens, use the DIR command to check the disk directory. Make sure that some version of BASIC is on the disk, note the proper name, and try again.

GW-BASIC begins with the opening screen shown in Figure 1-1, or a similar screen. At the top you see the name and version number ("GW-BASIC 3.22"), followed by the Microsoft copyright notice and the number of bytes of memory available for GW-BASIC programs and data. This information may be different on your computer screen.

On the next two lines you see "Ok" and the blinking cursor (_). Ok is the GW-BASIC prompt. When you see Ok and the blinking cursor, you know it is your turn to do something; GW-BASIC is ready to accept your instructions.

The bottom line on the opening screen is the *key line*. It has brief descriptive labels showing the functions assigned to *function keys* (F1) through (F10). You will learn how to use these function keys to eliminate keystrokes and save time.

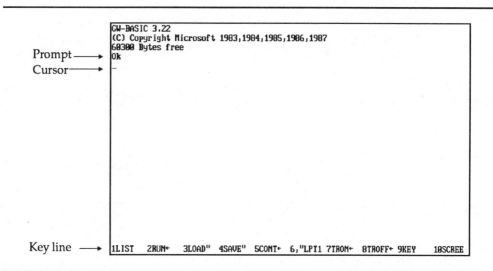

Prompt ⟶
Cursor ⟶

```
GW-BASIC 3.22
(C) Copyright Microsoft 1983,1984,1985,1986,1987
60300 Bytes free
Ok
_
```

Key line ⟶ `1LIST   2RUN←  3LOAD"  4SAVE"  5CONT←  6,"LPI1 7TRON←  8TROFF← 9KEY    10SCREE`

| FIGURE 1-1. | GW-BASIC opening screen |

Exercises

1. Suppose that the version of BASIC you want to use resides on the disk under the filename BASIC.EXE. How do you load it into the computer's memory?
2. What is the GW-BASIC prompt?
3. What does the GW-BASIC cursor look like?
4. What is the GW-BASIC key line?

LEARN HOW TO CLEAR THE SCREEN

1.5

It is a good idea to begin each GW-BASIC activity with a clear or almost clear screen. To clear the screen, hold down the (CTRL) key and press the (L) key. Do it now.

Press (CTRL)-(L)

This clears the screen of all information except the key line at the bottom of the screen and the blinking cursor in the top left corner of the screen, as shown in Figure 1-2.

REMEMBER: To clear the screen, press (CTRL)-(L) (hold down the (CTRL) key and press the (L) key).

1.6 LEARN ABOUT KEYWORDS AND DIRECT STATEMENTS

When you see the blinking cursor, you know that it is your turn to do something. The computer will (blink, blink) wait patiently (blink, blink) until you (blink, blink), **do** something. Do this:

Press (CTRL)-(L)   (*To clear the screen*)

Type *your name*
and press (ENTER)

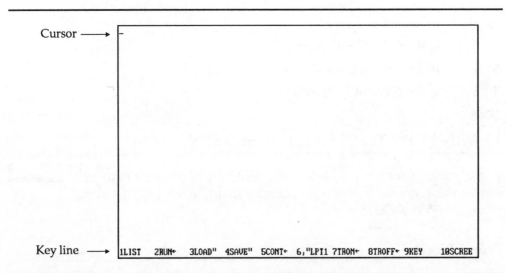

Cursor ⟶

Key line ⟶ `1LIST   2RUN+   3LOAD"  4SAVE"  5CONT+  6,"LPT1 7TRON+  8TROFF+ 9KEY     1ØSCREE`

FIGURE 1-2.   GW-BASIC screen after pressing (CTRL)-(L)

Here is what happened when Rory typed her name. As she typed the letters of her name, the cursor moved to the right, as shown here:

```
Rory_
```

Then she pressed the (ENTER) key. The computer printed "Syntax error," and then displayed the GW-BASIC prompt (Ok) and the blinking cursor. The screen looked like this:

```
Rory
Syntax error
Ok
_
```

Rory's name is not a word in GW-BASIC's vocabulary, so the computer did not understand. When the computer does not understand you, it prints an error message like "Syntax error," followed by the Ok prompt and the cursor.

To use GW-BASIC, you must learn a few of the words it understands. These are called *keywords*. You will next learn how to use keywords in GW-BASIC instructions called *direct statements*. A direct statement tells the computer to do something immediately. The computer executes (carries out) the instruction and then waits for your next command.

When you see the cursor blinking all alone at the beginning of a line, you can type a direct statement and press (ENTER). The computer will immediately execute your statement, as long as it is a valid GW-BASIC operation. For example, BEEP is a GW-BASIC keyword that you can use as a direct statement to tell the computer to sound a beep.

Press (CTRL)-(L)   (*To clear the screen*)

Type **BEEP**
and press (ENTER)

The computer beeps and the top of the screen displays

```
BEEP
Ok
_
```

In this book, GW-BASIC keywords, such as BEEP, are shown in uppercase letters. However, you can type **beep** or **Beep** or even **BeeP**. You can type keywords in upper- or lowercase, whichever you prefer.

If you type a word or phrase that GW-BASIC does not understand, you will see a syntax error message. To see this on the computer now, let's intentionally misspell the BEEP command. Clear the screen with (CTRL)-(L), and then

Type **BOOP**
and press (ENTER)

You won't hear a beep this time, but you will see a syntax error message, as follows:

```
BOOP
Syntax error
Ok
_
```

BOOP is not a valid GW-BASIC keyword, so GW-BASIC printed an error message, then Ok, and then displayed the blinking cursor. The computer is very patient and forgiving. It awaits your next instruction.

You already know one way to clear the screen, by holding down the (CTRL) key and pressing the (L) key. You can also clear the screen by using the keyword CLS as a direct statement. Do this now.

Type **CLS**
and press (ENTER)

This clears the screen in a slightly different way from using (CTRL)-(L). When you use CLS, you see Ok and the blinking cursor at the top of the screen. The bottom line of the screen displays the key line as usual. After completing a direct statement, the computer usually prints Ok, and then displays the cursor.

Remember these two ways to clear most of the screen:

- Hold down the (CTRL) key and press the (L) key ((CTRL)-(L)). This erases everything on the screen except the cursor and the key line.

- Type **CLS** and press (ENTER). This clears the screen except for the GW-BASIC prompt (Ok), the cursor, and the key line.

It is a good practice to clear the screen before beginning each example or programming activity.

Exercises

1. When you see the cursor blinking all alone at the beginning of a line, you can type a direct statement and press (ENTER). What is a direct statement?

2. You can press (CTRL)(L) to clear the screen. After doing so, the screen is empty except for two things. What are they?

3. You can clear the screen by using the keyword CLS as a direct statement. After doing so, what remains on the screen?

4. Suppose your fingers stumble and you type **CLZ** instead of **CLS**, and then press (ENTER). What will happen?

UNDERSTAND GW-BASIC'S DEFAULT ENVIRONMENT

1.7

When you first load GW-BASIC, you see its default *environment*, which includes the following attributes:

- On a color monitor, white letters appear on a black screen. White is the *foreground* color; black is the *background* color.

- On a monochrome monitor, the foreground color for text and the background (screen) color depend on the type of monochrome monitor you are using.

- The screen is a text screen that can display 25 lines of text, with up to 80 characters per line.

- The bottom line (line 25) is the key line, which displays information about function keys (F1) through (F10).

You can change this environment to suit your style. In the following sections, you will learn how to change the screen colors (on a color monitor), change the width of text characters, and turn the key line off and on. You will also learn how to use some of the function keys.

1.8 CHANGE THE SCREEN'S FOREGROUND COLOR

You can use the COLOR keyword in a direct statement to change the color in which text is displayed (foreground color) to any of 16 colors. To do so, you type the keyword **COLOR**, followed by a space and a color number, **0** to **15**. Then press (ENTER). Table 1-1 lists the 16 possible colors and their color numbers. Let's change the screen's foreground color to blue, as follows:

Type **COLOR 1**
and press (ENTER)

You will see the Ok prompt printed in blue, while the cursor remains white.

```
COLOR 1          (Sets the foreground color to blue)
Ok               (Ok is printed in blue)
_                (The cursor remains white)
```

Tell the computer to change the screen's foreground color to light green, color number 10.

Type **COLOR 10**   (*Sets foreground color to light green*)
and press (ENTER)

This COLOR statement, the prompt (Ok), and the cursor look like this:

```
COLOR 10              (Printed in blue)
Ok                    (Printed in light green)
_                     (Cursor remains white)
```

TABLE 1-1.	Foreground Colors and Color Numbers

Color	Number	Color	Number
Black	0	Gray	8
Blue	1	Light blue	9
Green	2	Light green	10
Cyan	3	Light cyan	11
Red	4	Light red	12
Magenta	5	Light magenta	13
Brown	6	Yellow	14
White	7	Bright white	15

You can save time and reduce the likelihood of a typing error by using one of GW-BASIC's handy shortcuts to type the keyword COLOR followed by a space. This shortcut uses the (ALT) key. You can use the (ALT) key and the (C) key to print the keyword COLOR, followed by a space, this way:

Press (ALT)(C)   *(Hold down (ALT) and press (C))*

After doing this, you will see the word COLOR, a space, and the blinking cursor, as shown here:

```
COLOR _
```

You can now type the rest of the direct COLOR statement to change the foreground color to yellow, color 14, as follows:

Type **14**
and press (ENTER)

The screen looks like this:

```
COLOR 14        (Sets the foreground color to yellow)
Ok              (Printed in yellow)

_
```

The default background color is black, color 0. If you set the foreground color to black, the printed text will be black on black, hence invisible. Try this.

Press (ALT)(C)   (*To type COLOR*)

Type **0**
and press (ENTER)

The COLOR statement appears as shown next. Notice that Ok is invisible.

```
COLOR 0           (Sets the foreground color to black)
                  (Ok is black on black, invisible)
_                 (The cursor remains white)
```

Ok is invisible, but you can still see the cursor. If you now type something, the cursor will move, but the text will be invisible. Using (ALT)(C) to type COLOR is especially useful in this situation.
    Now change the foreground color to white, color 7.

Press (ALT)(C)   (*To type COLOR*)

Type **7**
and press (ENTER)

If all goes well, the screen will look like this:

```
COLOR 0           (Sets the foreground color to black)
                  (Ok is invisible)
                  (COLOR 7 is invisible)
Ok                (Ok is white and again visible)

_
```

White, color 7, is the original (default) foreground color. The screen is now back to the original default colors: white foreground and black background.
    You can change the foreground color to a *blinking color* by adding 16 to the color number. Thus, color 17 is blinking blue, color 18 is blinking green, color 19 is blinking cyan, and so on. Color 13 is light

magenta. Set the foreground color to blinking light magenta, as shown here:

```
COLOR 29        (13 + 16 = 29, blinking light magenta)
Ok              (Blink, blink, blink,...)
_               (Still white)
```

Try some other colors. Color numbers 0 to 15 give you nonblinking colors; color numbers 16 to 31 give you blinking colors.

What happens if you use a negative color number or a color number greater than 31? What happens if you use a noninteger color number, such as 3.2 or 3.7? Try them and find out. When you finish experimenting, return the foreground color to white.

Press (ALT)(C)   *(To type COLOR)*

Type **7**
and press (ENTER)

Exercises

1. Instead of typing COLOR and a space, you can save time and reduce the chance of making a typing error by using a shortcut. Describe this shortcut.

2. Write a direct statement to set the foreground color to red, color 4.

3. Write a direct statement to set the foreground color to blinking red.

4. How do you return the foreground color to the default color (white)?

CHANGE THE SCREEN'S BACKGROUND COLOR | 1.9

You can use the COLOR keyword in a direct statement to set the screen's background color to any of eight colors. The colors and their color numbers are shown in Table 1-2. Notice that these background colors and color numbers are the same as the first eight foreground colors and color numbers.

TABLE 1-2.	Background Colors and Color Numbers

Color	Number
Black	0
Blue	1
Green	2
Cyan	3
Red	4
Magenta	5
Brown	6
White	7

You can set the background color without changing the foreground color, or you can use a single COLOR statement to set both the foreground color and the background color at the same time. In this section, you'll learn to change only the background color.

First make sure the foreground color is white, color 7, and clear the screen. To set the background color to blue, you type the keyword **COLOR**, a space, a comma, and the color number for blue. (Remember, you can press (ALT)-(C) to type COLOR and a space.) Be sure to include the comma between COLOR and the color number.

Type **COLOR , 1**   (*Sets background color to blue*)
and press (ENTER)

Most of the screen remains black. However, you will see Ok displayed on a small rectangle in the newly selected background color, blue. It looks like this:

```
COLOR , 1
Ok    ◄──────  Ok is printed on a blue background
─
```

Now clear the screen.

Press (CTRL)-(L)

This clears the screen to the new background color. You see a blue screen with only the cursor and the key line in white.

Here is a slightly different way to change the background color (to green), and then clear the screen to the new background color.

Type **COLOR , 2**   (*Remember to include the comma*)
and press (ENTER)
Type **CLS**
and press (ENTER)

This clears the screen to green. In the upper-left corner, you see Ok and the cursor. On the bottom line, you see the key line.

Return the screen's background color to the original (default) background color of black, color 0.

Type **COLOR , 0**   (*Sets the background color to black*)
and press (ENTER)

Type **CLS**   (*Clears the screen to the background color*)
and press (ENTER)

REMEMBER: To change the screen's background color, type the keyword **COLOR**, a comma, a space, and the color number (0 to 7), and then press (ENTER). The space following COLOR is optional, but is included automatically if you use (ALT)-(C) to type COLOR.

Exercises

1. Describe what happens if you

   Type **COLOR , 5**
   and press (ENTER)

2. After entering a direct COLOR statement to change the background color, what must you do to make the entire screen appear in the newly selected background color?

3. Fill in the blanks: There are _____ background colors, numbered _____ to _____.

4. In typing a direct COLOR statement to change the background color, what will happen if you forget to type the comma (,) following COLOR?

1.10   CHANGE BOTH THE FOREGROUND AND BACKGROUND COLORS

You can use a single COLOR statement to change both the foreground and background colors. For example, change the foreground color to yellow (color 14) and the background color to blue (color 1), as follows:

Type **COLOR 14, 1**   (*Yellow foreground, blue background*)
and press (ENTER)

Type **CLS**   (*Clear to the new colors*)
and press (ENTER)

The screen is cleared to blue, with Ok, the cursor, and the key line all appearing in yellow. The COLOR statement used to do this has the following general form:

COLOR *foreground, background*

Color number, 0 to 15   Color number, 0 to 7

EXPERIMENT: Try various foreground and background color combinations. Pick the ones you would like to use as you wend your way through this book.

Exercises

1. Write a direct COLOR statement to change the foreground color to magenta (color 5) and the background color to cyan (color 3).

2. Write a direct COLOR statement to change the screen colors to the original default colors of white foreground (color 7) on a black background (color 0).

CHANGE THE WIDTH OF TEXT CHARACTERS

1.11

The default GW-BASIC text screen can display lines up to 80 characters long. You can use the WIDTH keyword in a direct statement to tell the computer to print in double-width characters, 40 characters per line, as follows:

Type **WIDTH 40**
and press (ENTER)

The WIDTH 40 statement sets the screen to display 25 lines, with 40 double-width characters per line. The screen appears as shown in Figure 1-3. The key line now includes only function keys (F1) through (F5).

To change the screen back to a width of 80 characters, use a WIDTH statement with 80.

Type **WIDTH 80**
and press (ENTER)

The screen once again displays single-width characters, up to 80 per line, and the key line contains all ten function keys. Now try to change the screen width to 67.

Type **WIDTH 67**
and press (ENTER)

Since the only available screen widths are 40 or 80 characters, you will see an "Illegal function call" error message, as shown here:

```
WIDTH 67
Illegal function call
```

```
Ok
_




1LIST    2RUN←    3LOAD"    4SAVE"    5CONT←
```

FIGURE 1-3.	Screen after a WIDTH 40 statement

Since the WIDTH keyword is used frequently, GW-BASIC provides a shortcut you can use to type WIDTH followed by a space: (ALT)(W). For example, you can change to WIDTH 40 like this:

Press (ALT)(W)   (*Hold down* (ALT) *and press* (W))

Type **40**
and press (ENTER)

Now change back to WIDTH 80, like this:

Press (ALT)(W)   (*To type WIDTH*)

Type **80**
and press (ENTER)

Exercises

1. Fill in the blanks: When you first load GW-BASIC, the screen is a text screen that displays _____ lines with _____ characters per line.

2. How do you change the screen width so that it displays 40 double-width characters per line?

3. Describe a shortcut for typing WIDTH and a space.

LEARN HOW TO TURN THE KEY LINE OFF AND ON

1.12

You can turn off the key line at the bottom of the screen by using the keywords KEY and OFF. Clear the screen, and then turn off the key line.

Type **KEY OFF**
and press (ENTER)

The key line disappears, and the top of the screen displays

```
KEY OFF
Ok
_
```

Of course, if you misspell KEY or OFF, or forget to type a space between them, the key line will not disappear. Instead, you will see a syntax error message. For example:

```
KEYOFF            (No space between KEY and OFF)
Syntax error
Ok
_
```

The prompt and blinking cursor tell you that everything is all right. The computer is patiently waiting for you to try again.

You can turn the key line on again by using the keywords KEY and ON in a direct statement. Clear the screen, and then turn on the key line.

Type **KEY ON**
and press (ENTER)

GW-BASIC has many shortcuts designed to reduce the number of keystrokes required to tell the computer to do something. You use the function keys ((F1), (F2), (F3), and so on) for this purpose. For example, (F9) saves you time in turning the key line off or on. The key line itself reminds you of this; near the right end of the key line you see 9KEY. This tells you that function key (F9) is related to the keyword KEY in some way.

Now try using (F9) to enter direct statements to turn the key line off, and then on. First, clear the screen. Then press the (F9) key. The word KEY, a space, and the blinking cursor will appear on the screen, like this:

```
KEY _
```

Pressing (F9) caused the computer to type the first part of the KEY OFF statement. Now you do the rest.

Type **OFF**
and press (ENTER)

The key line disappears, and the top of the screen displays

```
KEY OFF
Ok
_
```

Exercises

1.   How do you turn off the key line? Describe two ways.

2.   How do you turn on the key line? Describe two ways.

1.13 LEARN ABOUT GW-BASIC PROGRAMS

A GW-BASIC program is written using the vocabulary and syntax (rules of grammar) of GW-BASIC. At the end of this paragraph, you'll find a short program that tells the computer to print a message over and over until you stop the computer. The program uses two keywords, PRINT and GOTO, that you will learn more about in the next chapters.

```
10 PRINT "To stop, hold down CTRL and press BREAK"
20 GOTO 10
```

This program has two *program lines*. Each program line begins with a line number (10 and 20), and contains a statement (PRINT and GOTO).

Previously, you used statements such as BEEP and COLOR as direct statements. You typed the direct statement without a line number and pressed (ENTER), and the computer executed the statement immediately. In contrast, when you type a statement with a line number (a program line), it is not executed immediately when you press (ENTER). Instead, it is stored in the computer's memory for later execution. After entering all the lines of your program, you can tell the computer to run (*execute*) the entire program. It does so, unless the program contains something the computer doesn't understand. If this happens, the computer prints an error message and, in some cases, displays the line that contains the error. It then waits for you to fix the mistake and tell it what to do next.

Exercises

1. A BASIC program consists of one or more program lines. Each line begins with a _____,
   which is followed by a _____.

2. What is the difference between a direct statement and a program line?

LEARN HOW TO ENTER A PROGRAM INTO THE COMPUTER'S MEMORY

1.14

You will soon enter the program described above into the computer's memory. Before doing so, tell the computer that you will enter a new program. To do this, use the NEW keyword as a direct statement. First, clear the screen with (CTRL)(L). Then

Type **NEW**
and press (ENTER)

The screen displays

```
NEW
Ok
_
```

NOTE: In this book, keywords such as NEW are always shown in uppercase letters. However, you may type **new**, **New**, or even **NeW**. The computer will recognize a keyword typed in any mixture of upper- and lowercase letters, as long as you spell it correctly.

The NEW statement clears (erases) the part of the computer's memory used to store a GW-BASIC program. You can verify this by telling the computer to list any program now in memory. The easiest way to do this is to press the (F1) function key, and then the (ENTER) key. Pressing (F1) causes the keyword LIST to appear on the screen, along with the blinking cursor. Pressing (ENTER) then causes the computer to execute LIST as a direct statement. Do this now, slowly, and watch what happens on the screen.

Press (F1)
and press (ENTER)

The computer lists any program resident in its memory, and then displays the prompt (Ok) and the cursor (_). Since there is no program in the memory, the screen should look like this:

```
LIST        (Since no program resides in memory,
Ok           nothing is listed between LIST and Ok.)
_
```

Now clear the screen and enter the first line of the program into the computer's memory.

Type:
10 PRINT "To stop, hold down CTRL and press BREAK"
and press (ENTER)

The screen looks like this:

```
10 PRINT "To stop, hold down CTRL and press BREAK"
_
```

Notice that the Ok prompt is not printed. The cursor blinks below the line you just entered. The line number (10) tells GW-BASIC that you are not entering a direct statement, but rather a program line to be stored for later execution. If you make a typing error, you will not see a "Syntax error" message. For now, ignore any errors you make in entering program lines.

Now enter the second line of the program.

Type **20 GOTO 10**
and press (ENTER)

The screen now shows the two lines of the program, as follows:

```
10 PRINT "To stop, hold down CTRL and press BREAK"
20 GOTO 10
_
```

You have entered the complete two-line program into the computer's memory. If your entries look somewhat different from those shown above, don't worry. You can easily correct any lines that contain errors.

To verify that the program is now resident in the computer's memory, clear the screen and list the program.

Press (F1)
and press (ENTER)

The computer lists the two-line program, as shown next.

```
LIST
10 PRINT "To stop, hold down CTRL and press BREAK"
20 GOTO 10
```

When you see a listed program line with an error, you can easily fix it—just retype the entire line, *including* the line number. The corrected line you enter will replace the line of the same number in the computer's memory. For example, suppose you list the program and it looks like this:

```
10 PRINT "To stop, hold down CTRL and press BREAK"
20 GOTO 19
```

Oops! Line 20 is incorrect. Correct it like this:

Type **20 GOTO 10**
and press (ENTER)

You can list the program again to see the corrected line as it is stored in memory.

REMEMBER: To correct a program line, simply type the correct line, including the line number.

Exercises

1. Before you enter a new program, you should first delete, or erase, any old program that might be in the computer's memory. How do you do this?

2. How do you list to the screen a program in the computer's memory?

3. How do you enter a program line into the computer's memory?

4. Suppose you make a typing error in line 10 of a program, so that the stored line contains the misspelled keyword PRINT, like this:

```
10 PTINT "To stop, hold down CTRL and press BREAK"
```

How do you correct this error?

RUN A GW-BASIC PROGRAM

1.15

You have now entered a program, listed it, and corrected any obvious errors. Let's run the program and see what it does. The key line tells you how to run the program, as shown here:

2RUN←

This key line item tells you that you can press the (F2) function key to run the program that is in the computer's memory. The little arrow (←) tells you that you don't even have to press (ENTER)—just press (F2) and the program begins. Try it.

Press (F2)

The screen quickly fills with line after line of the message printed by line 10. When you tire of watching this message endlessly repeated, stop the computer, as directed by the message on the screen (press (CTRL)(BREAK)). You will then see a screen similar to the one in Figure 1-4.

```
To stop, hold down CTRL and press BREAK
To stop, hold down CTRL and press BREAK
To stop, hold down CTRL and press BREAK
To stop, hold down CTRL and press BREAK
To stop, hold down CTRL and press BREAK
To stop, hold down CTRL and press BREAK
To stop, hold down CTRL and press BREAK
To stop, hold down CTRL and press BREAK
To stop, hold down CTRL and press BREAK
To stop, hold down CTRL and press BREAK
To stop, hold down CTRL and press BREAK
To stop, hold down CTRL and press BREAK
To stop, hold down CTRL and press BREAK
To stop, hold down CTRL and press BREAK
To stop, hold down CTRL and press BREAK
To stop, hold down CTRL and press BREAK
To stop, hold down CTRL and press BREAK
To stop, hold down CTRL and press BREAK
To stop, hold down CTRL and press BREAK

Break in 10
Ok

1LIST   2RUN←   3LOAD"   4SAVE"   5CONT←   6,"LPT1 7TRON←  8TROFF← 9KEY     10SCREE
```

FIGURE 1-4. | To stop the computer, do what it says on the screen

When you interrupt a program by pressing (CTRL)(BREAK), the computer stops what it's doing and tells you that it stopped because you pressed (CTRL)(BREAK). You will see the following message, or a similar one:

```
Break in line 10
```

The message "Break in line 10" tells you the computer stopped just after executing line 10 of the program. Run the program again (press (F2)), and then stop it (press (CTRL)(BREAK)).

REMEMBER: To stop a runaway program, hold down the (CTRL) key and press the (BREAK) key (press (CTRL)(BREAK)).

Exercises

1. How do you tell the computer to run a program already stored in its memory?

2. How do you stop a program that is running?

1.16 TRY MORE TINY PROGRAMS

Try each of the three programs shown below under "Examples." For each program:

- Use a NEW statement to erase the program previously stored in the computer's memory.
- Enter each line of the program.
- List the program and correct any errors.
- Run the program (with (F2)).
- Press (CTRL)(BREAK) to stop the program.

Remember that (ALT)(P) is a shortcut to type PRINT and a space. (ALT)(G) is a shortcut to type GOTO and a space.

Examples

These programs use two new keywords, RND and SOUND. You will
learn about these in Chapter 3.

1.
```
10 COLOR 16 * RND
20 PRINT "Rory ";   (Note the semicolon at the end)
30 GOTO 10
```

2.
```
10 COLOR 16 * RND, 8 * RND
20 PRINT "Rory ";
30 GOTO 10
```

3.
```
10 COLOR 16 * RND, 8 * RND
20 PRINT "Rory ";
30 SOUND 4000 * RND + 37, 1
40 GOTO 10
```

LEARN HOW TO LEAVE GW-BASIC AND RETURN TO DOS

1.17

After spending some time with GW-BASIC, you may wish to return
to DOS and its familiar DOS command line (A>_ or C>_). You can
do this by using the keyword SYSTEM in a direct statement.

Type **SYSTEM**
and press (ENTER)

This returns you to DOS, with the cursor blinking on the DOS
command line.

```
SYSTEM                        (Returns you to DOS)
A>_                           (The DOS command line)
```

REMEMBER: To leave GW-BASIC and return to DOS, type **SYS-
TEM** and press (ENTER).

INTEGRATING
SKILLS
CHECK

EXERCISES

1. In the spaces provided, fill in the letter of the item from the right column that best describes or illustrates the item in the left column.

    ___ BASIC   a. a set of instructions

    ___ syntax   b. instruction that is obeyed immediately

    ___ program   c. 1LIST, 2RUN←, 3LOAD", and so on

    ___ DOS command line   d. blinking underscore character (_)

    ___ BASIC prompt   e. word that GW-BASIC understands

    ___ cursor   f. the computer didn't understand

    ___ key line   g. computer language

    ___ syntax error   h. rules of grammar

    ___ keyword   i. A>_ or C>_

    ___ direct statement   j. Ok

2. Write a direct COLOR statement to set the foreground color to black and the background to white. (This color combination is the reverse of the default colors of white foreground on a black background.)

3. When you first load GW-BASIC, you see the default screen, which can display 25 lines with 80 characters per line. How do you change to a screen width of 40 double-width characters per line? How do you change the screen back to the default width of 80 characters per line?

4. How do you turn the key line off? When the key line is off, how do you turn it on?

5. What is the difference between a program line and a direct statement?

6. How do you enter a program into the computer's memory?

7. How do you list on the screen the program in the computer's memory?

8. How do you correct a program line that contains an error?

9. How do you run the program that is in the computer's memory?

10. How do you stop a program that is running?

11. Here is the program you used in sections 1.13 through 1.15.

```
10 PRINT "To stop, hold down CTRL and press BREAK"
20 GOTO 10
```

This program has a PRINT statement in line 10 and a GOTO statement in line 20. These statements will be explained in the next chapter. However, since you have seen the program in operation, perhaps you can already describe what each statement does.

a. What does the PRINT statement in line 10 tell the computer to do?

b. What does the GOTO statement in line 20 tell the computer to do?

12. How do you tell the computer to leave GW-BASIC and return to DOS?

You are off to a great start! Perhaps you would now like to take a break and do something physical: go for a nature walk, ride a bike, play tennis, whatever. Then, refreshed, plunge into Chapter 2 and learn more about GW-BASIC.

Do It Now: Direct Statements

▶2◀

CHAPTER OBJECTIVES

In this chapter, you will load GW-BASIC into your computer's memory, then choose the colors in which you like to work. You will learn how to print information on the screen and do simple arithmetic.

This chapter introduces GW-BASIC's graphics screen. You will use it to plot tiny points called *pixels* and to draw lines, boxes, and circles on the screen.

EXERCISES

SKILLS
CHECK

Before beginning Chapter 2, make sure you know how to do the following things you learned about in Chapter 1:

1. Load DOS, and then load GW-BASIC into your computer's memory.

2. Change the screen's foreground and background colors.

3. Set the screen width to 40 or 80 characters per line.

4. Use (ALT) key shortcuts: (ALT)(C) (COLOR) (ALT)(G) (GOTO)
    (ALT)(P) (PRINT) (ALT)(W) (WIDTH)

5. Leave GW-BASIC and return to DOS.

2.1   LOAD GW-BASIC AND CHOOSE YOUR COLORS

Load GW-BASIC into your computer's memory. The opening screen is shown in Figure 2-1. If you are using a color monitor, you can choose the foreground and background colors in which you would like to work. The author likes to use yellow text (foreground color) on a blue background. Here is a quick way to set both these colors on the screen. You type a COLOR statement and a CLS statement, separated by a colon (:), on one line.

Type **COLOR 14, 1: CLS**
and press (ENTER)

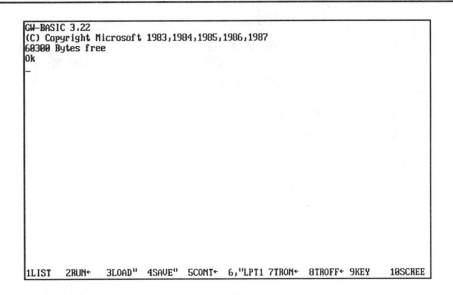

```
GW-BASIC 3.22
(C) Copyright Microsoft 1983,1984,1985,1986,1987
60300 Bytes free
Ok
_
```

```
1LIST   2RUN←   3LOAD"  4SAVE"  5CONT←  6,"LPT1 7TRON←  8TROFF← 9KEY     10SCREE
```

FIGURE 2-1.   The GW-BASIC opening screen is SCREEN 0

REMEMBER: You can type two statements on a single line. Use a colon (:) to separate the two statements. You can press (ALT)-(C) to type COLOR and a space.

Exercises

1. If you type two direct statements on one line, what character must you type between the two statements?

2. What do you think will happen if you do the following? (Try it and find out.)

    Type **COLOR 14, 1 CLS**
    and press (ENTER)

3. Choose and set the screen to the screen colors that you want to use.

| 2.2 | **PRINT THE DATE AND TIME** |

You can use the keywords PRINT and DATE$ in a direct statement to tell the computer to print the date on the screen. Note that the keyword DATE$ ends in a dollar sign ($).

Type **PRINT DATE$**
and press (ENTER)

A possible result is shown below. Of course, the date you see is probably different from the date shown here.

```
04-01-1991
```

DATE$ is a GW-BASIC keyword. It is a *string variable*. A string variable has a *value*. The value of DATE$ is the current date, according to the computer. If you leave your computer on, or if it has a battery-powered clock and calendar, it will advance the date one day at midnight.

You can type the keywords PRINT and DATE$ in upper- or lowercase letters, or a mixture of both. Be sure to spell both keywords correctly and put a space between them. If you misspell either word or omit the space, you will no doubt see the dreaded syntax error message. That's OK; just try again.

Now tell the computer to print the time.

Type **PRINT TIME$**
and press (ENTER)

The computer immediately prints the time in hours, minutes, and seconds like this:

```
PRINT TIME$
09:53:28                    (9:53 and 28 seconds)
```

The computer keeps time on a 24-hour clock. If you tell it to print the time in midafternoon, you might see something like this:

```
PRINT TIME$
15:29:46
```

The time shown is a few seconds before 3:30 P.M.

Like DATE$, TIME$ is a string variable. A string variable has a value. The value of TIME$ is the current time, according to the computer's clock.

You can print the date and time on one line, as shown below. Note that a comma separates the keywords DATE$ and TIME$.

Type **PRINT DATE$, TIME$**
and press (ENTER)

If you entered this command in the early evening of April Fools' Day, you might see the following:

```
PRINT DATE$, TIME$
04-01-1991    19:20:08
```

The time shown is eight seconds after 7:20 P.M.

Commas in a PRINT statement tell the computer to print values in *standard print positions*. In our example, the value of DATE$ was printed in the first standard print position; the value of TIME$ was printed in the second standard print position. There are five standard print positions across the screen: Position #1 begins at column 1 (the left edge of the screen), position #2 at column 15, position #3 at column 29, position #4 at column 43, and position #5 at column 57.

Exercises

1. Write a direct PRINT statement to print the time first, then the date, both on the same line.

2. Suppose the time is printed as 23:59:59. What time is it?

2.3 | PRINT YOUR NAME

You can use a direct PRINT statement to tell the computer to print your name. To do so, you type the keyword **PRINT**, a space, and your name enclosed in quotation marks ("). Laran Stardrake did it this way:

Laran typed **PRINT "Laran Stardrake"**
and pressed (ENTER)

The direct PRINT statement and its result appeared on the screen as shown here:

```
PRINT "Laran Stardrake"
Laran Stardrake
```

You can use the PRINT keyword to display the date, the time, and your name. The PRINT keyword can, in fact, be used to print almost any message. This is what makes PRINT one of the most used and useful keywords in GW-BASIC. To use PRINT to tell the computer to print a message, follow these steps:

1. Type the keyword **PRINT** and a space.

2. Type a quotation mark (").

3. Type your name or any desired message.

4. Type another quotation mark (").

5. Press (ENTER).

The information enclosed in quotation marks is called a *string*. A string can be a name, a message, a telephone number, or any group of characters:

```
PRINT "Laran Stardrake"
```
             This is a string. In a PRINT statement,
             a string is enclosed in quotation marks.

Exercises

1. When you use a PRINT statement to print a string of characters, the string to be printed must be enclosed in _____.

2. Write a PRINT statement to print George Firedrake's name.

USE SHORTCUTS FOR PRINT _____ | 2.4 |

Anything that reduces the amount of typing also reduces the likelihood of typing mistakes. GW-BASIC provides many shortcuts for typing keywords. You can use a question mark (?) as an abbreviation for PRINT. Just type a question mark followed by a space, and then whatever you want to print. For example:

Type **? "Laran Stardrake"**
and press (ENTER)

GW-BASIC provides another handy shortcut that works for many keywords, including PRINT. You first used this shortcut in Chapter 1. The shortcut uses (ALT) and (P) to print the keyword PRINT followed by a space, this way:

Press (ALT)-(P)   (*Hold down the* (ALT) *key and press* (P))

After doing this, you will see

```
PRINT _
```

You can now type the rest of the PRINT statement and press (ENTER).

REMEMBER: Press (ALT)-(P) to print the keyword PRINT followed by a space.

Exercises

1. Instead of typing the keyword PRINT, you can use a _____ as an abbreviation for PRINT.

2. A quick way to type the keyword PRINT followed by a space is to_____.

2.5 | SET THE DATE

You can set the date to a date of your choice. To do so, you type a statement that *assigns* the date as a string value to the string variable DATE$, as follows:

Type **DATE$ = "4-1-91"**
and press (ENTER)

After setting the date, verify that it has been set properly by using a direct PRINT statement.

Type **PRINT DATE$**
and press (ENTER)

If you set the date and print it as described above, the screen will display

```
DATE$ = "4-1-91"
Ok
PRINT DATE$
04-01-1991
```

The statement

```
DATE$ = "4-1-91"
```

tells the computer to assign the string 4-1-91 as the value of the string variable DATE$. The string itself (4-1-91) is enclosed in quotation marks. When assigning the string as the value of DATE$, the computer puts it into a standard format: 04-01-1991. This is the format in which the PRINT DATE$ statement prints.

You can set the date in several ways. Two ways are shown here:

```
DATE$ = "4/1/91"
DATE$ = "4-1-1991"
```

For both of these formats, the date will be printed as 04-01-1991 when you use PRINT DATE$ to print it.

Table 2-1 shows several ways to make a mistake while setting the date. In each case, the computer prints an error message, and then waits for your next try. The error message is shown directly below each incorrect direct statement.

The earliest valid date is 01-01-1980. The latest valid date is 12-31-2099. If you assign a two-digit year in the range 00 to 79, the computer assumes you mean 2000 to 2079. For example:

Type **DATE$ = "1-1-01"**
and press (ENTER)

Type **PRINT DATE$**
and press (ENTER)

| TABLE 2-1. | Possible Mistakes and Error Messages in Setting the Date |

Mistake and Error Message	Comments
DATE$ = 1-1-91 Type mismatch	The date is a string and must be enclosed in quotation marks.
DATE = "1-1-91" Type mismatch	The dollar sign ($) in DATE$ is missing.
DATE$ = "4-31-91" Illegal function call	Oops! Too many days in that month.
DATE$ = "13-1-91" Illegal function call	Oops! Too many months in that year.
DATE$ = "1 1 91" Illegal function call	Need slashes (/) or dashes (-) to separate month, day, and year.
DATE$ = "12-31-1979" Illegal function call	Earliest valid date is 01-01-1980.
DATE$ = "1-1-2100" Illegal function call	Latest valid date is 12-31-2099.

The date now displayed on the screen is the beginning of the year in which a computer named HAL goes to Jupiter.

```
DATE$ = "1-1-01"
Ok
PRINT DATE$
01-01-2001
```

Exercises

1. When assigning a date as the value of the string variable DATE$, you must enclose the date in _____.
2. Write a statement to assign July 15, 2010, as the value of DATE$.

2.6 SET THE TIME

The computer maintains a 24-hour clock. Time is measured from midnight, which is 00:00:00. Table 2-2 shows 24-hour clock times corresponding to selected ante meridiem (A.M.) and post meridiem (P.M.) times for a conventional 12-hour clock.

Set the time to exactly 1:00 P.M., as follows:

Type **TIME$ = "13"**
and press (ENTER)

The computer automatically sets the minutes and seconds to zero. Verify this by entering a direct PRINT statement.

Type **PRINT TIME$**
and press (ENTER)

After executing the above two direct statements, your screen will look like the following display. Of course, the time displayed depends on how much time elapsed between your entries.

```
TIME$ = "13"
Ok
PRINT TIME$
13:00:24
```

TABLE 2-2.	12-Hour and 24-Hour Clock Times

12-Hour Clock	24-Hour Clock	Comments
00:00:01 A.M.	00:00:01	One second after midnight
00:01:00 A.M.	00:01:00	One minute after midnight
01:00:00 A.M.	01:00:00	One hour after midnight
06:00:00 A.M.	06:00:00	Time to get up
09:00:00 A.M.	09:00:00	Many companies begin work
10:30:00 A.M.	10:30:00	Coffee break?
12:00:00 Noon	12:00:00	High noon
3:00:00 P.M.	15:00:00	School's out!

Now set the time to exactly 10:30 P.M.

Type **TIME$ = "22:30"**
and press (ENTER)

Verify your setting with a direct PRINT statement.

Table 2-3 shows several ways to make a mistake while setting the time. In each case, the computer prints an error message, and then waits for your next command. The error message is shown directly below each incorrect direct statement.

Exercises

1. Write a statement to set the time to 23 seconds after 7:30 A.M.

2. Write a statement to set the time to 23 seconds after 7:30 P.M.

TABLE 2-3.	Possible Mistakes and Error Messages in Setting the Time

Mistakes and Error Messages	Comments
TIME$ = 12:00:00 Type mismatch	The time is a string and must be enclosed in quotation marks.
TIME = "8:30" Type mismatch	The dollar sign ($) in TIME$ is missing.
TIME$ = "11:60" Illegal function call	Oops! Too many minutes.
TIME$ = "24:00:01" Illegal function call	Too many hours. One second after midnight is 00:00:01.
TIME$ = "12-30" Illegal function call	In setting time, use colons (:) instead of dashes (-).
TIME$ = "12/30" Illegal function call	In setting time, use colons (:) instead of slashes (/).

2.7 DO ARITHMETIC

If you misplace your $10 solar-powered calculator, relax—you can use your computer instead. Use +, −, *, and / to specify the arithmetic operations of addition, subtraction, multiplication, and division, as shown in Table 2-4.

You use the PRINT statement and the appropriate arithmetic operator to tell the computer to add, subtract, multiply, or divide numbers and display the result. Clear the screen, and then tell the computer to add two numbers, 3 and 4, and print the result.

Type **PRINT 3 + 4**
and press (ENTER)

TABLE 2-4.	GW-BASIC Arithmetic Operations

Operation	Operation Symbol	Example
Addition	+	3 + 4
Subtraction	−	3 − 4
Multiplication	*	3 * 4
Division	/	3 / 4

When you press the (ENTER) key, the computer first adds the numbers (3 plus 4), and then prints the result, as shown here:

```
PRINT 3 + 4
 7
```

Now try the other arithmetic operations: subtraction, multiplication, and division.

- To subtract a number from another number,

  Type **PRINT 3 − 4**
  and press (ENTER)

- To multiply two numbers,

  Type **PRINT 3 * 4**
  and press (ENTER)

- To divide a number by another number,

Type **PRINT 3 / 4**
and press (ENTER)

After entering all four of the preceding statements, the screen will
look like the following:

```
PRINT 3 + 4                        (Addition: +)
 7
Ok
PRINT 3 - 4                        (Subtraction: -)
-1
Ok
PRINT 3 * 4                        (Multiplication: *)
 12
Ok
PRINT 3 / 4                        (Division: /)
 .75
```

Each of the preceding direct PRINT statements consists of the
keyword PRINT followed by a *numerical expression* (3 + 4, 3 – 4, 3 * 4,
or 3 / 4). The computer first evaluates the numerical expression (does
the arithmetic), and then prints the result, a single number.

Notice how the four numbers are printed: the negative number
(–1) is printed beginning at the far left position (column of the
screen), but the positive numbers are printed with a blank space in
front. Positive numbers (and zero) are printed with a leading space,
while negative numbers are printed with a leading minus sign (–)
and no leading space.

You can put two or more numerical expressions in a single PRINT
statement. Use commas or semicolons between expressions as
delimiters (separators). For example, enter a PRINT statement that
contains the four numerical expressions shown previously,
separated by commas.

Type **PRINT 3 + 4, 3 – 4, 3 * 4, 3 / 4**
and press (ENTER)

The computer computes the four values and displays them in the first four standard print positions, as shown here:

```
PRINT 3 + 4, 3 - 4, 3 * 4, 3 / 4
 7              -1            12            .75
```

Each result is printed as a single number. The first result is a positive number. It is printed with a leading space, a digit (7), and a space. The comma in the PRINT statement then causes the computer to skip over to the next standard print position. The second result (–1) is printed with a minus sign, a digit, and a space. The computer then skips over to the third standard print position. The third result (12) is printed with a leading space, two digits, and a space. Finally, in the fourth standard print position, the computer prints the fourth result (.75) with a leading space, a decimal point, two digits, and a space.

You can also use semicolons as delimiters (separators) between numerical expressions.

Type **PRINT 3 + 4; 3 – 4; 3 * 4; 3 / 4**
and press (ENTER)

The results are printed close together, as shown here:

```
PRINT 3 + 4; 3 - 4; 3 * 4; 3 / 4
 7 -1  12   .75
```

This time results are not printed in standard print positions. Instead, they are printed contiguously. A positive number is printed with a space, the digits (and decimal point, if required), and a space. A negative number is printed with a minus sign (–), the digits (and decimal point, if required), and a space. Therefore, you see one space between the first two results (7 and –1), but two spaces between the second and third results (–1 and 12).

Exercises

1. The GW-BASIC symbols for addition (+) and subtraction (–) are the same as those used in mathematics literature. However, the symbols for multiplication and division are different. What symbol do you use for GW-BASIC multiplication? What symbol do you use for GW-BASIC division?

2. If you write a single PRINT statement to compute and print the values of two or more numerical expressions, you must use delimiters to separate the expressions. What delimiters can you use?

3. Write a single PRINT statement to compute and print the values of seven plus five, seven minus five, seven times five, and seven divided by five. Print the results in the standard print positions.

4. Write a single PRINT statement to compute and print the values of 39.95 * .06, and 39.95 + 39.95 * .06. Print the results contiguously, as close together as possible.

2.8 | MAKE SOME SOUNDS

The BEEP statement makes the computer beep. Every beep sounds the same, and lasts for the same length of time. You can make more interesting sounds by using SOUND statements.

The SOUND statement lets you control the *frequency* (or *pitch*) of the sound, as well as its *duration* (the length of time the sound is heard). For example, the following SOUND statement causes the computer to play the note middle C for 18 *ticks*, or about one second (18.2 ticks equal one second):

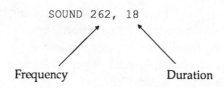

```
SOUND 262, 18
```

Frequency   Duration

Use this SOUND statement as a direct statement.

Type **SOUND 262, 18**
and press (ENTER)

You will hear middle C for about one second.
    The statement

```
SOUND 262, 18
```

tells the computer to sound a tone of frequency 262 Hertz (Hz)—or
cycles per second—for 18 ticks, or about one second. That tone is
middle C on a musical scale.
    Now tell the computer to make another sound.

Type **SOUND 440, 9**
and press (ENTER)

This statement tells the computer to sound a tone of frequency 440
Hz for a duration of nine ticks, or about one-half second. That tone
is the note A above middle C.
    Table 2-5 lists the frequencies of musical notes for four octaves in
the scale of C. The frequency of sounds may be any number from 37
to 32767. You will probably not hear the very high tones, but you
might attract dogs and other animals within earshot of your computer. A frequency less than 37 or greater than 32767 will cause an
error message.
    The duration of sounds may be any number from 0 to 65535, and
need not be an integer. Try a very short duration, such as 0.25 or
0.125. If the duration is zero, any sound in progress is turned off.
    Tell the computer to make a sound of frequency 523 (C above
middle C) for a duration of 65535 ticks (about 3600 seconds, or one
hour), as follows:

Type **SOUND 523, 65535**
and press (ENTER)

TABLE 2-5.	Hertz Frequencies for Musical Notes in the Scale of C

Note	Hz Frequency	Note	Hz Frequency
C	130.81	C	523.25
D	146.83	D	587.33
E	164.81	E	659.26
F	174.61	F	698.46
G	196.00	G	783.99
A	220.00	A	880.00
B	246.94	B	987.77
C*	261.63	C	1046.50
D	293.66	D	1174.70
E	329.63	E	1318.50
F	349.23	F	1396.90
G	392.00	G	1568.00
A	440.00	A	1760.00
B	493.88	B	1975.50

*Middle C

The sound begins. You can wait for an hour, or turn off the sound like this:

Type **SOUND 123, 0**
and press (ENTER)

To turn off an ongoing sound, use a duration of zero and any legal frequency, 37 to 32767. The frequency (123) was chosen for the previous command arbitrarily and is not significant.

Exercises

1. What is the highest frequency you can use in a SOUND statement? What is the lowest frequency?

2. Here are some durations in seconds or fractions of a second. For each one, how many ticks would you use in a SOUND statement?

   a. 1 second
   b. 2 seconds
   c. 1/2 second
   d. 1/4 second

3. Write a SOUND statement to sound a tone of frequency 5000 Hz for about one second.

4. Write a SOUND statement to play the lowest frequency tone. Use a duration of about 1/3 second.

UNDERSTAND SCREEN MODES

2.9

Your computer probably has at least three screen modes:

- text mode

- medium-resolution graphics mode

- high-resolution graphics mode

The *text mode* allows you to print *characters* on the screen: letters, numbers, punctuation, special characters like $, #, @, and so on, foreign alphabets, and some picture-like characters.

The *graphics modes* allow you to plot tiny rectangles called *pixels* (picture elements) in order to draw lines, boxes, circles, and more complex shapes on the screen. You can also print text and other characters in the graphics modes.

When you first load GW-BASIC, it begins in the text mode. This is SCREEN 0. In SCREEN 0 you can print text and other characters in 16 foreground colors, on a background selected from 8 background colors.

Text is normally printed on a screen of 25 lines with 80 characters per line. You learned in Chapter 1 to use a WIDTH 40 statement to tell the computer to print in 25 lines with 40 double-width characters per line.

If your computer has a Color Graphics Adapter (CGA), it has at least two color graphics screens:

- SCREEN 1 is a *medium-resolution* graphics screen with 16 background colors and four foreground colors at any one time. The *resolution* is 320 by 200. That is, you can think of the screen as being 320 pixels wide by 200 pixels high. Thus there are 64,000 (320 x 200 = 64,000) pixel positions in SCREEN 1. A text character occupies an 8-by-8 pixel "box." For printing text, SCREEN 1 has 25 lines with 40 character positions per line.

- SCREEN 2 is a *high-resolution* graphics screen with one background color (black) and one foreground color (white). The resolution is 640 by 200. You can think of SCREEN 2 as being 640 pixels wide by 200 pixels high. Thus there are 128,000 (640 x 200 = 128,000) pixel positions in SCREEN 2. A text character occupies an 8-by-8 pixel "box," so you can print up to 80 characters per line on any of 25 lines. SCREEN 2 is not covered in this book.

If your computer has an Extended Graphics Adapter (EGA) or Video Graphics Array (VGA), it has additional screen modes.

Exercises

1. When you first load GW-BASIC, it begins in SCREEN 0. Describe this screen mode.

2. If your computer has a color graphics card (CGA), it has a medium-resolution graphics screen called SCREEN 1.

   a. SCREEN 1 can display pixels. What is a pixel?
   b. How many pixels can you plot horizontally in SCREEN 1?
   c. How many pixels can you plot vertically in SCREEN 1?
   d. For text, what is the screen width of SCREEN 1?

PLOT PIXELS IN SCREEN 1 ————————— 2.10

You can use a direct SCREEN statement to select SCREEN 0, SCREEN 1, or SCREEN 2. Select SCREEN 1.

Type **SCREEN 1**
and press (ENTER)

SCREEN 1 appears as shown in Figure 2-2. This screen looks like SCREEN 0 with the width set to 40, except for one thing. Notice that the SCREEN 1 cursor is a nonblinking solid rectangular block (■) instead of the underline character (_) used in SCREEN 0.

For graphics, SCREEN 1 is divided into 64,000 tiny rectangles called pixels (picture elements). A pixel position is identified by two *coordinates*: a column number (0 to 319) and a row number (0 to 199), as shown in Figure 2-3.

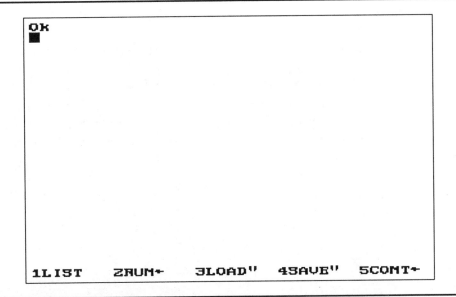

FIGURE 2-2. ▌ SCREEN 1

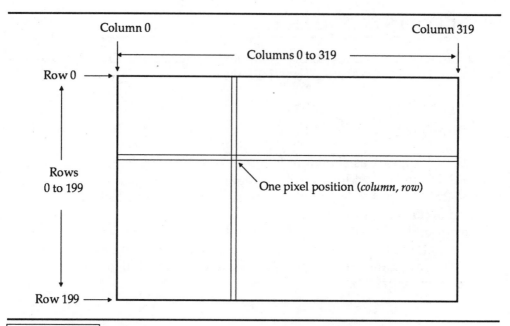

FIGURE 2-3. Columns, rows, and pixel positions in SCREEN 1

In SCREEN 1, the default background color is black (color 0). You can use a COLOR statement to select any of 16 background colors, shown in Table 2-6. The SCREEN 1 background colors are the same as the SCREEN 0 foreground colors (see Table 1-1 in Chapter 1). Use a COLOR statement to set the background color to the color of your choice. For example, you can set the background color to blue, as follows:

Type **COLOR 1**
and press (ENTER)

In SCREEN 1, the COLOR statement sets the *background* color to blue. In SCREEN 0, this statement sets the *foreground* color to blue.
    Now return the background to black.

Type **COLOR 0**
and press (ENTER)

TABLE 2-6.	SCREEN 1 Background Colors and Color Numbers

Color	Color Number	Color	Color Number
Black	0	Gray	8
Blue	1	Light blue	9
Green	2	Light green	10
Cyan	3	Light cyan	11
Red	4	Light red	12
Magenta	5	Light magenta	13
Brown	6	Yellow	14
White	7	Bright white	15

Think of SCREEN 1 as a canvas available in 16 background colors. You can pick a *palette* of foreground colors for plotting pixels or drawing shapes on the screen. SCREEN 1 provides two palettes, each with four colors numbered 0, 1, 2, and 3.

- Palette 0 has the following colors:

  0 is the current background color
  1 is green
  2 is red
  3 is brown (orange on some monitors)

- Palette 1 has the following colors:

  0 is the background color
  1 is cyan
  2 is magenta
  3 is bright white

Remember, these are *palette* color numbers for the foreground colors, not to be confused with the numbers that represent background colors. You pick a palette by including the palette number, 0 or 1, in a COLOR statement.

The statement

```
COLOR 0, 1
```

picks black (0) as the background color and palette 1 for the foreground colors. So the foreground colors will be 0 for black, 1 for cyan, 2 for magenta, and 3 for bright white.

The statement

```
COLOR 15, 0
```

picks bright white (15) for the background color and palette 0 for the foreground colors. The foreground colors will thus be 0 for bright white, 1 for green, 2 for red, and 3 for brown.

NOTE: In palette 0, text is printed in palette color 3, brown. In palette 1, text is printed in bright white.

A COLOR statement to select both a background color and a palette consists of the keyword COLOR, a space, a number from 0 to 15, a comma, and 0 or 1:

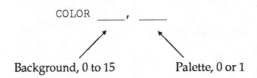

A pixel is a picture element, a tiny rectangle on the screen. Use a PSET statement to plot a pixel. PSET means *pixel set*. If you want to plot a pixel, you must tell the computer where to put it by naming the column and row. You also indicate what color you want (0, 1, 2, or 3 from a previously selected palette).

For example, the statement

```
PSET (0, 0), 1
```

tells the computer to plot a pixel at column 0, row 0 in palette color 1. In palette 0, this is green; in palette 1, it is cyan. Column 0, row 0 is the upper-left corner of the screen.

The statement

```
PSET (319, 199), 2
```

tells the computer to plot a pixel at column 319, row 199 in palette color 2. In palette 0, this is red; in palette 1, it is magenta. Column 319, row 199 is the bottom-right corner of the screen.

Clear the screen (press (CTRL)(L)); then select a black background and palette 1.

Type **COLOR 0, 1**
and press (ENTER)

Now plot a pixel near the center of the screen in palette color 1.

Type **PSET (160, 100), 1**
and press (ENTER)

You should see a tiny cyan pixel in the center of the screen, as shown in Figure 2-4. The pixel is very small, so you may have trouble discerning its shape and color. Plot another pixel in palette color 2, a little up and to the left of the pixel already on the screen.

Type **PSET (150, 90), 2**
and press (ENTER)

You now see two pixels, one cyan and the other magenta. Plot a third pixel in palette color 3, a little down and to the right of the first pixel.

Type **PSET (170, 110), 3**
and press (ENTER)

You now see the screen shown in Figure 2-5. The COLOR and PSET statements are in the upper-left part of the screen. Three pixels are shown near the center of the screen. Arrows show you which pixel is plotted by each PSET statement.

If you plot a pixel using palette color 0 (the background color), the pixel will be invisible. So why bother? Well, you can use palette

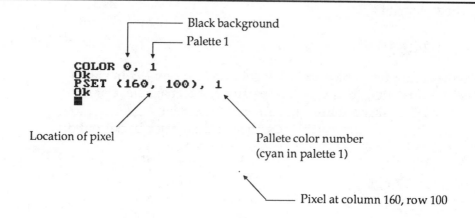

Black background

Palette 1

```
COLOR 0, 1
Ok
PSET (160, 100), 1
Ok
```

Location of pixel

Pallete color number
(cyan in palette 1)

Pixel at column 160, row 100

```
1LIST   2RUN↵   3LOAD"  4SAVE"  5CONT↵
```

FIGURE 2-4.   A plotted pixel in SCREEN 1

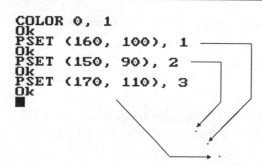

```
COLOR 0, 1
Ok
PSET (160, 100), 1
Ok
PSET (150, 90), 2
Ok
PSET (170, 110), 3
Ok
```

```
1LIST   2RUN↵   3LOAD"  4SAVE"  5CONT↵
```

FIGURE 2-5.   Three pixels in three palette 1 colors

color 0 to erase a previously plotted pixel, for example. Do it now. Erase the pixel located at column 160, row 100.

Type **PSET (160, 100), 0**
and press (ENTER)

This erases the pixel that was in the center of the screen. Go ahead and erase the other two pixels.

Type **PSET (150, 90), 0**
and press (ENTER)

Type **PSET (170, 110), 0**
and press (ENTER)

After working in SCREEN 1, you can return to SCREEN 0 by typing **SCREEN 0**. When you return to SCREEN 0, the screen will still be set to a text width of 40 characters per line. If you prefer a text width of 80 characters per line, use a WIDTH 80 statement to obtain it.

You know you can press (ALT)-(S) as a shortcut for typing the keyword SCREEN. However, there is an even faster way to return from SCREEN 1 to SCREEN 0. You can simply press the (F10) function key. Try it.

Type **SCREEN 1**   (*To go to SCREEN 1*)
and press (ENTER)

Press (F10)   (*To return to SCREEN 0*)

Exercises

1. In SCREEN 1, pixel positions are identified by a column number and a row number. A column number can be any integer from _____ to _____. A row number can be any integer from _____ to _____.

2. Select SCREEN 1 and clear it (press (CTRL)-(L)), and then do the following:

    a. Set the background to bright white (15) and select palette 0.
    b. Plot a pixel at column 160, row 100, in palette color 1.
    c. Plot a pixel at column 150, row 90, in palette color 2.
    d. Plot a pixel at column 170, row 110, in palette color 3.
    e. Plot a pixel at column 160, row 100, in palette color 0. (This should erase a previously plotted pixel.)

3. After you finish working in SCREEN 1, what is the easiest way to return to SCREEN 0?

2.11 DRAW LINES AND BOXES IN SCREEN 1

Make sure that your computer is in GW-BASIC's SCREEN 1 mode. You can use a LINE statement to draw a line from any point on the screen to any other point on the screen. Before doing so, select the background color and palette in which you want to draw lines. The author suggests a black background and palette 1.

Type **COLOR 0, 1**   (*Use* (ALT)-(C) *to type COLOR*)
and press (ENTER)

Next, clear the screen (press (CTRL)-(L)). Now draw a line from the upper-left corner of the screen (column 0, row 0) to the bottom-right corner (column 319, row 199). Use palette color 1.

Type **LINE (0, 0) – (319, 199), 1**
and press (ENTER)

Draw another line from the lower-left corner (column 0, row 199) to the upper-right corner (column 319, row 0), in palette color 2, like this:

Type **LINE (0, 199) – (319, 0), 2**
and press (ENTER)

The screen should now appear as shown in Figure 2-6.

If you wish, draw another line. You pick the starting and ending points, and the palette color number; then complete the LINE statement shown here:

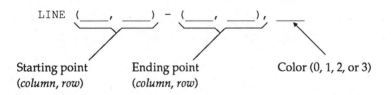

Starting point (*column, row*)   Ending point (*column, row*)   Color (0, 1, 2, or 3)

If you use a column number less than zero or greater than 319, you will see a "Syntax error" message. You will also see this message if you use a row number less than zero or greater than 199. For

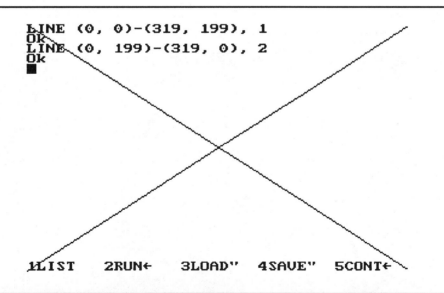

| FIGURE 2-6. | Two lines in SCREEN 1 |

example, both of the following LINE statements will cause a syntax error:

```
LINE (0, 0) - (320, 199), 1
LINE (0, 200) - (319, 0), 2
```

You can also use a LINE statement to draw a box (an open rectangle). Clear the screen and draw a box enclosing the entire SCREEN 1 pixel area.

Type **LINE (0, 0) – (319, 199), 3, B**
and press (ENTER)

The B on the right end of this LINE statement causes a box to be drawn, as shown in Figure 2-7. One corner of the box is at column 0, row 0; the opposite corner is at column 319, row 199. The box is drawn in palette color 3 (bright white) in palette 1.

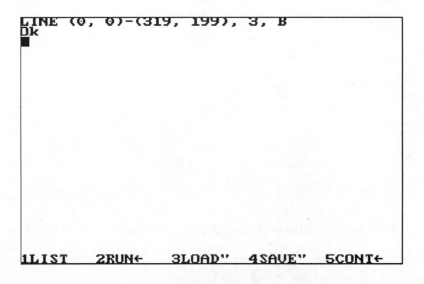

FIGURE 2-7. A box is drawn around SCREEN 1

By using *BF* instead of *B*, you can draw a box and fill it with color. Clear the screen and then draw three boxes, as follows:

Type **LINE (20, 100) – (100, 150), 1, BF**
and press (ENTER)

Type **LINE (120, 100) – (200, 150), 2, BF**
and press (ENTER)

Type **LINE (220, 100) – (300, 150), 3, BF**
and press (ENTER)

These three statements draw a row of three solid-colored boxes—a cyan box on the left, a magenta box in the middle, and a bright white box on the right, as shown in Figure 2-8.

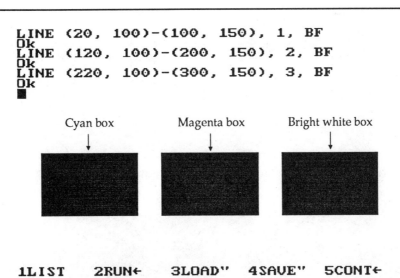

FIGURE 2-8. ▮ Three boxes filled with color

To erase a filled box, draw the same box and fill it with the background color, palette color 0. Erase the middle box now, like this:

Type **LINE (120, 100) – (200, 150), 0, BF**
and press (ENTER)

Poof! The middle box disappears. Go ahead and erase the other two boxes.

Exercises

1. Write a LINE statement to draw a horizontal line across the middle of the screen. Use palette color 1.

2. Write a LINE statement to draw a vertical line down the middle of the screen. Use color 2.

3. Clear the screen. Write LINE statements to draw three nested boxes, as shown here:

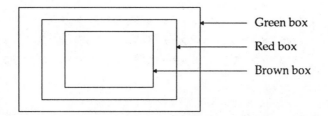

4. Clear the screen. Write three LINE statements to draw the "flag" shown here. This flag has three equal-sized, solid-color areas.

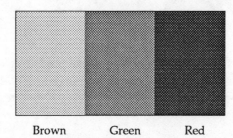

Brown   Green   Red

5. How would you erase

    a. a line from (100, 50) to (200, 75)?
    b. an open box with opposite corners at (80, 60) and (160, 120)?
    c. a filled box with opposite corners at (20, 30) and (50, 80)?

DRAW CIRCLES IN SCREEN 1   2.12

The CIRCLE statement is your tool for drawing roundish shapes (circles and ellipses) on the screen. In a CIRCLE statement, you provide the coordinates (column, row) of the center; the radius; and the color in which to draw the circle:

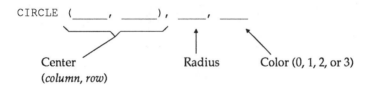

    Clear the screen. Select a background color and palette 1 for the foreground color. Draw a circle with its center at column 160, row 100, with a radius of 16, and in color 1.

Type **CIRCLE (160, 100), 16, 1**
and press (ENTER)

This circle is shown in Figure 2-9. It is 32 pixels high and 32 pixels wide.
    Draw another circle with the same center (160, 100), a radius of 24, and in palette color 2.

Type **CIRCLE (160, 100), 24, 2**
and press (ENTER)

Both circles are shown in Figure 2-10. They are *concentric circles*, both having the same center.
    To erase an existing circle, draw the same circle using the background color, palette color 0. To erase the inner circle in Figure 2-10,

```
COLOR 0, 1
Ok
CIRCLE (160, 100), 16, 1
Ok
■
```

```
1LIST    2RUN←    3LOAD"  4SAVE"  5CONT←
```

FIGURE 2-9. A circle in SCREEN 1

```
COLOR 0, 1
Ok
CIRCLE (160, 100), 16, 1
Ok
CIRCLE (160, 100), 24, 2
Ok
■
```

```
1LIST    2RUN←    3LOAD"  4SAVE"  5CONT←
```

FIGURE 2-10. Concentric circles in SCREEN 1

Type **CIRCLE (160, 100), 16, 0**
and press (ENTER)

Clear the screen. Draw a bright white circle with its center at (160, 100) and a radius of 32.

Type **CIRCLE (160, 100), 32, 3**
and press (ENTER)

You can use a PAINT statement to fill this circle with color. Fill it with magenta, as follows:

Type **PAINT (160, 100), 2, 3**
and press (ENTER)

You should now see a bright white circle filled with magenta. The bright white circle is the *boundary* of the figure. The *interior* is filled with solid magenta.
The statement

```
PAINT (160, 100), 2, 3
```

tells the computer to start at (160, 100) and paint outward in color 2 until a boundary in color 3 is encountered. This PAINT statement is of the general form shown here:

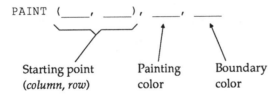

PAINT (____ , ____), ____ , ____

Starting point Painting Boundary
(*column, row*) color color

The starting point for PAINT can be any interior point of the shape being painted. The computer starts at the starting point and paints outward in the painting color until it reaches the boundary color. If you do not specify a boundary color, the computer uses the painting color as the boundary color.
Now erase the interior color (magenta), but not the bright white boundary, like this:

Type **PAINT (160, 100), 0, 3**
and press (ENTER)

This fills the interior of the circle with the background color, thus erasing the magenta that was there previously. Next, fill the interior with cyan.

Type **PAINT (160, 100), 1, 3**
and press (ENTER)

You should now see a bright white (boundary color) circle with a cyan interior.

You can erase the entire circle by using black as both the painting color and the boundary color, as follows:

Type **PAINT (160, 100), 0, 0**
and press (ENTER)

This statement tells the computer to begin at (160, 100) and paint outward in black until a black boundary is encountered. Thus, the circle's cyan interior and bright white boundary are both erased.

Exercises

1. Write CIRCLE statements and use them to draw the following set of interlocking circles on the screen.

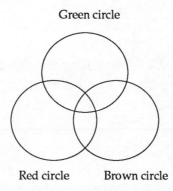

Green circle

Red circle   Brown circle

2. Use the CIRCLE and PAINT statements to draw the following "target" on the screen.

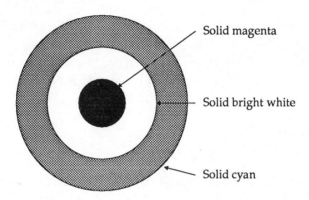

Solid magenta

Solid bright white

Solid cyan

EXERCISES

MASTERY
SKILLS
CHECK

1. Write a sequence of direct statements to

   - set the date to January 1, 1992.

   - set the time to one second after midnight.

   - print the date, time, and the message "Happy New Year!" on one screen line.

2. Write a PRINT statement to print the numbers 1, 2, 3, 4, and 5 in the five standard print positions on one line.

3. Write a PRINT statement to print the numbers 1, 22, 333, 4444, and 55555 on one line as close together as possible.

4. For each of the following PRINT statements, predict what the computer will print. Then try it on the computer.

   a. `PRINT "3 + 4 ="; 3 + 4`
   b. `PRINT "The sales tax is"; 30 * 0.06`

5. Write a SOUND statement to make a sound of frequency 800 Hz for a duration of 1/4 second.

6. Suppose the computer has just begun executing this statement:

```
SOUND 440, 65535
```

This sound will go on for an hour, unless you turn it off. How do you turn off the sound?

7. In SCREEN 1, you can choose any of 16 background colors and a palette with four foreground colors. What are the foreground colors and color numbers for:

a. palette 0?
b. palette 1?

8. Write a COLOR statement to select a green background and palette 1.

9. Write a PSET statement to plot a pixel at column 100, row 120, in palette color 2.

10. Select the background color and palette of your choice; then draw a triangle on SCREEN 1, as shown here. Use palette color 3.

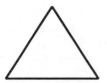

11. You have used the PAINT statement to fill the interior of a circle with color. You can also use it to fill the interior of the triangle you drew in the previous exercise. Complete the following PAINT statement to fill the interior of the triangle with the color you choose.

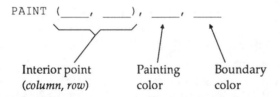

Interior point   Painting   Boundary
(*column, row*)   color   color

12. Write LINE statements to draw the following figure. Make the large box solid color 3, and the small boxes solid colors 1 and 2.

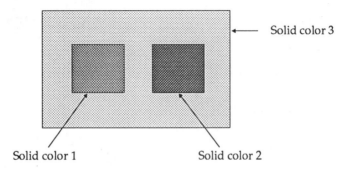

13. Write CIRCLE statements to draw the following figure. Then use PAINT statements to fill it with three colors, as shown.

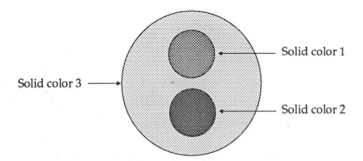

14. Describe how to erase the following:

a. Pixel located at (123, 45)
b. Line from (50, 50) to (80, 50)
c. Box with opposite corners at (160, 100) and (319, 199)
d. Unfilled circle with center at (160, 100) and radius 40
e. Filled (solid color) circle with center at (160, 100) and radius 40

15. How do you leave SCREEN 1 and return to SCREEN 0?

GW-BASIC Programs

▶3◀

CHAPTER OBJECTIVES

▶ Understand a GW-BASIC progam   3.1

▶ Fix a mistrake   3.2

▶ Enter and run a four-line program   3.3

▶ Save the program to a disk   3.4

▶ Save a program to a designated disk drive   3.5

▶ Load a program   3.6

▶ List a program on the printer   3.7

▶ Add program lines   3.8

▶ Save a program in ASCII format   3.9

▶ Try programs that go round and round   3.10

In this chapter, you will learn to understand and use simple GW-BASIC programs. A program is a set of instructions that tells the computer what to do and how to do it. You will enter a program into the computer's memory, and then tell the computer to run (execute) the entire program automatically. You will learn how to save a program to a disk and how to load a program into the computer's memory from the disk on which it has been saved.

EXERCISES

Before you start this chapter, you should know something about, or know how to do, the following things:

1. Select GW-BASIC's text screen (SCREEN 0) and the graphics screen called SCREEN 1.

2. Select foreground and background colors in SCREEN 0.

3. Select a background color and a palette of foreground colors in SCREEN 1.

4. Use the PRINT statement to print the date, the time, a string, or the value of a numerical expression.

5. Plot pixels and draw lines, boxes, and circles in SCREEN 1.

UNDERSTAND A GW-BASIC PROGRAM

3.1

A GW-BASIC program is written using the vocabulary (keywords) and syntax (rules of grammar) of GW-BASIC. The simple four-line program shown below tells the computer to beep, print the date, print the time, and print Laran Stardrake's name. The program uses these keywords introduced in Chapters 1 and 2: BEEP, PRINT, DATE$, and TIME$.

```
10 BEEP
20 PRINT DATE$
30 PRINT TIME$
40 PRINT "Laran Stardrake"
```

This program has four program lines. Each line consists of a *line number* (10, 20, 30, 40), followed by a statement (such as BEEP or PRINT DATE$):

First line:	`10 BEEP`
Second line:	`20 PRINT DATE$`
Third line:	`30 PRINT TIME$`
Fourth line:	`40 PRINT "Laran Stardrake"`

Line numbers

In Chapters 1 and 2, you used statements such as BEEP and PRINT DATE$ as direct statements. When you type a direct statement and press (ENTER), the computer executes the statement immediately.

When you type a statement with a line number, however, the statement is not executed immediately when you press (ENTER). Instead, it is stored in the computer's memory for later execution. After entering all the lines of your program, you can tell the computer to run the entire program. It will do so, unless the program contains something the computer doesn't understand. In this case, it prints an error message, and then waits for you to fix the mistake and tell it what to do next.

Exercises

1. How does a program line differ from a direct statement?

2. In the following program line, circle the line number.

```
30 PRINT TIME$
```

FIX A MISTRAKE

For this activity, use SCREEN 0 in WIDTH 80.

You will soon enter the program discussed in section 3.1. Before doing so, tell the computer you will enter a new program. Clear the screen, and then

Type **NEW**
and press (ENTER)

After you do this, the screen displays

```
NEW
Ok
—
```

The NEW statement clears (erases) the part of the computer's memory used to store a GW-BASIC program. You can verify this by telling the computer to list any program now in memory. The easiest way to do this is to press the (F1) function key, and then press the (ENTER) key.

Press (F1)
and then press (ENTER)

The computer lists any program resident in its memory, and then displays the prompt (Ok) and the cursor (_). Since there is no program in memory, your screen should look like this:

```
LIST            (Since no program resides in memory,
Ok              nothing is listed between LIST and Ok.)
—
```

REMEMBER: To list the program in the computer's memory, press (F1), and then (ENTER). From now on, this sequence of two keystrokes will be abbreviated as shown here:

Press (F1), (ENTER)

Now clear the screen and enter the first line of the program into the computer's memory.

Type **10 BEEP**
and press (ENTER)

The screen looks like this:

```
10 BEEP
_
```

Notice that you do not hear a beep. The line number (10) tells GW-BASIC that this is a program line, not a direct statement. There is now a one-line program in the computer's memory. Verify this by telling the computer to list the program.

Press (F1), (ENTER)

The computer lists the one-line program this way:

```
LIST              (The one-line program is listed
10 BEEP           between LIST and Ok.)
Ok
_
```

If your screen matches what is shown above, your program is correct and you can now run it. The easiest way to do this is to press (F2). The computer will print the word RUN on the screen and immediately execute the program.

Press (F2)

Of course, this one-line program doesn't do much. It just tells the computer to beep. You will hear the beep immediately after you press (F2).

This BEEP program works if there is no error in the program. But errors do happen. That's all right. GW-BASIC has several ways to help you find and fix errors.

Clear the screen, and then enter the following line 10, which contains an error. (The keyword BEEP is intentionally misspelled as BOOP.) When you enter this line, it will replace the line 10 currently in memory.

Type **10 BOOP**
and press (ENTER)

Verify that the above line 10 is now in memory. List the program (press (F1), (ENTER)). You will then see the following:

```
LIST
10 BOOP
Ok
_
```

Now run the program (press (F2)). Instead of hearing a beep, you will see a syntax error message, as shown here:

```
RUN
Syntax error in 10
Ok
10 BOOP_
```

The computer tells you there is a syntax error in line 10, and then displays line 10 with the cursor blinking to the right of the word it did not understand (BOOP).
    You can easily correct the error, as shown here:

Do This   **See This**
1. Press (BACKSPACE) three times   10 B_
2. Type **EEP**   10 BEEP_
3. Press (ENTER)   10 BEEP
                                         _

That's one way. Here's another way, beginning from the error as originally shown (10 BOOP_). Use the arrow keys to move the cursor.

Do This	See This
1. Move cursor to first O	10 B<u>O</u>OP
2. Type **EE**	10 BEE<u>P</u>
3. Press (ENTER)	10 BEEP —

After making a correction, list the program to make sure it is all right. Then run it.

REMEMBER: To list a program, press (F1), (ENTER); to run a program, press (F2).

Exercises

1. Before entering a GW-BASIC program, you should usually type **NEW** and press (ENTER). Why?

2. What happens when you type a line that begins with a line number, and then press (ENTER)?

3. How do you tell the computer to display on the screen a listing of a program stored in its memory?

4. How do you run a program?

5. Suppose line 10 is stored incorrectly, as follows. How do you fix it?

    ```
    10 BEAP
    ```

3.3 ENTER AND RUN A FOUR-LINE PROGRAM

Here again is the four-line program you saw in Section 3.1:

```
10 BEEP
20 PRINT DATE$
30 PRINT TIME$
40 PRINT "Laran Stardrake"
```

Clear the screen and enter this program, as follows:

Type **NEW**
and press (ENTER)

Type **10 BEEP**
and press (ENTER)

Type **20 PRINT DATE$**
and press (ENTER)

Type **30 PRINT TIME$**
and press (ENTER)

Type **40 PRINT "Laran Stardrake"**
and press (ENTER)

If you entered all four lines of the program without a typing mistake, the screen now displays

```
NEW
10 BEEP
20 PRINT DATE$
30 PRINT TIME$
40 PRINT "Laran Stardrake"
—
```

If you see a mistake, however, use the arrow keys to position the cursor, fix the mistake, and press the (ENTER) key. When you press (ENTER), the corrected line is stored in memory, replacing the previously stored incorrect line. When you are satisfied that everything is all right, clear the screen and list the program.

You can also correct a program line by simply retyping it, including its line number. The new line you type replaces the old one in the computer's memory.

Suppose you mistyped a line number. For example, it is easy to type a 9 instead of a 0. Here line 20 is mistyped as line 29:

```
29 PRINT DATE$
```

When you correct the mistake by either of the two ways previously described and then list the program, you will see something like this:

```
LIST
10 BEEP
20 PRINT DATE$
29 PRINT DATE$
30 PRINT TIME$
40 PRINT "Laran Stardrake"
```

Now there are two PRINT DATE$ statements, in lines 20 and 29. You can erase line 29 by typing only the line number and pressing (ENTER).

Type **29**
and press (ENTER)

Line 29 is now deleted. (If there were no line 29, you would see an "Undefined line number" error message.) As usual, list the program to see what it now looks like.

REMEMBER: To delete a program line already stored in memory, type only its line number and press (ENTER).

Clear the screen and run the program (press (F2)). If all goes well, you will hear a beep and see information on the screen similar to the following:

```
RUN
01-01-1991
07:37:28
Laran Stardrake
```

If the program did not run properly, list it and fix any errors, as you have learned how to do in this chapter. Remember that you can correct or change a line by simply retyping the line.

Exercises

1. How do you enter a program into the computer's memory?
2. Describe two ways to run a program.

3. Suppose a program contains a misspelled keyword. What will probably happen when you run the program?

4. Suppose the program is correct except for one little thing: Laran's name is misspelled as "Loren Stardrake." What will happen when you run the program?

SAVE THE PROGRAM TO A DISK

You have now entered a short GW-BASIC program into the computer's memory, listed the program, and run it. If you save the program to a disk, you can load it back into memory whenever you wish. Let's save the program now to a disk in drive A or, if you prefer, to a disk in another drive.

To save a program, you must first give it a name, called a *filename*. A filename can have up to eight characters (letters and numbers). The first character must be a letter. Name this program LARAN01.

Now save the program to the default drive, using the filename LARAN01. To do this, use the keyword SAVE in a direct statement. You can do this the long way or the short way; look at both ways before deciding how you want to save your program. First, here is the long way:

Type **SAVE"LARAN01"**
and press (ENTER)

You have probably guessed that the short way involves a function key. You can use the (F4) function key to type the keyword SAVE and a quotation mark.

Press (F4)

The keyword SAVE, a quotation mark ("), and the cursor appear on the screen:

```
SAVE"_
```

You complete the SAVE statement by supplying the filename, LARAN01, and a quotation mark, like this:

Type **LARAN01"**
and press (ENTER)

The completed SAVE statement should appear as shown here:

```
SAVE"LARAN01"
```

You may type the filename in lowercase or a mixture of upper- and lowercase. GW-BASIC recognizes LARAN01, laran01, or Laran01 as the same filename. Also, you may omit the closing quotation mark (") at the right side of LARAN01.

You can use either the long way or the short way to save the program to your default drive. GW-BASIC will add a *filename extension* (.BAS) to the filename. Thus, the program is actually stored as LARAN01.BAS. The filename extension .BAS identifies a file as a BASIC program.

Is the program really stored on the disk in the default drive? Use the keyword FILES as a direct statement to find out what is on the disk.

Type **FILES**
and press (ENTER)

The computer displays the names of all files on the disk in the default drive (assumed to be drive A). For example, the author's disk now contains the following files:

```
FILES
A:\
COMMAND .COM     GWBASIC .EXE     LARAN01 .BAS
```

If the disk in the default drive contains many files, you may wish to list the names of only the BASIC programs—the files with a .BAS filename extension. To do this, use the following FILES statement:

```
FILES "*.BAS"
```

This FILES statement tells the computer to list the names of all files that have the extension .BAS. The asterisk (*) is called a *wildcard*. It can be used in certain DOS commands, as well as in GW-BASIC. Consult your DOS Reference Manual for more information on the use of the asterisk as a wildcard.

Exercises

1. Change the program used in this section so that it prints your name instead of Laran's name. How do you save the program to the default disk drive under the filename MYNAME.BAS?

2. Write a FILES statement to list the names of all files on the default drive that have the filename extension .BAS.

SAVE A PROGRAM TO A DESIGNATED DISK DRIVE

3.5

You can save a program to any disk drive by designating the drive in the SAVE statement. For example, to save Program LARAN01 to a disk in drive B,

Type **SAVE"B:LARAN01"**
and press (ENTER)

where B is the disk drive designation.

Be sure to include a colon (:) between the drive designation (B) and the name of the program (LARAN01). The program is saved to drive B with the filename LARAN01.BAS.

You can list the names of the files on any disk drive by using a FILES statement with a drive designation. For example, suppose you want to see the names of all files on drive B.

Type **FILES "B:"**
and press (ENTER)

Remember to enclose the drive designation (B:) in quotation marks. If you want to list only the names of BASIC programs with a .BAS extension,

Type **FILES "B:*.BAS"**
and press (ENTER)

The wildcard (*) and .BAS extension following the drive designation (B:) tell the computer to list only files on drive B that have the .BAS extension.

Exercises

1. Suppose that you are working out of a hard disk drive. Your default drive is drive C. How do you save a program called MYNAME to the disk in drive A?

2. Assume that your default drive is drive C. Write a FILES statement to display a list of all files on the disk in drive A that end in the filename extension .BAS.

3.6 | LOAD A PROGRAM

To load a program stored on a disk into the computer's memory, use the keyword LOAD in a direct statement. For example, suppose you want to load Program LARAN01 from the default disk drive. Do it the short way. Use the (F3) function key as a shortcut for typing LOAD".

Press (F3)

The keyword LOAD, a quotation mark, and the cursor appear on the screen, as shown here:

```
LOAD"_
```

Type **LARAN01"**
and press (ENTER)

List the program (press (F1), (ENTER)). The screen displays:

```
LOAD"LARAN01"
Ok
LIST
10 BEEP
20 PRINT DATE$
30 PRINT TIME$
40 PRINT "Laran Stardrake"
```

The program is in memory, ready for your use. Note that you do not have to type the extension (.BAS) as part of the filename, although it is all right to do so. A space between LOAD and the first quotation mark (") is optional. You may omit the final quotation mark (after the filename).

You can load a program from any disk drive by designating that drive in the LOAD statement. For example, to load Program LARAN01 from drive B,

Type **LOAD"B:LARAN01"**
and press (ENTER)

where B is the drive designation.

Exercises

1. Write a LOAD statement to load a program called MYNAME.BAS from the default disk drive.

2. Write a LOAD statement to load a program called MYNAME.BAS from drive B.

3.7 | LIST A PROGRAM ON THE PRINTER

If you have a printer, you can list a program on the printer. To do so, use the keyword LLIST as a direct statement. An LLIST statement tells the computer to list on the printer the program in memory. One way to do it is shown below. (Remember, there are two Ls in LLIST.)

Type **LLIST**
and press (ENTER)

Here is another way, using the handy (F1) function key to type LIST:

Type **L**
Press (F1), (ENTER)

REMEMBER: To list a program on the screen, use LIST; to list a program on the printer, use LLIST.

Exercises

1. Describe the long way to list a program on the printer.

2. For the short way to list a program on the printer, you need press only three keys (fill in the blanks):

   Type _____ and press _____ , _____

3.8 | ADD PROGRAM LINES

Perhaps you wonder why the lines in Program LARAN01 are numbered 10, 20, 30, 40 instead of 1, 2, 3, 4. The program could have been written as shown here:

```
1 BEEP
2 PRINT DATE$
3 PRINT TIME$
4 PRINT "Laran Stardrake"
```

However, it is better to space the line numbers as shown here:

```
10 BEEP
20 PRINT DATE$
30 PRINT TIME$
40 PRINT "Laran Stardrake"
```

This line number spacing (10, 20, 30, 40) provides room for inserting additional lines. For example, between lines 10 and 20, you can insert up to nine lines (lines 11, 12, 13, 14, 15, 16, 17, 18, and 19). To insert a line between two existing lines, simply type it with a line number that is between the two existing line numbers.

Do this now. Insert a CLS statement between lines 10 and 20 of the LARAN01 program. Use line number 15, which is halfway between line 10 and line 20.

Type **15 CLS**
and press (ENTER)

Now list the program again. You will see line 15 in its proper place between lines 10 and 20, as shown here:

```
LIST
10 BEEP
15 CLS  ←——————— Line 15
20 PRINT DATE$
30 PRINT TIME$
40 PRINT "Laran Stardrake"
```

When you run the program, it causes the computer to beep (line 10), clear the screen (line 15), and then print the date, time, and Laran's name (lines 20, 30, and 40). Run the program now; press (F2).

In the top part of the screen, you see the information printed by the program, as shown here:

```
01-01-1991
08:02:37
Laran Stardrake
```

Now add another line to the program. Make it line 50 so it will be added to the bottom of the program, after the current line 40. As usual, first clear the screen, and then type the line to be added.

Type **50 PRINT "Happy New Year!"**
and press (ENTER)

List the program. You should see line 50 in its proper place, as shown here:

```
LIST
10 BEEP
15 CLS
20 PRINT DATE$
30 PRINT TIME$
40 PRINT "Laran Stardrake"
50 PRINT "Happy New Year!"
```

REMEMBER: To *insert* a line into a program, use a line number between two existing line numbers. To *append* a line to the end of a program, use a line number greater than the highest line number in the program. To *append* a line at the beginning of a program (as the first line), use a line number less than the lowest line number in the program. To *replace* a line in the program, type a new line with the same line number as the line you want to replace.

Exercises

1. How do you insert a new program line between two existing program lines?

2. How do you insert a program line so that it becomes the first line in the program? The last line?

SAVE A PROGRAM IN ASCII FORMAT

Earlier, you saved Program LARAN01 to a disk. It is saved in *compressed binary format*. This format is very efficient, using a minimum amount of space on the disk.

You can also save a program in BASIC as an ASCII file. This method is less efficient; the program occupies more room on the disk. There is an advantage, however: the program can be read by a word processor. Also, you can use the DOS TYPE command to display an ASCII program on the screen.

To store the current program as Program LARAN02 in ASCII format,

Type **SAVE"LARAN02", A**
and press (ENTER)

The letter A tells the computer to save the program as an ASCII file:

```
SAVE"LARAN02", A
```

────── Save as an ASCII file

Use a FILES statement to verify that Program LARAN02 is on the disk.

Type **FILES**
and press (ENTER)

The result of your FILES statement will be similar to the following:

```
FILES
A:\
COMMAND .COM    GWBASIC .EXE    LARAN01 .BAS    LARAN02 .BAS
```

The filename, LARAN02.BAS, does not tell you that this is an ASCII file. This presents no problem to GW-BASIC. You can load an ASCII program into memory the same way you load a program stored in compressed binary format. Just type **LOAD"LARAN02"** and press (ENTER).

You can also store Program LARAN02 as an ASCII file with a filename extension that tells you it is an ASCII file. For example, you can use .ASC as an explicit filename extension. Do so now.

Press (F4)   (*To type SAVE"*)

Type **LARAN02.ASC", A**
and press (ENTER)

Program LARAN02 is now saved under two filenames, LARAN02.BAS and LARAN02.ASC. Use a FILES statement to verify this.

Type **FILES**
and press (ENTER)

The list of filenames now includes LARAN02.ASC:

```
FILES
A:\
COMMAND.COM      GWBASIC.EXE      LARAN01.BAS      LARAN02.BAS
LARAN02.ASC
```

When you load a program that has a .BAS extension, you may omit the extension in typing the filename. However, to load a program whose extension is not .BAS, you must include the filename extension in the LOAD statement. For example,

Press (F3)   (*To type LOAD"*)

Type **LARAN02.ASC**   (*Ok to omit closing quotation mark*)
and press (ENTER)

Now list the program (press (F1), (ENTER)). The author's version looks like this:

```
LIST
10 BEEP
15 CLS
20 PRINT DATE$
30 PRINT TIME$
40 PRINT "Laran Stardrake"
50 PRINT "Happy New Year!"
```

If you run this program on New Year's Day, the message printed by line 50 is appropriate. However, on any other day of the year the message is not appropriate. Go ahead and delete line 50, or change it to another message you want to print. Remember, though, that your change does not delete line 50 in the program as it is stored on the disk. After making your changes, save your final version to the disk.

NOTE: Unless stated otherwise, all programs in this book are saved as ASCII files. The author has prepared a Convenience Disk that contains all the programs and other files described in this book, plus additional files of related interest. Using the Convenience Disk saves you the time required to enter programs, and lets you move through the tutorials more rapidly. For information about obtaining the Convenience Disk, see the disk order form included in the "Introduction" section of this book.

Exercises

1. Suppose you have written a program that prints a birthday message on the screen and also plays the birthday song. Call this program BIRTHDAY. How do you save it as

   a. a compressed binary file with a .BAS extension?

   b. an ASCII file with a .BAS extension?

   c. an ASCII file with an .ASC extension?

2. How do you load the program if it is saved with

   a. a .BAS file extension?

   b. an .ASC file extension?

3.10 TRY PROGRAMS THAT GO ROUND AND ROUND

In Chapter 1 you saw some very short programs that produced a lot of action on the screen. A modified version of one of those programs is shown below. Erase the program now in memory, and enter the one shown here:

```
10 COLOR 7, 0: CLS
20 COLOR 16 * RND
30 PRINT "Rory ";
40 GOTO 20
```

This is a "never-ending" program. It goes round and round, printing Rory's name in many colors, until you press (CTRL)-(BREAK) to stop the action.

Run the program: Press (F2)

Stop the program: Press (CTRL)-(BREAK)

When you stop the program, the screen will be similar to Figure 3-1. Rory's name appears in random foreground colors, including black (invisible on the black background). It is possible that the program may stop with the foreground color set to black. In this case, the message "Break in 30" will be invisible. If this happens, set the foreground color to white.

Press (ALT)-(C)   *(To type COLOR)*

Type **7**
and press (ENTER)

This program introduces a new keyword, GOTO, and a program *control structure* called a GOTO loop.
The program line

```
40 GOTO 20
```

```
Rory Rory        Rory Rory Rory Rory Rory Rory Rory Rory Rory Rory Rory Rory Rory
Rory        Rory Rory Rory Rory Rory Rory Rory Rory Rory Rory Rory Rory Rory Rory
Rory Rory Rory Rory Rory Rory Rory Rory        Rory Rory Rory Rory Rory Rory Rory
Rory Rory Rory Rory Rory Rory Rory Rory Rory Rory Rory        Rory Rory Rory
Rory Rory Rory Rory Rory Rory Rory Rory Rory Rory        Rory Rory Rory        Rory
Rory Rory Rory Rory Rory Rory Rory Rory Rory Rory Rory Rory Rory Rory Rory Rory
Rory Rory        Rory Rory Rory Rory Rory        Rory Rory Rory Rory Rory Rory Rory
Rory Rory Rory Rory Rory        Rory Rory Rory Rory Rory Rory Rory Rory Rory Rory
Rory Rory Rory Rory Rory Rory Rory Rory        Rory Rory Rory Rory Rory Rory Rory
Rory Rory Rory Rory Rory Rory Rory Rory Rory Rory Rory Rory Rory Rory Rory Rory
Rory Rory        Rory Rory Rory Rory Rory Rory Rory Rory Rory Rory Rory Rory Rory
Rory Rory Rory Rory Rory Rory Rory Rory Rory Rory Rory Rory Rory        Rory Rory
Rory Rory Rory Rory Rory Rory Rory Rory Rory Rory Rory Rory Rory Rory Rory Rory
Rory Rory Rory Rory Rory Rory Rory Rory Rory Rory Rory Rory Rory Rory Rory Rory
     Rory Rory Rory Rory Rory Rory Rory Rory Rory Rory Rory Rory Rory        Rory
Rory Rory Rory Rory Rory Rory        Rory Rory Rory Rory Rory Rory Rory Rory Rory
Rory Rory Rory Rory Rory Rory Rory        Rory Rory Rory Rory Rory Rory Rory Rory
Rory        Rory Rory Rory Rory Rory Rory Rory Rory Rory Rory Rory Rory Rory
Rory Rory Rory Rory Rory Rory Rory Rory Rory Rory Rory Rory Rory Rory Rory Rory
Rory Rory Rory Rory Rory Rory Rory Rory Rory Rory Rory Rory Rory Rory Rory Rory
Rory Rory Rory Rory Rory Rory Rory Rory Rory        Rory
Break in 30
Ok
_
1LIST  2RUN←  3LOAD"  4SAVE"  5CONT←  6,"LPT1 7TRON←  8TROFF← 9KEY    10SCREE
```

FIGURE 3-1.   Rory's name is printed in randomly selected colors

tells the computer to go to line 20 and continue from there. When you run the program, it begins with line 10, then goes to line 20, then to line 30, and then to line 40. Line 40 tells the computer to go to line 20 and continue. This continuing process is illustrated in Figure 3-2. Lines 20, 30, and 40 are in a GOTO loop. The computer goes around and around in this loop until you press (CTRL)(BREAK) to stop it.

Line 20 selects a random foreground color by using GW-BASIC's RND keyword. You will learn more about RND in the next section.

Now add some sound to the program. Add line 35, as follows:

Type **35 SOUND 4000 * RND + 37, 1**
and press (ENTER)

List the modified program. Look for line 35 in its proper place between lines 30 and 40, as shown next.

```
LIST
10 COLOR 7, 0: CLS
20 COLOR 16 * RND
30 PRINT "Rory ";
35 SOUND 4000 * RND + 37, 1
40 GOTO 20
```

Run the program. You will see Rory's name printed in random colors, accompanied by random "music." Enjoy, and then stop the program and return the foreground color to white or to a color of your choice.

The program line

```
35 SOUND 4000 * RND + 37, 1
```

tells the computer to make a sound with a random frequency in the range 37 to 4037, for a duration of one tick. (You will learn how to use the RND keyword in the next section.)

3.11 USE RND TO MAKE RANDOM NUMBERS

In the programs that print Rory's name, GW-BASIC's RND keyword is used in program lines to select random foreground colors and

```
RUN
 ↓
10 COLOR 7, 0: CLS
 ↓
20 COLOR 16 * RND ←──────┐
 ↓                       │
30 PRINT "RORY ";        │
 ↓                       │
40 GOTO 20 ──────────────┘
```

FIGURE 3-2. Lines 20, 30, and 40 comprise a GOTO loop

random sound frequencies. The program lines in which RND appears are shown here:

```
20 COLOR 16 * RND
35 SOUND 4000 * RND + 37, 1
```

RND is a GW-BASIC *function*. A function is a keyword that, when used, returns a *value;* this value is the result computed by the function. RND is a *numeric function*. Its value is a *random number* between 0 and 1. The numbers generated by the RND function are not truly random, however, as are numbers obtained, for example, by rolling dice. Rather, RND generates *pseudorandom numbers*.

To see the difference between truly random and pseudorandom numbers, run the following short program at least twice:

```
10 CLS
20 PRINT RND, RND, RND, RND
```

Two runs are shown here. Note that both runs produced the same set of numbers. First run:

```
.1213501     .651861     .8688611     .7297625
```

Second run:

```
.1213501     .651861     .8688611     .7927625
```

RND generates the same sequence of four numbers each time you run the program. These numbers are pseudorandom; if RND generated truly random numbers, the numbers produced would be unpredictable.

You can avoid this replication of so-called random numbers by using the RANDOMIZE statement with the TIMER function, as shown in this program:

```
10 RANDOMIZE TIMER
20 CLS
30 PRINT RND, RND, RND, RND
```

The program line

```
10 RANDOMIZE TIMER
```

tells the computer to start the random number generator in a place that depends on the value of the TIMER function. TIMER is a numeric function. This function returns the number of elapsed seconds since midnight, according to the computer's clock. At midnight, the value of TIMER is zero (0). At high noon, the value of TIMER is 43200. At one second before midnight, the value of TIMER is 86399.

Two runs of this program are shown next. Notice that these two runs produced different sets of random numbers. First run:

```
.6274775      .4732618      .3228105      .8009587
```

Next run:

```
.3198908      .9272718      .3670305      .4495488
```

The RND function generates a random number between 0 and 1, but never 0 or 1. That is, RND generates a random number greater than 0 and less than 1. Thus:

0 < RND < 1

To obtain random numbers in another range of values, just multiply RND by an appropriate number. For example, 10 * RND is a random number between 0 and 10, but never 0 or 10. That is, 10 * RND is a random number greater than 0 and less than 10. So:

0 < 10 * RND < 10

The program line

```
20 COLOR 16 * RND
```

first generates a random number (16 * RND) between 0 and 16, but not 0 or 16. However, color numbers must be integers, so the random number is rounded to the nearest integer. After rounding, a value of 0 or 16 is possible. A value of 0 gives a foreground color of black; a value of 16 gives a foreground color of blinking black. Black and blinking black are both invisible on the black background.

The program line

```
35 SOUND 4000 * RND + 37, 1
```

generates a random frequency between 37 and 4037. The number 37 is the lowest valid frequency for the SOUND statement; 4037 was chosen arbitrarily. The result of 4000 * RND is a random number between 0 and 4000. Add 37 to get a random number between 37 and 4037. Thus:

```
0 < 4000 * RND < 4000
37 < 4000 * RND + 37 < 4037
```

These frequency values may be integer or noninteger.

Exercises

1. RND is a GW-BASIC _____. Its value is a _____

    _____ between _____ and _____.

2. The value of 16 * RND is a random number between _____ and

    _____.

ENJOY A VISIT FROM ZAPPY ARTIST

3.12

While this book was being written, Zappy Artist stopped by. Zappy likes to zap around the screen, plotting random pixels and drawing random lines, boxes, and circles. Zappy spent an hour or so humming to himself and entering programs. Then, "Gotta go," said Zappy. Without further ado, he handed the author a disk and left, promising to return soon and explain how his programs work.

One of Zappy's programs is shown below. Although he uses SCREEN 1, you can enter it from SCREEN 0. Save it as ZAPPY01.

```
10 SCREEN 1: CLS
20 RANDOMIZE TIMER
30 COLOR 0, 1
40 PSET (319 * RND, 199 * RND), 3 * RND
50 SOUND 3000 * RND + 1000, 9
60 GOTO 40
```

Run Program ZAPPY01. You will see a cyan, magenta, or white pixel appear in a random place on the screen about every half second. Each pixel is accompanied by a sound of random frequency between 1000 and 4000 Hz.

Line 10 selects SCREEN 1 and clears the screen. Line 20 "scrambles" the RND function so that you will see a different arrangement of pixels each time you run the program. Line 30 selects black (0) as the background color, and palette 1 for the foreground colors.

The pixels are plotted by the GOTO loop in lines 40, 50, and 60. This loop operates as shown here:

```
40 PSET (319 * RND, 199 * RND), 3 * RND  ◄─────┐
   │                                           │
   ▼                                           │
50 SOUND 3000 * RND + 1000, 9                  │
   │                                           │
   ▼                                           │
60 GOTO 40  ───────────────────────────────────┘
```

The program line

```
40 PSET (319 * RND, 199 * RND), 3 * RND
```

plots a pixel at a random column (319 * RND) and random row (199 * RND), in a random color (3 * RND) chosen from palette 1, previously selected in line 30.

After stopping the program, you can return to SCREEN 0.

Press (F10)

SCREEN 0 will be in WIDTH 40. Change it to WIDTH 80 the easy way.

Press (ALT)-(W)   (*To type WIDTH*)

Type **80**
and press (ENTER)

Exercises

1. When using program ZAPPY01, can a pixel appear anywhere on SCREEN 1?
2. Modify Program ZAPPY01, as follows:
   a. Use a bright white background and palette 0.
   b. Plot pixels in only the top-left quarter of SCREEN 1.
   c. Use a duration of 0.25 tick in the SOUND statement.

   Save this program as ZAPPY02.

EXERCISES

MASTERY
SKILLS
CHECK

Congratulations! You have completed another chapter. Now test yourself to renew your knowledge of what you learned in this chapter.

1. A program consists of one or more program lines. What is a program line?
2. Describe the result of using each of the following direct statements:
   a. NEW
   b. LIST
   c. LLIST
   d. RUN
3. For each of these GW-BASIC keywords, show a shortcut way to type it, using only one or two keys.
   a. COLOR
   b. GOTO
   c. LIST
   d. LLIST
   e. LOAD
   f. PRINT

g. RUN

h. SAVE

i. SCREEN

j. WIDTH

4. Draw arrows to show the path the computer follows in executing this program.

```
RUN
10 COLOR 15 * RND, 7 * RND
20 PRINT "Rory ";
30 GOTO 10
```

5. How do you save a program as an ASCII file?

6. If you play a musical instrument, you know about scales. You may have spent many joyful (?) hours practicing scales on a piano, guitar, flute, or other instrument. And, if you saw *The Sound of Music*, you know that it all begins with DO, RE, MI! Here are the frequencies for one octave of notes in the scale of C.

DO	RE	MI	FA	SOL	LA	TI	DO
262	294	330	349	392	440	494	523

Write a program to play the scale of C from frequency 262 to frequency 523, and then stop.

7. Write a program to play the scale of C repeatedly, until someone presses (CTRL)-(BREAK). Play each note while displaying an empty screen in a different background color, as follows:

Note	Background Color	Color Number
DO	Blue	1
RE	Green	2
MI	Cyan	3
FA	Red	4
SOL	Magenta	5
LA	Brown	6
TI	White	7
DO	Blue	1

Save this program as SOUND01.

8. How do you obtain a list of names of files stored on a disk, while still in GW-BASIC?

9. How do you load a GW-BASIC program from a disk into the computer's memory?

10. How do you insert a program line in a program so that it is:

    a. the first program line in the program?

    b. the last program line in the program?

    c. between existing program lines 20 and 30?

11. How do you delete line 15 from a program?

12. Complete the following:

    a. The value of RND is a random number between _____ and _____.

    b. The value of 10 * RND is a random number between _____ and _____.

    c. The value of 261 * RND + 262 is a random number between _____ and _____.

13. Write a program to plot pixels in random places in the center part of the screen, between columns 80 and 239, and rows 50 and 149. Use palette 1 on a black background.

Number Crunching

▶4◀

CHAPTER OBJECTIVES

- ▶ Do arithmetic with direct statements   4.1
- ▶ Compute the integer quotient and remainder   4.2
- ▶ Calculate powers of numbers   4.3
- ▶ Understand floating point numbers   4.4
- ▶ Define types of numbers   4.5
- ▶ Understand numeric variables   4.6
- ▶ Use variables in programming   4.7

In this chapter, you will learn how to use the computer to do calculations. You will use direct statements for simple calculations, and programs for more complex number crunching. You will use the arithmetic operation symbols (+, −, *, /), and the exponentiation symbol (^).

You will also learn about GW-BASIC *variables* and various ways to assign or acquire values of variables. You will use variables in direct statements and in programs.

SKILLS
CHECK

EXERCISES

Before beginning this chapter, you should know something about, or know how to do, the following things:

1. Use direct statements to print the date, the time, the results of numerical calculations, and strings.

2. Use direct statements to set the date and time.

3. Enter, list, and run a program.

4. Save a program to a disk.

5. Load a program from a disk.

4.1 | DO ARITHMETIC WITH DIRECT STATEMENTS

In Chapter 2 you learned how to use your computer as a calculator. You used the arithmetic operation symbols +, −, *, and / to specify the operations of addition, subtraction, multiplication, and division.

To tell the computer to do arithmetic, use a direct PRINT statement consisting of the keyword PRINT followed by a numerical expression (such as 3 + 4, or 3 − 4). The computer evaluates the numeric expression (does the arithmetic), and then prints the result. For example, tell the computer to add the numbers 3 and 4, and then print the result.

Type **PRINT 3 + 4**
and press (ENTER)

The computer prints

```
7
```

Now try the following examples. Press (ENTER) after typing a direct PRINT statement. Remember, you can press (ALT)(P) to type PRINT followed by a space.

Examples

1. Mariko is 63 inches tall. Convert her height to centimeters. One inch equals 2.54 centimeters.

```
PRINT 63 * 2.54
 160.02
```

2. An ancient ruler named Zalabar measured 100 centimeters from the tip of his nose to the end of his outstretched arm. How long is that in inches?

```
PRINT 100 / 2.54
 39.37008
```

Does that number look familiar? Perhaps you recall that 100 centimeters equals one meter. One meter equals 39.37008 inches, a little more than one yard.

3. People ususlly give their height in feet and inches. If you ask Mariko how tall she is, she will probably tell you she is 5 feet, 3 inches tall. It is easy to write a PRINT statement to convert feet and inches to inches.

```
PRINT 5 * 12 + 3
 63
```

The computer first does the multiplication (5 times 12), and then the addition (plus 3). In evaluating an expression, the computer does multiplications and divisions first, and then additions and subtractions.

4. Almost everyone gets a monthly bill from a utility company. Gas is measured in therms, and electricity in kilowatt-hours. Suppose gas is charged at the rate of $0.44826 per therm for the first 84 therms, and $0.84849 per therm for additional therms. Compute the amount paid for 97 therms of gas (84 therms at the lower rate, plus 13 therms at the higher rate).

```
PRINT 84 * .44826 + 13 * .84849
 48.68421
```

In evaluating this expression, the computer first does both multiplications, and then adds the two results to get the final result. Rounded to the nearest penny, the result is $48.68.

5. Before he reached his full stature, King Kong was once 37 feet, 8 inches tall. How tall was he in meters?

```
PRINT (37 * 12 + 8) * 2.54 / 100
 11.4808
```

Note the use of parentheses. The computer does the arithmetic inside the parentheses first, then multiplies that result by 2.54, and then divides by 100.

6. At the beginning of an auto trip, the odometer showed 41,832 miles. At the end of the trip it read 42,219 miles. The car used 9.3 gallons of gas. How many miles per gallon did the car get on the trip?

```
PRINT (42219 - 41832) / 9.3
 41.6129
```

7. Suppose your favorite team has won 38 and lost 24 games. You can compute its win percentage like this:

```
PRINT 38 / (38 + 24)
 .6129033
```

The computer first does the arithmetic inside the parentheses, adding 38 and 24 to obtain 62. It then divides 38 by this result. Newspapers usually round a team's percentage to three places after the decimal point, so this result would be reported as .613. Your team is doing very well!

Exercises

1. Write a direct PRINT statement to compute and display the answer for each of the following:

   a. The sum of 19.95, 6.59, and 2.50.

   b. Your checkbook balance is $123.45. What is the balance after subtracting checks in the amounts of $24.95 and $12.23?

   c. Convert 53 kilograms to pounds (1 kilogram = 2.2 pounds).

   d. Convert 1000 kilometers to miles (1 mile = 1.609344 kilometers).

   e. Compute the number of ounces in 23 pounds, 14 ounces.

   f. Compute the number of seconds in 12 hours, 36 minutes, and 47 seconds.

   g. Compute the cost of electricity: 846 kwh at $0.08882 per kwh, plus 589 kwh at $0.13524 per kwh.

2. Write a direct PRINT statement to compute and display the answer for each of the following. Use parentheses where appropriate.

   a. Convert 23 pounds, 14 ounces to grams (1 ounce = 28.3495 grams).

   b. In his first three games, Christopher scored 19, 17, and 24 points. What is his average number of points per game?

4.2 COMPUTE THE INTEGER QUOTIENT AND REMAINDER

Some applications require the use of *integer division* that computes an integer quotient and an integer remainder. For example, suppose you want to convert 73 ounces to pounds and ounces. With paper and pencil, you could do it like this:

$$
\begin{array}{r}
4 \longleftarrow \text{Integer quotient (number of pounds)} \\
16 \overline{\smash{)}\,73} \\
64 \\
\hline
9 \longleftarrow \text{Integer remainder (number of ounces)}
\end{array}
$$

GW-BASIC provides two operations you can use for this type of calculation. Use the backslash (\) to obtain the integer quotient, and the MOD operation to obtain the integer remainder. The MOD operation is also known as *modulus arithmetic*.

Integer quotient: 73 \ 16

Integer remainder: 73 MOD 16

Use a direct PRINT statement to compute and display the integer quotient and remainder on dividing 73 by 16, as shown here:

```
PRINT 73 \ 16, 73 MOD 16
 4              9
```

In this example, the numbers 73 and 16 are integers. Operands such as these, used in integer division and integer remainder operations, must be integers in the range -32768 to 32767. Numbers outside this range cause an error message to be printed, as shown here:

```
PRINT 33000 \ 16
Overflow
Ok
```

```
PRINT 33000 MOD 16
Overflow
```

If an operand is within the range –32768 to 32767, but is not an integer, it is rounded to the nearest integer prior to the computation. For example:

```
PRINT 72.9 \ 16,  72.9 MOD 16
 4               9
Ok
PRINT 72.4 \ 16,  72.4 MOD 16
 4               8
```

In the above operations, 72.9 was first rounded to 73, and 72.4 was rounded to 72. Note that the remainder is 9 in the first line of results and 8 in the second line.

Examples

1. Suppose you have 200 eggs to pack in cartons, each carton containing one dozen eggs. How many cartons do you need, and how many eggs will be left over?

   ```
   PRINT 200 \ 12,  200 MOD 12
    16              8
   ```

   Looks like you will need 17 cartons, with 16 of them full and one carton two-thirds full.

2. Convert 12,345 seconds to hours, minutes, and seconds. First, convert 12,345 seconds to hours and seconds, and then convert the leftover seconds to minutes and seconds.

   ```
   PRINT 12345 \ 3600,  12345 MOD 3600
    3                   1545
   Ok
   PRINT 1545 \ 60,  1545 MOD 60
    25               45
   ```

You can see that 12,345 seconds equals 3 hours, 25 minutes, and 45 seconds.

3. Perhaps you would like to identify the results, as follows:

```
PRINT 73 \ 16; "pounds,"; 73 MOD 16; "ounces"
 4 pounds, 9 ounces
```

The computer prints the value of 73 \ 16, then prints the string "pounds,", then prints the value of 73 MOD 16, and then prints the string "ounces".

Exercises

1. Angles are usually given in degrees from 0 to 360, where 0 degrees and 360 degrees are actually the same angle. Angles greater than 360 degrees can be reduced to *cycles* and degrees from 0 to 359. For example, 900 degrees is the same as 2 cycles, 180 degrees (2 times 360 plus 180 equals 900). Write a direct PRINT statement to convert 1250 degrees to cycles and degrees.

2. Convert 12,345 seconds to hours, minutes, and seconds in a different way from that shown in Example 2. First, convert 12,345 seconds to minutes and seconds. Then convert minutes to hours and minutes.

3. Write direct PRINT statements to convert 10,000 inches to yards, feet, and inches.

4.3 CALCULATE POWERS OF NUMBERS

You have used the arithmetic operation symbols (+, −, *, /, \, and MOD) to add, subtract, multiply, and divide numbers. Now you will use another symbol, the *exponentiation operator* (^), to compute a *power* of a number.

A room has a floor that is 12 feet square. That is, the floor is square, and each side of the square is 12 feet long. What is the area of the room in square feet? Here are two ways to compute it.

The first method uses multiplication:

```
PRINT 12 * 12
 144
```

The second method uses the exponentiation operator (^) to compute the square of 12, also called the second power of 12:

```
PRINT 12 ^ 2
 144
```

To type the exponentiation symbol (^), hold down a (SHIFT) key and press the key that has both the number 6 and the exponentiation symbol (^).

Now suppose the room has a rather lofty ceiling, exactly 12 feet high. A fortuitous coincidence! The room is 12 by 12 by 12 feet; therefore, the volume of the room is 12 times 12 times 12, or 12 cubed. Another way to say "12 cubed" is "12 to the third power, or the third power of 12." You can compute the volume in cubic feet in two ways.

Use multiplication (*):

```
PRINT 12 * 12 * 12
 1728
```

Or, use exponentiation (^):

```
PRINT 12 ^ 3
 1728
```

In math books, squares and cubes of numbers are indicated by means of superscript numbers. The numbers 12 squared and 12 cubed are shown here in both standard math notation and in GW-BASIC notation

Math Notation	GW-BASIC Notation	Meaning
12^2	12 ^ 2	12 squared, or 12 to the second power
12^3	12 ^ 3	12 cubed, or 12 to the third power

In an expression such as 12 ^ 3, the number 12 is the *base*, and 3 is the *exponent*. The exponent tells how many times the base is to be used as a factor. Here are some examples.

Expression	Base	Exponent	Multiplication Equivalent
12 ^ 2	12	2	12 * 12
12 ^ 3	12	3	12 * 12 * 12
2 ^ 10	2	10	2 * 2 * 2 * 2 * 2 * 2 * 2 * 2 * 2 * 2

Exponents can be very useful. It is much easier to write 2 ^ 10 (2 to the tenth power) than to write 2 * 2 * 2 * 2 * 2 * 2 * 2 * 2 * 2 * 2. Consider, also, the expression of computer memory capacities. People say a computer has 256K, 512K, 640K, or more bytes of memory. *K* is an abbreviation of the metric term *kilo*, which means 1000. A kilogram is 1000 grams; a kilometer is 1000 meters. However, 1K bytes actually means 2 ^ 10 bytes.

The following examples use the exponentiation operator (^) to compute the number of bytes in 1K and 640K.

Examples

1. Compute the number of bytes in 1K bytes.

```
PRINT 2 ^ 10
 1024
```

2. The author's computer has a memory capacity of 640K bytes:

```
PRINT 640 * 2 ^ 10
  655360
```

In evaluating the numeric expression, 640 * 2 ^ 10, the computer first calculates the value of 2 ^ 10 and then multiplies that result by 640.

Exercises

1. The area of a circle is given by this formula:

Area = πr^2 where r is the radius of the circle
                         π is equal to approximately 3.14159

Write a direct PRINT statement to compute the area of a circle whose radius is 7. Use both multiplication and exponentiation to compute r^2, and print both results.

2. The volume of a sphere is given by this formula:

Volume = $\frac{4}{3}\pi r^3$ where r is the radius of the sphere
                          π is approximately equal to 3.14159

Write a direct PRINT statement to compute the volume of a sphere whose radius is 5.

UNDERSTAND FLOATING POINT NUMBERS   4.4

Computer memories are getting bigger. Memories of one, two, or more megabytes are increasingly common. The term *mega* is also borrowed from the metric system; it means one million. When referring to the size of computer memories or hard disk storage capacity, however, it means 2 ^ 20 (2 to the twentieth power, or the twentieth power of 2).

How many bytes are in a megabyte? Use GW-BASIC to find out.

```
PRINT 2 ^ 20
 1048576
```

One megabyte equals 1,048,576 bytes, not 1,000,000 bytes.

Next, compute the number of bytes in a 40-megabyte (40MB) hard disk.

```
PRINT 40 * 2 ^ 20
 4.194304E+07
```

GW-BASIC prints this large number as a *floating point number*. Read it like this: 4.194304E+07 is 4.194304 times 10 to the seventh power. Floating point notation is similar to *scientific notation*, used in math, science, and engineering books, as shown here:

Floating point notation: 4.194304E+07
Scientific notation: 4.194304×10^7

Floating point notation is simply a shorthand way of expressing large numbers. A floating point number has two parts: a *mantissa* and an *exponent*. The mantissa and exponent are separated by the capital letter E (for exponent), as shown here:

Floating point number: 4.194304E+07

Mantissa   E   Exponent

In a floating point number, the exponent is always a power of 10. Here are more examples of large numbers shown in "ordinary" notation, floating point notation, and scientific notation.

Number	Ordinary Notation	Floating Point	Scientific
Population of the earth	5000000000	5E+09	5×10^9
Three trillion	3000000000000	3E+12	3×10^{12}
Miles in one light year	5865566000000	5.865696E+12	5.865696×10^{12}

The national debt of the United States is about three trillion dollars, and the population is about 250 million. You can use floating point numbers to compute the debt for each person, as shown here:

```
PRINT 3E12 / 250E6
 12000
```

The debt for each person in this country is $12,000! Three trillion equals 3 times 10 ^ 12. In floating point notation, this is 3E+12. Two hundred fifty million equals 250 times 10 ^ 6. In floating point notation, this is 250E+06. Note that you can write three trillion as 3E12 instead of 3E+12. Also, 250 million can be written as 250E6 instead of 250E+06.

As you have seen, GW-BASIC does a good job representing large numbers by means of floating point notation. It is equally adept at representing very small numbers.

A recent experiment has determined that a frightened snail moves at the speed of one inch every four seconds. How fast is that in miles per second? Let's see now, the snail moves at 0.25 inches per second. Divide that number by the number of inches in a mile. There are 5280 feet in a mile, so first compute the number of inches.

```
PRINT 12 * 5280
 63360
```

Now divide the snail's speed in inches per second by 63360.

```
PRINT 0.25 / 63360
 3.945707E-06
```

You can combine these operations into a single PRINT statement, as shown below. Note the use of parentheses to force the computer to compute the value of 12 * 5280 first.

```
PRINT 0.25 / (12 * 5280)
 3.945707E-06
```

GW-BASIC prints this very small number as a floating point number with a mantissa (3.945707) and a negative exponent (–06). The mantissa and exponent are separated by the capital letter E. Read it this way: three point nine four five seven zero seven, times ten to the minus six. In scientific notation, you might see this number written as 3.945707×10^{-6}.

Floating point notation:	3.945707E-06
Scientific notation:	3.945707×10^{-6}

Hydrogen is universal stuff. It began with the Big Bang that created the universe. It is here, there, everywhere. The hydrogen atom is very small and light, with a mass of about 1.67×10^{-27} kilograms.

Floating point notation:	1.67E-27
Scientific notation:	1.67×10^{-27}
Ordinary notation:	.00000000000000000000000000167

As you can see, you can type this number much more quickly in floating point than in ordinary notation, and with far less chance of a typing mistake.

Exercises

1. Write each number as a floating point number.

    a. 123 billion

    b. 0.000000000000123

2. Write each of these floating point numbers as an "ordinary" number, without using the letter E and an exponent.

    a. 6.643E-24

    b. 10E10

4.5 DEFINE TYPES OF NUMBERS

GW-BASIC has several types of numbers: integers, single precision numbers, double precision numbers, and floating point numbers. So far, you have seen three types—integers, single precision numbers, and floating point numbers, examples of which are shown here:

Integers: 3 4 –1 12

Single precision numbers: 2.54 11.4808 655360

Floating point numbers: 4.194304E+07 250E6 3.945707E-06

- An *integer* is a whole number in the range –32768 to +32767. It is stored in two bytes of memory.

- A *single precision number* can be an integer or noninteger with up to seven digits. A single precision number is stored in four bytes of memory. It is actually stored as a floating point number, described next.

- A *floating point number* is a number with a mantissa and an exponent. The mantissa can have up to seven digits. The exponent is in the range –39 to +38. A floating point number is stored in four bytes of memory.

Now let's explore a number pattern. Clear the screen and enter the following four PRINT statements.

Type **PRINT 11 * 11**
and press (ENTER)
Type **PRINT 111 * 111**
and press (ENTER)
Type **PRINT 1111 * 1111**
and press (ENTER)
Type **PRINT 11111 * 11111**
and press (ENTER)

After you enter these four statements, the screen should appear as shown in Figure 4-1.

The first two results (121 and 12321) can be thought of as integers or single precision numbers. The third result (1234321) is a single precision number. The fourth result (1.234543E+07) is a floating point number. It is not the exact answer, however, which is 123454321, but rather a seven-digit approximation of the true result.

```
PRINT 11 * 11
 121
Ok
PRINT 111 * 111
 12321
Ok
PRINT 1111 * 1111
 1234321
Ok
PRINT 11111 * 11111
 1.234543E+08
Ok
—
```

FIGURE 4-1.	Exploring a number pattern

Fortunately, there is another number type that you can use to correctly represent numbers with more than seven digits.

A *double precision number* can have up to 16 digits. You can specify a number as double precision by appending a number symbol (#) to it. You can use double precision numbers to compute the correct result of multiplying 11111 by 11111:

```
PRINT 11111 * 11111#
 123454321
```

The number 11111# is a double precision number. Therefore, the expression 11111 * 11111# is evaluated as a double precision result, and the answer (123454321) is printed correctly. You can also write the expression in the following manner:

```
PRINT 11111# * 11111
 123454321
```

When any operand in an expression is double precision, the computer treats the entire expression as double precision.

Now continue the pattern:

```
PRINT 111111 * 111111#
 12345654321
```

If you keep going, you will soon see a double precision floating point number, as shown here:

```
PRINT 111111111 * 111111111#
 1.234567898765432D+16
```

A *double precision floating point number* consists of a mantissa and an exponent separated by the letter D. The mantissa can have up to 16 digits. The exponent has the same range as single precision numbers, –39 to +38. A double precision number is stored in eight bytes of memory.

REMEMBER: Integers are whole numbers (no decimal point) in the range –32768 to 32767. An integer is stored in two bytes of memory. Single precision numbers are real numbers (integer or noninteger) with up to seven digits and, possibly, a decimal point. A single precision number can appear as a floating point number consisting of a mantissa, the letter E, and an exponent. A double precision number is a real number (integer or noninteger) with up to 16 digits and a decimal point. A double precision number can appear as a double precision floating point number consisting of a mantissa, the letter D, and an exponent.

Examples

1. The result of a calculation might be outside GW-BASIC's range of numbers. If a result is too large, GW-BASIC prints an "Overflow" error message and then prints the largest allowable number.

    ```
    PRINT 1E40
    Overflow
     1.701412E+38
    ```

    The number 1E40 (1 times 10 to the fortieth power) is too big for GW-BASIC to handle. You see the "Overflow" error message and also the largest allowable number, 1.701412E+38.

2. Division by zero is not allowed. If you try to divide by zero, you will see a "Division by zero" error message followed by the largest allowable number, 1.701412E+38.

```
PRINT 1 / 0
Division by zero
 1.701412E+38
```

3. GW-BASIC also has a smallest positive number. If a result is smaller than this number, then the result is replaced by zero.

```
PRINT 1E-40
 0
```

The number 1E–40 is nonzero, and smaller than the smallest positive number that GW-BASIC can handle. Therefore, this too-small number is replaced by zero.

Exercises

1. In mathematics, integers are the counting numbers (1, 2, 3, and so on); the opposites, or negatives, of the counting numbers (–1, –2, –3, and so on); and the number zero (0). GW-BASIC integers are integers in a finite range from _____ to _____.

2. Which of the following numbers can be stored exactly as a single precision number?

   12345678   1234567

3. Complete the following PRINT statement to divide the number 1 by the number 7 and display the result as shown in both single precision and double precision.

```
PRINT _____, _____
 .1428572      .14285714248571429
```

UNDERSTAND NUMERIC VARIABLES

4.6

Imagine that, in the computer's memory, there are many "number boxes." Each number box can hold one number at any one time. A number box can hold, or store, different numbers at different times. Each number box has a name. This illustration contains number boxes called *a*, *diameter*, and *Price*:

a | 7 | *diameter* | 24 | *Price* | 19.95 |

Each number box contains a number. The number 7 is in number box *a*; 24 is in the number box called *diameter*; the number box labeled *Price* contains the number 19.95.

In GW-BASIC, a number box is called a *numeric variable*. The number in a number box is the *value* of the variable that identifies the box. Therefore,

- The value of the variable *a* is 7.
- The value of the variable *diameter* is 24.
- The value of the variable *Price* is 19.95.

You can create variable names, subject to the following limitations:

- A variable name can be a single letter, or any combination of up to 40 letters and digits.
- The first character of a variable name must be a letter.
- You cannot use a GW-BASIC keyword (such as BEEP, CLS, or PRINT) as a variable, but a keyword can be part of a variable. For example, *beeper* is all right even though it contains *beep*.

Here are seven sample variable names:

a diameter price pi Qty R2D2 GasRate

Note that letters may be uppercase (A, B, C) or lowercase (a, b, c). GW-BASIC does not distinguish between upper- and lowercase in variables. Therefore, *a* and *A* are the same variable; *pi* and *PI* are the same variable; *GasRate*, *gasrate*, and *GASRATE* are the same variable. Nevertheless, in this book, variable names appear in lowercase or a mixture of lowercase and uppercase letters. This makes it easy to distinguish variables from keywords (BEEP, CLS, PRINT, and so on), which always appear in uppercase letters

Since GW-BASIC has three types of numbers, it also has three types of numeric variables: *integer variables, single precision variables,* and *double precision variables.* An integer variable can have only integer values. A single precision variable can have single precision numbers as values.

- An integer variable consists of a variable name followed by a percent sign (%). The percent sign designates the variable as an integer variable.

  Integer variables: *n% Qty% Year%*

- A double precision variable consists of a variable name followed by a number symbol (#).

  Double precision variables: *BigNumber# LotsaBucks# pi#*

- A single precision variable consists of a variable name followed by no designator, or by an exclamation point (!).

  Single precision variables: *x Price Price! pi pi!*

REMEMBER: A variable name without a designator (%, !, or #) is automatically a single precision variable. Single precision variables suffice for most programming. Other variables are used when necessary. For example, double precision variables are necessary for problems involving large amounts of money.

You can use direct statements to assign a value to a variable and then print the value of that variable. Do it now. Clear the screen and assign the value 7 to the variable *a.*

Type **a = 7**
and press (ENTER)

You will see this on the screen:

```
a = 7
Ok
_
```

GW-BASIC has now reserved a small part of memory (four bytes) as a single precision variable named *a*, and assigned the number 7 as the value of *a*. When you type **a = 7** and press (ENTER), you tell the computer to assign the value 7 to the variable named *a*.

Now use a direct PRINT statement to tell the computer to print the value of *a*.

Type **PRINT a**
and press (ENTER)

The computer prints the value of *a*, which is 7. On the screen you see the statement (PRINT *a*) and the value of *a* that was printed:

```
PRINT a
 7
```

The value of a variable remains the same until you change it. You can verify this by repeating the previous statement.

Type **PRINT a**
and press (ENTER)

Again the computer prints 7, the value of *a*. Now assign a different number as the value of *a*, and then print it. Your new number will replace the old value of *a*.

Type **a = 1.23**
and press (ENTER)

Then type **PRINT a**
and press (ENTER)

These last two statements, and their result, look like this:

```
a = 1.23
Ok
PRINT a
 1.23
```

Let's assign the value 3.14 to a new variable, *pi*, and print the value of *pi*:

```
pi = 3.14
Ok
PRINT pi
 3.14
```

Both *pi* and *a* will maintain their values until changed. Confirm this by printing both variables. You can do this with a single PRINT statement, using a comma (,) between the two variables:

```
PRINT pi, a
 3.14          1.23
```

You can use variables in *arithmetic expressions*. Assign values to the variables *a* and *b*, and then add, subtract, multiply, and divide the values of *a* and *b*.

Type **a = 7**
and press (ENTER)

Type **b = 5**
and press (ENTER)

Type **PRINT a + b, a − b, a * b, a / b**
and press (ENTER)

After these entries, you will see the following results on the screen:

```
a = 7
Ok
b = 5
Ok
PRINT a + b, a - b, a * b, a / b
 12          2          35          1.4
```

Examples

1. Two bicycles have wheels with diameters of 21 and 24 inches, respectively. How far does each bike travel in one turn of its wheels? The distance is the diameter multiplied by *pi* (π), where *pi* is approximately equal to 3.14. First, assign the value 3.14 to *pi*; then compute and print the two distances.

```
pi = 3.14
Ok
PRINT pi * 21, pi * 24
 65.94           75.36
```

2. The local sales tax rate is 6%. Assign this value to the variable *TaxRate*.

   Type **TaxRate = .06**
   and press (ENTER)

   The value of *TaxRate* is .06, since 6% is 6/100, or .06 when stated as a decimal. You can assign the value of *TaxRate* another way.

   Type **TaxRate = 6 / 100**
   and press (ENTER)

   You can now use *TaxRate* to compute the amount of sales tax for various amounts of money. Here is an example.
   You buy a computer game that costs $39.95. How much is the sales tax?

```
PRINT 39.95 * TaxRate
 2.397
```

   Rounded to the nearest cent, the tax on the $39.95 computer game is $2.40. In the next chapter, you will learn how to print results that are rounded to the nearest cent.

Exercises

1. Suppose your utilities company charges these rates for electricity:

   $0.08882 per kwh for the first 846 kwh

   $0.13524 per kwh for any amount over 846 kwh

   a. Write a statement to assign .08882 as the value of the variable *LoRate*.

   b. Write a statement to assign .13524 as the value of the variable *HiRate*.

   c. Use the variables *LoRate* and *HiRate* in a PRINT statement to compute the cost of 846 kwh at the low rate, plus 589 kwh at the high rate.

2. Suppose the values of *LoRate* and *HiRate* are assigned as in Exercise 1. Write statements to assign 846 as the value of the variable *BaseKwh*, and 589 as the value of the variable *XtraKwh*. Then write a PRINT statement using all four variables to compute the cost of electricity used.

| 4.7 | ## USE VARIABLES IN PROGRAMMING |

The computer becomes a much more powerful and useful tool if you create programs that use variables. Values of variables can be entered as needed from the keyboard. The program can then do most of the work automatically.

The INPUT statement provides the means for entering values of variables as needed by a program. In its simplest form, an INPUT statement consists of the keyword INPUT followed by a variable.

Program 4-1, KWH01, illustrates the use of the INPUT statement to acquire a value of the variable *kwh*. Enter this program into the computer's memory.

1. Type **NEW** and press (ENTER).

2. Type each line of the program, pressing (ENTER) after each line. You can use (ALT)(P) as a shortcut for typing PRINT and (ALT)(I) as a shortcut for typing INPUT.

3. List the program on the screen. It will appear as shown here:

```
LIST
10 CLS
20 LORATE = 0.08882
30 INPUT KWH
40 PRINT KWH * LORATE
```

As you can see from the listing of the program, GW-BASIC converts variable names to all uppercase letters, no matter how they were typed. It also converts keywords typed in lowercase letters to uppercase. Nevertheless, in this book, variables are shown in either lowercase or a mixture of uppercase and lowercase, except in listings. This is done to make programs easier to read.

```
10 CLS
20 LoRate = .08882
30 INPUT kwh
40 PRINT kwh * LoRate
```

PROGRAM 4-1. Cost of Electricity with INPUT Statement #1

Press (F2) to run the program. The program first clears the screen (line 10), and then sets the value of *LoRate* to .08882 (line 20). It executes the INPUT statement in line 30. Now the program prints a question mark on the screen, displays the blinking cursor, and waits. The top of the screen looks like this:

```
? _
```

The computer is waiting for you to enter the value of *kwh* and press (ENTER). If you type 846 and press (ENTER), the computer will accept that number as the value of *kwh*, then compute and print the cost of electricity (line 40), and stop, as shown here:

```
? 846
 75.14173
```

Run the program again and enter the *kwh* value of your choice. Try entering numbers such as 1, 10, or 100, so you can easily verify that the program is running correctly and producing the right answers. Then examine the program; it works as described in Table 4-1.

Examples

1. The following program computes the amount of sales tax on the value of the variable *SalesAmount* entered in response to an INPUT statement. Line 20 assigns the sales tax rate of 6% to the variable *TaxRate*.

    ```
    10 CLS
    20 TaxRate = 6 / 100
    30 INPUT SalesAmount
    40 PRINT SalesAmount * TaxRate
    ```

    Three runs are shown here:

Run #1	Run #2	Run #3
? 1	? 39.95	? 1000000000
.06	2.397	6E+07
Ok	Ok	Ok
—	—	—

| TABLE 4-1. | The Cost of Electricity Program Explained |

Program Line	Explanation
10 CLS	Clears the screen
20 LoRate = .08882	Assigns .08882 as the value of the variable *LoRate*
30 INPUT kwh	Displays a question mark and waits for a value of *kwh* to be entered
40 PRINT kwh * LoRate	Computes the cost of electricity and prints it

Oops! The sales amount of 1000000000 is too big to be handled properly with single precision numbers and variables. For large numbers, it is better to use double precision, as in the next example.

2. The following program uses double precision numbers and variables to compute the sales tax and the total amount of the sale for large values of *SalesAmount#*. The computed sales tax is assigned to the variable *SalesTax#* in line 40. The total amount of the sale is computed and assigned to the variable *TotalAmount#* in line 50. Then both the sales tax and the total amount are printed by line 60.

```
10 CLS
20 TaxRate# = 6 / 100#
30 INPUT SalesAmount#
40 SalesTax# = SalesAmount# * TaxRate#
50 TotalAmount# = SalesAmount# + SalesTax#
60 PRINT SalesTax#, Total Amount#
```

This program handles a sale of one billion dollars quite nicely, as shown here:

```
? 1000000000
  60000000        1060000000
```

Note the following things about this program:

- The double precision variables are *TaxRate#*, *SalesAmount#*, *SalesTax#*, and *TotalAmount#*.

- In line 20, a double precision number (100#) is used to ensure that the value of *TaxRate#* will be as precise as possible. Numbers in GW-BASIC are stored as *binary* (base 2) numbers. Because the decimal number .06 cannot be stored exactly as a binary number, a small "round-off error" occurs. This error is much less when the computation is done using a double precision number.

Exercises

1. Supply the missing elements in the following program that computes the distance a bicycle wheel travels in one rotation (the circumference of the wheel). Print the distance in both inches and feet, if *diameter* is entered in inches.

```
10 CLS
20 pi = _____
30 INPUT diameter
40 PRINT _____, _____
```

2. Supply the missing elements in the following program that computes the value of a block of stock given the number of shares and the price per share. Allow for big numbers.

```
10 CLS
20 INPUT NumberOfShares#
30 INPUT _____
40 Value# = _____
50 PRINT Value#
```

MASTERY
SKILLS
CHECK

EXERCISES

1. Write direct statements to perform the following calculations and print the results.

   a. Convert 13 hours, 28 minutes to minutes.

b. Convert 8 hours, 37 minutes, 42 seconds to seconds.

c. Compute the average of three temperature measurements: 68, 73, and 77 degrees Fahrenheit. (Add the temperatures and divide by 3.)

d. A computer game, usually priced at $59.95, is offered at a 15% discount. What is its price?

2. Use the backslash (\) and the MOD operator in a direct PRINT statement to compute the integer quotient and remainder, on dividing

a. 73 by 10

b. –100 by 3

c. 99 by 100

d. 125 by –5

3. The population of Earth is increasing at the rate of 1.8% per year. If this rate holds steady, the population 20 years from now can be obtained by multiplying the present population by the twentieth power of 1.018, like this:

$$(1 + .018)^{20}$$

The present population is 5.3 billion. Write a direct PRINT statement to compute the projected population, 20 years hence.

4. The formula to convert temperature from degrees Fahrenheit (F) to degrees Celsius (C) is

$$C = \frac{5}{9}(F - 32)$$

Write a program to convert temperature from degrees F to degrees C.

5. Congratulations! You are the big winner on a TV game show. To select your prize, a number from 1 to 1000 is chosen at random. Call it n. You then select one, and only one, of the following prizes. You have 30 seconds to make your selection.

Prize Number 1: You receive n dollars

Prize Number 2: You receive 1.01^n dollars

For some values of *n*, Prize 1 is larger; for other values of *n*, Prize 2 is larger. Write a program to tell you the values of both prizes. Runs of the author's program are shown for *n* = 100 (take Prize 1) and *n* = 700 (take Prize 2).

```
? 100                    ? 700
 100                      700
 2.704813                1059.158
```

6. Write a program to compute the cost of electricity. Your program should:

   a. Clear the screen.

   b. Assign .08882 as the value of *LoRate*.

   c. Assign .13524 as the value of *HiRate*.

   d. Acquire the number of kilowatt-hours to be charged at the low rate. Call it *BaseKwh*.

   e. Acquire the number of kilowatt-hours to be charged at the high rate. Call it *XtraKwh*.

   f. Compute the total cost of electricity and assign it as the value of *KwhCost*.

   g. Print the total cost of electricity.

   A sample run is shown below. In this run, only 789 kwh were used—less than the baseline amount of 846 kwh. Therefore, the entire number of kilowatt-hours is charged at the low rate. Zero (0) is entered for the number of kwh charged at the high rate.

```
? 789                    (Kilowatt-hours at low rate)
? 0                      (Kilowatt-hours at high rate)
 70.07898
```

   In a second run, 846 kwh are to be charged at the low rate, and 123 kwh at the high rate.

```
? 846                    (Kilowatt-hours at low rate)
? 123                    (Kilowatt-hours at high rate)
 91.77624
```

Making Programs More Useful

▶5◀

In this chapter you will learn how to make your programs more useful. You will learn about the "enhanced" INPUT statement and use it to clearly specify information to be entered by someone who uses your program. You will learn how to identify and format the information printed by your program.

You will also learn how to make your programs more readable by including comments within the program that provide information about the program. This is part of good programming style, which makes your programs easy to read and understand by others, and by yourself, a year later.

SKILLS
CHECK

EXERCISES

Before starting this chapter, you should know something about, or know how to do, the following things:

1. Load GW-BASIC with the /D option, so that the exponentiation operation (^) can be done with double precision results. Some activities in this chapter require double precision exponentiation, so load GW-BASIC as shown here:

    Type **GWBASIC /D**
    and press (ENTER)

2. Use integer, single precision, and double precision numbers and variables in direct statements and in programs.

3. Use the arithmetic operations of addition (+), subtraction (–), multiplication (*), division (/), integer division (\), integer remainder (MOD), and exponentiation (^).

5.1 | USE REMARKS IN YOUR PROGRAMS

It is good practice to put information at the beginning of a program to tell people something about the program. The REM (REMark) statement allows you to do this. Any text that follows REM in a program line is ignored when you run the program. You can use an apostrophe (') as an abbreviation for REM.

Let's add four REM lines to Program 4-1, KWH01, from the previous chapter, as shown here:

```
1 REM ** Cost of Electricity with INPUT **
2 ' Teach Yourself GW-BASIC, Chapter 5. Filename: KWH03.BAS
3 ' Written on a balmy day in May
9 '
10 CLS
20 LoRate = .08882
30 Input kwh
40 PRINT kwh * LoRate
```

Line 1 is a REM statement that briefly describes the program. Line 2 uses an apostrophe (') instead of the word REM. It tells where the program originated (TeachYourself GW-BASIC, Chapter 5) and gives the filename (KWH03.BAS) under which it is saved on a disk. Line 3 is optional. You can put whatever comments you want in these first few lines. In our example, line 9 is blank, separating this block of descriptive information from the rest of the program, which does the actual work.

From now on, programs will usually be shown in this book with blank lines to enhance readability. You will not see these blank lines when you list a program. If you wish, when you enter a program, you can include lines that have only a line number and an apostrophe (for example, 9 ') in order to make the listed program have the same line spacing shown in the book.

The information in REM statements is for people; the computer ignores it. From now on, most programs in this book will have REM statements to help you identify and understand the programs.

WRITE MORE USEFUL PROGRAMS — 5.2

The INPUT statement tells the computer to put a question mark on the screen and wait for something to be entered. This is useful, but it would be more useful if the computer identified what sort of input it wanted. There is an easy way to do this.

Program 5-1, SALETX02 (Sales Tax with Enhanced INPUT Statement), is an improved sales tax program. It features an "enhanced"
INPUT statement. Two sample runs are shown side by side here:

```
Amount of sale? 39.95          Amount of sale? 269
  2.397          42.347          16.14          285.14
```

The program line

```
30 INPUT "Amount of sale"; SalesAmount#
```

tells the computer to do the following:

1. Print the string "Amount of sale."
2. Print a question mark.
3. Wait for something to be entered and assign it as the value of the
    SalesAmount# variable.

Note that the message to be displayed (Amount of sale) is enclosed
in quotation marks and followed by a semicolon.

Now change the program so that it identifies the printed results
as the amount of sales tax and the total amount of sale, as shown in

```
1 REM ** Sales Tax with Enhanced INPUT Statement **
2 ' Teach Yourself GW-BASIC, Chapter 5.  Filename: SALETX02.BAS

10 CLS
20 TaxRate# = 6 / 100#

30 INPUT "Amount of sale"; SalesAmount#

40 SalesTax# = SalesAmount# * TaxRate#
50 TotalAmount# = SalesAmount# + SalesTax#
60 PRINT SalesTax#, TotalAmount#
```

PROGRAM 5-1.   Sales Tax with Enhanced INPUT Statement

Program 5-2, SALETX03 (Sales Tax with Enhanced INPUT & PRINT Statements). Be sure to type all punctuation, including quotation marks ("). A sample run is shown here:

```
Amount of sale? 39.95
Amount of sales tax is 2.397
Total amount is 42.347
```

Notice that the program now identifies the required data to be entered (amount of sale) and the two results (amount of sales tax and total amount). Each result is printed by a PRINT statement that also identifies the printed result.

The program line

```
60 PRINT "Amount of sales tax is"; SalesTax#
```

tells the computer to first print the string "Amount of sales tax is," and then print the value of the *SalesTax#* variable. The string and the variable are separated by a semicolon. Thus, the value of *SalesTax#* is printed as close as possible to the string.

```
1 REM ** Sales Tax with Enhanced INPUT & PRINT Statements **
2 ' Teach Yourself GW-BASIC, Chapter 5.  Filename: SALETX03.BAS

10 CLS
20 TaxRate# = 6 / 100#

30 INPUT "Amount of sale"; SalesAmount#

40 SalesTax# = SalesAmount# * TaxRate#
50 TotalAmount# = SalesAmount# + SalesTax#
60 PRINT "Amount of sales tax is"; SalesTax#
70 PRINT "Total amount is"; TotalAmount#
```

PROGRAM 5-2.   Sales Tax with Enhanced INPUT & PRINT Statements

Examples

1. You can use the following program to compute the cost of electricity for values of *kwh* charged at the low rate of $0.08882. The program identifies the required data to be entered (Kilowatt-hours at low rate) and the result (The cost of electricity is).

```
1 REM ** Cost of Electricity with Enhanced INPUT & PRINT **
2 ' Teach Yourself GW-BASIC, Chapter 5. Filename: KWH04.BAS

10 CLS
20 LoRate = .08882
30 INPUT "Kilowatt-hours at low rate"; kwh
40 PRINT "The cost of electricity is"; kwh * LoRate
```

A sample run is shown here:

```
Kilowatt-hours at low rate? 789
The cost of electricity is 70.07898
```

2. In 1990, the population of Earth was about 5.3 billion people, increasing at the rate of 1.8% per year. The following program uses these values to estimate the population *n* years from 1990.

```
1 REM ** Projected World Population **
2 ' Teach Yourself GW-BASIC, Chapter 5. Filename: POPUL01.BAS

10 CLS
20 Pop1990 = 5.3E+09
30 GrowthRate = 1.8 / 100
40 INPUT "Number of years after 1990"; n
50 PRINT "Projected population:"; Pop1990 * (1 + GrowthRate) ^ n
```

Suppose you want to estimate the world population in the year 2010. Enter **20** for the value of *n*, as in the following sample run.

```
Number of years after 1990? 20
Projected population: 7.572365E+09
```

This shows that the projected world population in 2010 (20 years after 1990) will be about 7.6 billion. Note that Program POPUL01 does not use double precision variables or numbers, even though large numbers are involved. These current world population and growth rate figures are only estimates. Single precision arithmetic is adequate for these calculations.

3. For a given value of n, which is greater, n dollars or 1.01^n dollars? Use the program shown here to find out.

```
1 REM ** Big Winner on a TV Game Show **
2 ' Teach Yourself GW-BASIC, Chapter 5. Filename: TVSHOW02.BAS

10 CLS
20 INPUT "Enter an integer from 1 to 1000: ", n
40 PRINT "Prize #1:"; n
50 PRINT "Prize #2:"; 1.01 ^ n
```

In the program line

```
20 INPUT "Enter an integer from 1 to 1000: ", n
```

a comma (,) separates the string "Enter an integer from 1 to 1000: " from the variable n. This comma suppresses printing of the question mark normally supplied by the INPUT statement, as shown in the following sample run.

```
Enter an integer from 1 to 1000: 700
Prize #1: 700
Prize #2: 1059.158
```

In an INPUT statement, use a semicolon if you want a question mark printed; use a comma if you don't want a question mark printed.

Exercises

1. Program BIKE01 (Distance a Bike Travels in One Wheel Turn) is shown here. Complete the program by adding REM statements in lines 1 and 2.

1 _____

2 _____

```
10 CLS
20 pi = 3.14
30 INPUT "Diameter of wheel in inches"; diameter
40 distance = pi * diameter / 12
50 PRINT "Distance in one wheel-turn is"; distance; "feet."
```

2. Write Program KWH05 (Cost of Electricity at Low & High Rates). Your program should do all of the following:

   a. Begin with identifying REM statements.

   b. Clear the screen.

   c. Assign .08882 as the value of *LoRate* and .13524 as the value of *HiRate*.

   d. Acquire the number of kilowatt-hours to be charged at the low rate. Call it *BaseKwh*.

   e. Acquire the number of kilowatt-hours to be charged at the high rate. Call it *XtraKwh*.

   f. Compute the total cost of electricity and assign it as the value of *KwhCost*.

   g. Print the total cost of electricity.

   In the following sample run, only 789 kilowatt-hours were used—less than the baseline amount of 846 kwh. Therefore, the entire number of kilowatt-hours is charged at the low rate. Zero (0) is entered for the number of hours charged at the high rate.

```
Enter kwh charged at low rate: 789
Enter kwh charged at high rate: 0
Total cost of electricity is 70.07898
```

5.3   FORMAT THE PRINTED RESULTS

Program 5-3, SALETX04 (Sales Tax with TAB Function), prints the amount of the sale entered from the keyboard, the amount of the sales tax, and the total amount of the sale. Note two new things in this program.

• Line 60 is an "empty" PRINT statement. It prints a blank line.

- In lines 70, 80, and 90, the TAB function tells the computer to move the cursor to the column specified in parentheses. The TAB(30) function moves the cursor to column 30.

A sample run of Program SALETX04 is shown here:

```
Amount of sale? 1

Amount of sale is          1
Amount of sales tax is     .06
Total amount is            1.06
```

Although the values of *SalesAmount#*, *SalesTax#*, and *TotalAmount#* are all printed beginning in column 30, the decimal points do not line up correctly. To solve this problem, use a variation of PRINT, called PRINT USING. The PRINT USING statement lets you specify the appearance and position of numbers. It also provides the means for rounding numbers to a given number of decimal places.

```
1 REM ** Sales Tax with TAB Function **
2 ' Teach Yourself GW-BASIC, Chapter 5. Filename: SALETX04.BAS

10 CLS
20 TaxRate# = 6 / 100#

30 INPUT "Amount of Sale"; SalesAmount#

40 SalesTax# = SalesAmount# * TaxRate#
50 TotalAmount# = SalesAmount# + SalesTax#

60 PRINT
70 PRINT "Amount of sale is"; TAB(30); SalesAmount#
80 PRINT "Amount of sales tax is"; TAB(30); SalesTax#
90 PRINT "Total amount is"; TAB(30); TotalAmount#
```

PROGRAM 5-3.　Sales Tax with TAB Function

The following statement tells the computer to print the value of *SalesAmount#* with up to nine digits before the decimal point, and two digits following the decimal point, rounded if necessary:

```
PRINT USING "#########.##"; SalesAmount#
```

Program 5-4, SALETX05 (Sales Tax with PRINT USING), uses three PRINT USING statements, in lines 75, 85, and 95. Since all three numbers are printed with the same PRINT USING format string (#########.##), they line up vertically along the decimal point, as shown in the following run:

```
Amount of sale? 39.95

Amount of sale is               39.95
Amount of sales tax is           2.40
Total amount is                 42.35
```

```
1 REM ** Sales Tax with PRINT USING **
2 ' Teach Yourself GW-BASIC, Chapter 5. Filename: SALETX05.BAS

10 CLS
20 TaxRate# = 6 / 100#

30 INPUT "Amount of Sale"; SalesAmount#

40 SalesTax# = SalesAmount# * TaxRate#
50 TotalAmount# = SalesAmount# + SalesTax#

60 PRINT
70 PRINT "Amount of sale is"; TAB(30);
75 PRINT USING "#########.##"; SalesAmount#

80 PRINT "Amount of sales tax is"; TAB(30);
85 PRINT USING "#########.##"; SalesTax#

90 PRINT "Total amount is"; TAB(30);
95 PRINT USING "#########.##"; TotalAmount#
```

PROGRAM 5-4.   Sales Tax with PRINT USING

The following pair of statements from this program prints one line on the screen:

```
70 PRINT "Amount of sale is"; TAB(30);
75 PRINT USING "#########.##"; SalesAmount#
```

Line 70 prints the string "Amount of sale is," and then tabs to column 30. Line 75 prints the value of *SalesAmount#* as specified by the format string "#########.##":

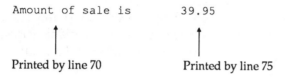

```
        Amount of sale is        39.95
```

Printed by line 70   Printed by line 75

Lines 80 and 85 also work together to produce one line of print, just as lines 90 and 95 do. Numbers are printed with two decimal places, as specified by the format string in the PRINT USING statement. The format string limits the printed number to, at most, nine digits before the decimal point. If a printed number is more than 999999999.99, a percent sign (%) is printed in front of the number, as shown here:

```
Amount of sale? 1000000000

Amount of sale is        %1000000000.00
Amount of sales tax is    60000000.00
Total amount is          %1060000000.00
```

This format problem has an easy solution. Use a format string that allows more digits before the decimal point. For example, the following PRINT statement allows up to 12 digits before the decimal point:

```
70 PRINT USING "############.##"; SalesAmount#
```

Examples

1. Program 5-5, TVSHOW03 (Big Winner on a TV Game Show with PRINT USING), assigns a format string ("#####.##") to the string

variable *format$*, and then uses *format$* in two PRINT USING statements. Here is a sample run:

```
Enter an integer from 1 to 1000: 700

Prize #1:           700.00
Prize #2:          1059.16
```

You can invent your own string variables, such as *format$*. Note that a string variable ends in a dollar sign ($). In Program 5-5, TVSHOW03, line 40 assigns a format string enclosed in quotation marks as the value of the string variable *format$*. This format string is then used in the PRINT USING statements in lines 70 and 90.

2. World population is frequently stated in billions, rounded to the nearest tenth of a billion, as in Program 5-6, POPUL02 (Projected World Population with PRINT USING). Line 20 assigns 5.3 as the value of *Pop1990*. This is the number of billions of people. The

---

```
1 REM ** Big Winner on a TV Game Show with PRINT USING **
2 ' Teach Yourself GW-BASIC, Chapter 5. Filename: TVSHOW03.BAS

10 CLS

20 INPUT "Enter an integer from 1 to 1000: ", n

40 format$ = "#####.##"

50 PRINT

60 PRINT "Prize #1:"; TAB(20);
70 PRINT USING format$; n

80 PRINT "Prize #2:"; TAB(20);
90 PRINT USING format$; 1.01 ^ n
```

PROGRAM 5-5.   Big Winner on a TV Game Show with PRINT USING

```
1 REM ** Projected World Population with PRINT USING **
2 ' Teach Yourself GW-BASIC, Chapter 5. Filename: POPUL02.BAS

10 CLS
20 Pop1990 = 5.3
30 GrowthRate = 1.8 / 100
40 format$ = "##.#"

50 INPUT "Number of years after 1990"; n

60 People = Pop1990 * (1 + GrowthRate) ^ n

70 PRINT "Projected population: ";
80 PRINT USING format$; People;
90 PRINT " billion people"
```

PROGRAM 5-6.	Projected World Population with PRINT USING

format string in line 40 allows a number up to 99.9 billion to be printed by line 80. Lines 70, 80, and 90 work together to print one line, as follows:

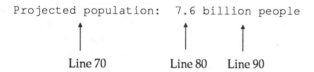

```
      Projected population:   7.6 billion people
```
Line 70   Line 80   Line 90

Exercises

1. Replace the program line shown below with two lines so that the value of *KwhCost* is printed with up to four digits before the decimal point and two digits after the decimal point.

   ```
   70 PRINT "Total cost of electricity is"; KwhCost
   ```

2. Complete the blanks in the following program exerpt. Print the value of *distance* with up to two places before the decimal point and two digits after the decimal point.

```
50 format$ = _____

60 PRINT "Distance in one wheel-turn is ";

70 PRINT _____

80 PRINT " feet."
```

5.4 — LEARN MORE ABOUT THE PRINT USING STATEMENT

The PRINT USING statement has many variations. Among the most useful of these are printing dollar signs ($) before numbers, and automatically putting commas in very large numbers. These features are shown in lines 75, 85, and 95 of Program 5-7, SALETX06 (Sales Tax with Dollars and Commas in Printout). In the following sample run, note the dollar sign ($) before each number, and the commas embedded in the number.

```
Amount of sale? 1000000000

Amount of sale is            $1,000,000,000.00
Amount of sales tax is          $60,000,000.00
Total amount is              $1,060,000,000.00
```

Program line 60 assigns the format string "$$###,###,###,###.##" to the string variable *format$*. This format string, used in lines 75, 85, and 95, tells the computer to print a number as follows:

- The double dollar sign ($$) causes a space and a dollar sign to be printed to the left of the number.

- The 12 number signs (#) separated by commas allow up to 12 digits of the number to be printed, with commas inserted every three digits. If fewer than 12 digits are printed, spaces are printed in the unused locations to the left of the dollar sign.

```
1 REM ** Sales Tax with Dollars & Commas in Printout **
2 ' Teach Yourself GW-BASIC, Chapter 5. Filename: SALETX06.BAS

10 CLS
20 TaxRate# = 6 / 100#

30 INPUT "Amount of sale"; SalesAmount#

40 SalesTax# = SalesAmount# * TaxRate#
50 TotalAmount# = SalesAmount# + SalesTax#

60 format$ = "$$###,###,###,###.##"

65 PRINT
70 PRINT "Amount of sale is"; TAB(30);
75 PRINT USING format$; SalesAmount#

80 PRINT "Amount of sales tax is"; TAB(30);
85 PRINT USING format$; SalesTax#

90 PRINT "Total amount is"; TAB(30);
95 PRINT USING format$; TotalAmount#
```

| PROGRAM 5-7. | Sales Tax with Dollars & Commas in Printout |

- The decimal point causes a decimal point to be printed in the number.

- The two number signs to the right of the decimal point cause two digits to be printed to the right of the decimal point. If necessary, the number being printed is rounded to two decimal places.

Exercises

1. Complete the following program to compute the percentage of games won, and print it rounded to the third decimal place.

```
10 CLS
20 INPUT "Number of games won "; won
```

```
30 INPUT "Number of games lost"; oops
40 PctWon = won / (won + oops)
50 PRINT "Win percentage is ";

60 PRINT USING _____
```

2. Here are lines 40, 70, and 90 of Program TVSHOW03:

```
40 format$ = "#####.##"

70 PRINT USING format$; n

90 PRINT USING format$; 1.01 ^ n
```

Rewrite line 40 so that the numbers printed by lines 70 and 90 are preceded by a dollar sign, and so that they include a comma for amounts of $1,000 or more, like this:

```
Prize #1:    $700.00
Prize #2:    $1,059.16
```

5.5 | USE REM STATEMENTS TO OUTLINE YOUR PROGRAMS

In this section you will use programs that require exponentiation (^) with double precision numbers. In order to obtain double precision results, you must load GW-BASIC with the /D (double precision) option. If you did not do so at the beginning of the chapter, reload BASIC now with this option. At the DOS A prompt (A>) or C prompt (C>),

Type **GWBASIC /D**
and press (ENTER)

Let's suppose you keep your money in a bank account that pays regular interest, compounded periodically. Program 5-8, INTRST01 (Future Value of Money—Compound Interest), computes the value of money (principal) invested at a particular interest rate per period, compounded for a given number of periods.

Before looking at the program, examine the following sample runs and think about how you would write the program. The first sample is for $1 invested at 1% interest, compounded for one period. This is used to test the program. The answer should be $1.01.

```
Principal amount invested ($)? 1
Interest rate per period (%) ? 1
Number of interest periods   ? 1

At maturity, the value will be              $1.01
```

Now suppose you have a balance of $500 on a credit card that charges 1.5% interest per month, and you put off paying it for 12 months.

```
Principal amount invested ($)? -500
Interest rate per period (%) ? 1.5
Number of interest periods   ? 12

At maturity, the value will be             -$597.81
```

```
1 REM ** Future Value of Money-Compound Interest **
2 ' Teach Yourself GW-BASIC, Chapter 5. Filename: INTRST01.BAS

100 REM ** Set up **
110 CLS
120 format$ = "$$###,###,###,###.##"

200 REM ** Get principal, interest rate, number of periods **
210 INPUT "Principal amount invested ($)"; Principal#
220 INPUT "Interest rate per period (%) "; Rate#
230 INPUT "Number of interest periods   "; Periods#

300 REM ** Compute future value **
310 Rate# = Rate# / 100
320 FutureValue# = Principal# * (1 + Rate#) ^ Periods#

400 REM ** Print the future value **
410 PRINT
420 PRINT "At maturity, the value will be ";
430 PRINT USING format$; FutureValue#
```

PROGRAM 5-8. Future Value of Money-Compound Interest

The "investment" is entered as –500 as an indicator that you owe $500 and that you are paying the interest. The result is –$597.81, the amount you will owe if you procrastinate for 12 months.

You might find it helpful to first write an outline of the program in REM statements. A possible outline is shown here:

```
1 REM ** Future Value of Money-Compound Interest **
2 ' Teach Yourself GW-BASIC, Chapter 5. Filename: INTRST01.BAS

100 REM ** Set up **

200 REM ** Get principal, interest rate, number of periods **

300 REM ** Compute future value **

400 REM ** Print the future value **
```

Once you have an outline for your program, you can expand it as shown in Program 5-8, INTRST01.

The program has five blocks. Each block begins with a REM statement that tells what the block does. The first block (line 1 REM) gives the name of the program, where it was first published, and the filename of the program as stored on a disk.

The second block (line 100 REM) clears the screen and assigns a format string to a string variable. If there were any other program setup to be done, this block would include those instructions as well.

The third block (line 200 REM) has INPUT statements to get values for the three variables used to compute the amount of interest and future value. All variables are double precision.

- *Principal#* is the amount invested, in dollars and cents.
- *Rate#* is the interest rate per interest period. Enter **1** for 1%, **1.5** for 1.5%, and so on.
- *Period#* is the number of periods over which the interest is compounded. For example, if the interest is compounded monthly for one year, enter **12** as the value of *Period#*.

The fourth block (line 300 REM) calculates the future value of the principal. The interest rate is first converted to a decimal fraction (line 310), which is used in the formula to compute the future value. Note the use of the exponentiation operation (^).

The fifth and final block (line 400 REM) prints the future value, preceded by the string "At maturity, the value will be." The format string assigned to the string variable *format$* causes the number to be printed with a leading dollar sign and commas every three digits.

Examples

1. In Chapter 3, you learned how to use the LLIST statement to list a program to the printer. You can also use LPRINT or LPRINT USING in a program to print information to the printer. Program 5-9, INTRST02 (Future Value of Money-Print to Printer), prints the values you enter and the final result on the printer. Here is a sample run, as printed on the printer.

   ```
   Principal amount invested:          $1,000.00
   Interest rate per period:                1.00
   Number of interest periods              12.00

   At maturity, the value will be:     $1,126.83
   ```

   Notice that the values of *Principal#* and *FutureValue#* are printed with dollar signs, while the values of *RatePerPeriod#* and *Periods#* are printed without dollar signs. The format string assigned to *format1$* in line 120 causes a space and a dollar sign to be printed when this variable is used in lines 420 and 490. The format string assigned to *format2$* in line 130 does not do this. The values in the TAB functions in block 400 are chosen to make sure that the decimal points line up vertically.

2. Program 5-10, POPUL03 (Projected World Population with REM Statements), is a revision of Program 5-6, POPUL02. Here is a REM outline of Program 5-10, POPUL03:

   ```
   1 REM ** Projected World Population with REM Statements **
   2 ' Teach Yourself GW-BASIC, Chapter 5. Filename: POPUL03.BAS
   ```

```
100 REM ** Set up **

200 REM ** Get the number of years after 1990 **

300 REM ** Compute projected population in billions of people **

400 REM ** Print projected population in billions of people **
```

```
1 REM ** Future Value of Money-Print to Printer **
2 ' Teach Yourself GW-BASIC, Chapter 5. Filename: INTRST02.BAS

100 REM ** Set up **
110 CLS
120 format1$ = "$$###,###,###,###.##"
130 format2$ = "###,###,###,###.##"

200 REM ** Get principal, interest rate, number of periods **
210 INPUT "Principal amount invested ($)"; Principal#
220 INPUT "Interest rate per period (%)"; RatePerPeriod#
230 INPUT "Number of interest periods "; Periods#

300 REM ** Compute future value **
310 Rate# = RatePerPeriod# / 100
320 FutureValue# = Principal# * (1 + Rate#) ^ Periods#

400 REM ** Print all values to the printer **
410 LPRINT "Principal amount invested:"; TAB(32);
420 LPRINT USING format1$; Principal#
430 LPRINT "Interest rate per period:"; TAB(34);
440 LPRINT USING format2$; RatePerPeriod#
450 LPRINT "Number of interest periods"; TAB(34);
460 LPRINT USING format2$; Periods#
470 LPRINT
480 LPRINT "At maturity, the value will be:"; TAB(32);
490 LPRINT USING format1$; FutureValue#
```

PROGRAM 5-9. Future Value of Money-Print to Printer

```
1 REM ** Projected World Population with REM Statements **
2 ' Teach Yourself GW-BASIC, Chapter 5. Filename: POPUL03.BAS

100 REM ** Set up **
110 CLS
120 Pop1990 = 5.3
130 GrowthRate = 1.8 / 100
140 format$ = "##.#"

200 REM ** Get the number of years after 1990 **
210 INPUT "Number of years after 1990"; n

300 REM ** Compute projected population in billions of people **
310 People = Pop1990 * (1 + GrowthRate) ^ n

400 REM ** Print projected poulation in billions of people **
410 PRINT "Projected population: ";
420 PRINT USING format$; People;
430 PRINT " billion people"
```

PROGRAM 5-10.   Projected World Population with REM Statements

---

Exercises

1. Write a program called STOCKS01 (Value of Stocks with REM
    Statements) according to the following REM outline:

```
1 REM ** Value of Stocks with REM Statements **
2 ' Teach Yourself GW-BASIC, Chapter 5. Filename: STOCKS01.BAS

100 REM ** Set up **

200 REM ** Get number of shares and price per share **

300 REM ** Compute value of this block of stock **

400 REM ** Print the value of this block of stock **
```

2. All you Alex P. Keaton fans will love this one. Write a program to compute and print a grade point average, given the number of hours of A, B, C, D, and F, according to the following point schedule. Save it as GPA01.

Grade	Points
A	4
B	3
C	2
D	1
F	0

The grade point average (gpa) is computed as follows:

$$gpa = \frac{4A + 3B + 2C + D}{A + B + C + D + F}$$

Here is a sample run with some fictitious data—definitely not Alex's grades.

```
For each letter grade, enter the number of hours.

Hours of A? 5
Hours of B? 8
Hours of C? 3
Hours of D? 0
Hours of F? 0

Total grade points:      50.000
Total number of hours:   16.000
Grade point average:      3.125
```

5.6   ENJOY SOME PROGRAMS BY ZAPPY ARTIST

In Chapter 3 you saw one of Zappy Artist's programs. Zappy, you may recall, likes to zap around SCREEN 1 plotting random pixels and drawing random lines, boxes, and circles. Program 5-11, ZAPPY03 (Zappy Artist Plots Pixels Pixilatedly), is a revision of Program ZAPPY01, which appeared in Chapter 3.

```
1 REM ** Zappy Artist Plots Pixels Pixilatedly **
2 ' Teach Yourself GW-BASIC, Chapter 5. Filename: ZAPPPY03.BAS

100 REM ** Set up **
110 SCREEN 1: CLS
120 RANDOMIZE TIMER
130 COLOR 0, 1

200 REM ** Use a GOTO loop to plot random pixels **
210 PSET (319 * RND, 199 * RND), 3 * RND
220 SOUND 3000 * RND + 1000, 9
230 GOTO 210
```

PROGRAM 5-11.   Zappy Artist Plots Pixels Pixilatedly

Enter and run Program 5-11, ZAPPY03. You will see a cyan, magenta, or white pixel appear in a random place on the screen about every half second. Each pixel is accompanied by a sound of random frequency between 1000 and 4000 Hz and a duration of nine ticks (about a half second).

Block 100 is a setup block. It selects SCREEN 1 and clears it (line 110). Line 120 "scrambles" the RND function so that you see a different arrangement of pixels when you run the program at different times. Line 130 selects black (0) as the background color and palette 1 for the foreground colors.

The program line

```
210 PSET (319 * RND, 199 * RND), 3 * RND
```

plots a pixel at a random column (319 * RND) and random row (199 * RND), in a random color (3 * RND) selected from palette 1, which was chosen in line 130.

The program repeats lines 210, 220, and 230 endlessly, or until you press (CTRL)-(BREAK). The program stops with the computer still in SCREEN 1 mode. You can return to SCREEN 0 like this:

Press (F10)

SCREEN 0 will be in WIDTH 40. Change it to WIDTH 80 the easy way, as follows:

Press (ALT)(W)   (*To type WIDTH*)

Type **80**
and press (ENTER)

Examples

Now enjoy two more of Zappy's programs.

1. Program 5-12, ZAPPY04 (Zappy Artist Draws Random Lines), draws random lines here, there, anywhere on the screen. Each line is drawn from a random point (*a*, *b*) to another random point (*c*, *d*). The speed at which lines are drawn is controlled by the duration in the SOUND statement in line 320, which causes a delay of about a half second (nine ticks) between lines. If you want to see Zappy really zap around the screen, and hear a different kind of "music," change line 320 to

    ```
    320 SOUND 3000 * RND + 1000, .25
    ```

    Of course, another way to speed up the action, and also rest your ears, is to zap, er, delete line 320. Just type **320** and press (ENTER).

2. You can easily and quickly edit Program 5-12, ZAPPY04, to obtain Program 5-13, Zappy05 (Zappy Artist Draws Random Boxes). The changes are in lines 1, 2, and 310. The modified line 310 is shown here. Note that it ends with the B option to tell the computer to draw a box instead of a line.

    ```
    310 LINE (a, b)-(c, d), Lcolor, B
    ```

Exercise

Modify Program 5-13, ZAPPY05, so that the boxes on the screen are filled with color. You need change only lines 1, 2, and 310. Save this

```
1 REM ** Zappy Artist Draws Random Lines **
2 ' Teach Yourself GW-BASIC, Chapter 5. Filename: ZAPPPY04.BAS

100 REM ** Set up **
110 SCREEN 1: CLS
120 RANDOMIZE TIMER
130 COLOR 0, 1

200 REM ** Compute random coordinates & line color **
210 a = 319 * RND
220 b = 199 * RND
230 c = 319 * RND
240 d = 199 * RND
250 Lcolor = 3 * RND

300 REM ** Draw a line from (a, b) to (c, d) in Lcolor **
310 LINE (a, b)-(c, d), Lcolor
320 SOUND 3000 * RND + 1000, 9

400 REM ** Go back for new coordinates and color **
410 GOTO 210
```

PROGRAM 5-12.   Zappy Artist Draws Random Lines

as Program ZAPPY06 (Zappy Artist Draws Random Boxes Filled with Color).

CUSTOMIZE THE KEY LINE   5.7

The key line indicates the current assignments to the function keys (F1) through (F10). You can use the KEY and LIST keywords together in a direct statement to list the complete key line assignments to the screen, as follows:

Press (F9), (F1), (ENTER)   *(Three keystrokes)*

```
1 REM ** Zappy Artist Draws Random Boxes**
2 ' Teach Yourself GW-BASIC, Chapter 5. Filename: ZAPPPY05.BAS

100 REM ** Set up **
110 SCREEN 1: CLS
120 RANDOMIZE TIMER
130 COLOR 0, 1

200 REM ** Compute random coordinates & line color **
210 a = 319 * RND
220 b = 199 * RND
230 c = 319 * RND
240 d = 199 * RND
250 Lcolor = 3 * RND

300 REM ** Draw a box from (a, b) to (c, d) in Lcolor **
310 LINE (a, b)-(c, d), Lcolor, B
320 SOUND 3000 * RND + 1000, 9

400 REM ** Go back for new coordinates and color **
410 GOTO 210
```

PROGRAM 5-13.   Zappy Artist Draws Random Boxes

The key line assignments are listed to the screen, as shown in Figure 5-1. Notice that assignments are shown for function keys (F1) through (F10), but not for (F11) and (F12).

You can assign a function of your choice to function keys (F1) through (F10). Do so now. Assign a WIDTH 80 statement as a string to function key (F7), like this:

Type **KEY 7, "WIDTH 80"**
and press (ENTER)

You can see part of the new assignment in the key line, as follows:

```
7WIDTH
```

```
KEY LIST
F1 LIST
F2 RUN←
F3 LOAD"
F4 SAVE"
F5 CONT←
F6 ,"LPT1:"
F7 TRON←
F8 TROFF←
F9 KEY
F10 SCREEN 0, 0, 0←
F11
F12
Ok

_
```

FIGURE 5-1.	Use KEY LIST to list the key line assignments

To see the complete key assignment, do a KEY LIST statement ((F9),
(F1), (ENTER)). You will see the following assignment for (F7).

```
F7 WIDTH 80
```

Now try it out. First change the screen width to 40 characters per
line. Then,

Press (F7)

Pressing (F7) causes this key's assigned string to be printed on the
screen. The cursor is blinking to the right of the string. It looks like
this:

```
WIDTH 80_
```

Now press (ENTER), and the WIDTH 80 statement is executed as if you
had typed it. From now on, you can change to WIDTH 80 by pressing
two keys, as follows:

Press (F7), (ENTER)

Unfortunately, this new key line assignment is lost when you leave GW-BASIC. When you next load GW-BASIC from DOS, the original (default) settings will appear. So why not write a short program to customize the key line to your taste? Then, whenever you load GW-BASIC, you can load this program and run it to set your personal key line assignments.

The program to customize the key line is shown next. It assigns WIDTH 80 to function key (F7), and COLOR 14, 1 to function key (F8).

```
1 REM ** Customize Key Line **
2 ' Teach Yourself GW-BASIC, Chapter 5. Filename: KEY.BAS

10 KEY 7, "WIDTH 80"
20 KEY 8, "Color 14, 1"
```

From now on, you can load this program (or your own version) and run it to customize the key line.

NOTE: You can include an (ENTER) keypress as part of a function key assignment. This has already been done in the default assignments for some function keys, such as (F2) (2RUN ←). The little arrow (←) tells you that the function of (F2) is carried out immediately when you press the key—you don't have to press (ENTER). If you wish to include this feature in your new assignments for (F7) and (F8), write lines 10 and 20 in Program KEY like this:

```
10 KEY 7, "WIDTH 80" + CHR$(13)
20 KEY 8, "COLOR 14, 1" + CHR$(13)
```

You will learn more about the CHR$ *string* function in Chapter 7.

MASTERY
SKILLS
CHECK

EXERCISES

1. The following program has an "enhanced" INPUT statement in line 20. Describe what happens when the computer executes line 20.

```
10 CLS
20 INPUT "Frequency"; frequency
40 SOUND frequency, 18
```

2. Add line 30 to the program in Exercise 1, so that the program asks for both the frequency and the duration of the sound. Modify line 40 appropriately.

3. Write a program, similar to the one in Exercises 1 and 2, that asks for values of *frequency* and *duration,* then sounds a tone using these values. Provide information to the user about the range of values allowed for *frequency* and *duration.* A sample run might look like the one shown here. Note that no question mark appears.

```
Enter a frequency from 37 to 32767:   262
Enter a duration between 0 and 65535: 18
```

After you enter both numbers, you hear the sound.

4. Show the result printed by the computer following execution of the following direct statements.

```
n = 73
Ok
d = 5
Ok
PRINT "The integer quotient of"; n; "divided by "; d; "is"; n \ d
```

5. Write a program that would result in the following two runs:

```
How many sentient beings live on Mars? 3
The population of Mars is 3 little green people.

How many sentient beings live on Mars? 1000000000
The population of Mars is 1E+09 little green people.
```

6. For each of these direct PRINT USING statements, show what the computer will print, including any spaces. Afterwards, enter the direct statement to verify your answer.
   a. PRINT USING "###"; 12
   b. PRINT USING "###"; –12
   c. PRINT USING "###"; 123

d. PRINT USING "###"; -123
e. PRINT USING "###"; 1234
f. PRINT USING "###"; .7
g. PRINT USING "###"; .3
h. PRINT USING "###"; -.3

7. For each of these direct PRINT USING statements, show what the computer will print, including any spaces. Afterwards, enter the direct statement to verify your answer.

a. PRINT USING "$$#,###.##"; 1234.567
b. PRINT USING "$$#,###.##"; -1234.567
c. PRINT USING "$$#,###.##"; 123.455
d. PRINT USING "$$#,###.##"; 123.4525
e. PRINT USING "$$#,###.##"; .999
f. PRINT USING "$$#,###.##"; .993

8. Write a program called METRIC01 (Convert Feet and Inches to Centimeters). Round the result to the nearest hundredth of a centimeter. In your program, use the fact that 1 inch equals 2.54 centimeters. Allow for up to 999.99 centimeters. Here is a sample run of the desired program.

```
Feet   ? 5
Inches? 3

Centimeters: 160.02
```

9. For this exercise, you must load GW-BASIC with the double precision function option, if you haven't already done so. Use the /D option when you load GW-BASIC from DOS.

If n is a positive integer, then the nth power of n is also a positive integer. The nth power of n is also called "n to the n." In mathematics books, it appears as n^n. Here are examples for $n = 1, 2,$ and 3.

$$1^1 = 1$$
$$2^2 = 4$$
$$3^3 = 27$$

Write a program called NPWRN01 (Compute the nth Power of n in Double Precision). Request a value of $n\#$, and then compute and print the value of $n\# \wedge n\#$. Note that $n\#$ is a double precision variable.

Two sample runs are shown next. For the first run, the printed result is exactly correct. It has eight digits, so it can be printed in double precision. The second result is printed as a double precision floating point number. It is a 16-digit approximation of the true result, which has 21 digits.

```
Positive integer, please: 8

 8 to the 8 is 16777216


Positive integer, please: 17

 17 to the 17 is 8.272402618863368D+20
```

Use your program to answer these questions: What is the largest integer for which the printed result is exactly correct? What is the corresponding result?

Strings, Decisions, and Loops

▶6◀

CHECKLIST ✓

CHAPTER OBJECTIVES

- ▶ Learn more about strings and string variables — 6.1
- ▶ Use INPUT with string variables — 6.2
- ▶ Use the IF statement for decision making — 6.3
- ▶ Learn about WHILE...WEND loops — 6.4
- ▶ Use FOR...NEXT loops for easy counting — 6.5
- ▶ Make sound effects — 6.6

GW-BASIC has several *control structures* you can use to make your programs more useful. In this chapter, you will learn how to use the IF statement for making decisions. You will also learn how to use two loop structures: WHILE...WEND and FOR...NEXT.

Previous chapters have introduced strings and string variables. You will explore them more in this chapter and use them in several programs.

SKILLS
CHECK

EXERCISES

Before beginning this chapter, you should know something about, or know how to do, the following things:

1. Use REM statements to annotate programs and make them easier for humans to read and understand.

2. Use INPUT statements to acquire information entered from the keyboard while a program is running.

3. Use strings in INPUT statements to identify desired information to be entered.

4. Use strings in PRINT statements to identify printed results.

5. Use PRINT USING statements with format strings to control the appearance of printed results.

6. Understand the use of GOTO loops to repeat a set of program lines. A GOTO loop is a control structure—you will learn how to use more powerful control structures in this chapter.

6.1 LEARN MORE ABOUT STRINGS AND STRING VARIABLES

A string is a group of characters, one after another in, well, a string. A string can be a

• name: Christopher

• telephone number: 707-555-1212

- message: Trust your psychic tailwind

- date: 1-1-91

- format string: $$###,###,###.##

You have seen strings enclosed in quotation marks:

```
DATE$ = "1-1-91"

PRINT "Laran Stardrake"

PRINT USING "$$###,###,###.##"; TotalAmount#
```

The quotation marks enclose the string, but are not part of the string. They tell the computer where the string begins and ends.

A *string variable* is specified by a name followed by a dollar sign ($). The name can be any combination of letters and numbers, but the first character must be a letter. Here are some examples of string variables:

DATE$ TIME$ *format$*   *Naym$*

The string variable *format$* was created for use in programs that appeared in previous chapters. Two of these, DATE$ and TIME$, are special string variables—they are GW-BASIC keywords.

NOTE: Most keywords may not be used as variables. For example, you may not use *Name$* as a string variable, because NAME is a GW-BASIC keyword. However, you can use *Naym$*, as shown above, as a string variable that sounds and looks like Name$.

In this book, string variables are shown in lowercase letters, or a mixture of lowercase and uppercase letters (except DATE$ and TIME$). No matter how you enter them, GW-BASIC will print all variables in uppercase when you list a program.

You can assign a value to a string variable in the same way that you assign a value to a numeric variable. For example, assign a value to the string variable *Naym$*, as shown next.

Type **Naym$ = "Laran Stardrake"**
and press (ENTER)

Verify that Laran's name is now the value of *Naym$*.

Type **PRINT Naym$**
and press (ENTER)

After executing the above direct statements, you will see the following on the screen:

```
Naym$ = "Laran Stardrake"

PRINT Naym$
Laran Stardrake
```

Assign a value to the string variable *PhoneNumber$*, and then verify it.

Type **PhoneNumber$ = "707-555-1212"**
and press (ENTER)

Type **PRINT PhoneNumber$**
and press (ENTER)

The last two direct statements and the information printed by the PRINT statement appear as shown here:

```
PhoneNumber$ = "707-555-1212"

PRINT PhoneNumber$
707-555-1212
```

Program 6-1, STRNGS01 (Print Two Strings in Various Ways), demonstrates several ways to print two strings with a single PRINT statement. Lines 310 through 370 introduce the use of an apostrophe (') to include a remark at the end of a program line. This remark is ignored by the computer, but provides information about the line for you to read.

The program prints the values of *FirstName$* and *LastName$* in seven ways. Table 6-1 shows each PRINT statement with its result.

```
1 REM ** Print Two Strings in Various Ways **
2 ' Teach Yourself GW-BASIC, Chapter 6. Filename: STRNGS01.BAS

100 REM ** Set up **
110 CLS

200 REM ** Assign values to string variables **
210 FirstName$ = "Laran"
220 LastName$ = "Stardrake"

300 REM ** Print values of 2 string variables in various ways **

310 PRINT FirstName$, LastName$          'Note comma
320 PRINT FirstName$; LastName$          'Note semicolon
330 PRINT FirstName$; " "; LastName$     'Put in a space
340 PRINT FirstName$ + LastName$         'Use + to join 2 strings
350 PRINT FirstName$ + " " + LastName$   'Use + to join 3 strings
360 PRINT LastName$; ", "; FirstName$    'Reverse order
370 PRINT LastName$ + ", " + FirstName$  'Another way to do it
```

PROGRAM 6-1.   Print Two Strings in Various Ways

Study the program and the printed results to learn more about the role of strings, commas, and semicolons in PRINT statements, and the use of a plus sign (+) to *catenate* (join) strings.

TABLE 6-1.   PRINT Statements and Their Printed Results

PRINT Statement	Printed Result
PRINT FirstName$, LastName$	Laran Stardrake
PRINT FirstName$; LastName$	LaranStardrake
PRINT FirstName$; " "; LastName$	Laran Stardrake
PRINT FirstName$ + LastName$	LaranStardrake
PRINT FirstName$ + " " + LastName$	Laran Stardrake
PRINT LastName$; ", "; FirstName$	Stardrake, Laran
PRINT LastName$ + ", " + FirstName$	Stardrake, Laran

The program line

```
310 PRINT FirstName$, LastName$     'Note comma
```

contains a remark ('Note comma). You can annotate your programs this way to make them more readable. The computer ignores the apostrophe and everything to its right on that line.

Examples

1. You can assign the value of a variable to another variable. After doing so, both variables have the same value. For example, assign the value of DATE$ to the string variable *Today$*, and then print the values of both DATE$ and *Today$*.

```
Today$ = DATE$

PRINT Today$, DATE$
01-24-1991    01-24-1991
```

You can assign the value of TIME$ to a variable called, say, *StartTime$*. For an instant, these two variables will have the same value. However, TIME$ marches on, while *StartTime$* remains the same.

```
StartTime$ = TIME$

PRINT StartTime$, TIME$
07:59:53      08:01:06
```

2. You can use a plus sign (+) to catenate (join) strings and assign the result to a variable. The example shown below catenates the value of DATE$, two spaces, and the value of TIME$. It then assigns the result to the variable *DateTime$*.

```
DateTime$ = DATE$ + "  " + TIME$

PRINT DateTime$
01-24-1991  08:06:35
```

In a PRINT statement, you can use either the plus sign (+) or a semicolon (;) to catenate strings, as shown here:

```
PRINT DATE$ + "   " + TIME$
01-24-1991  08:16:01

PRINT DATE$; "   "; TIME$
01-24-1991  08:16:17
```

Exercises

1. Assign these values to strings:

   ```
   FirstName$ = "Christopher"

   MiddleName$ = "John"

   LastName$ = "Hassenpfeffer"
   ```

   Then complete each of the following, showing what the computer prints:

   ```
   PRINT FirstName$, MiddleName$, LastName$
   ```
   _____

   ```
   PRINT FirstName$; MiddleName$; LastName$
   ```
   _____

   ```
   PRINT FirstName$ + MiddleName$ + LastName$
   ```
   _____

2. Assume that values have been assigned to *FirstName$*, *Middle-Name$*, and *LastName$*, as in Exercise 1. Use these three variables in PRINT statements to produce the following results:

   a. `Christopher John Hassenpfeffer`
   b. `Hassenpfeffer, Christopher John`

6.2 | USE INPUT WITH STRING VARIABLES

You can use INPUT to acquire a value for a string variable. In the following program, an INPUT statement is used to acquire a value for the string variable *Strng$*. This variable is used in lieu of String$, which is a GW-BASIC keyword (STRING$).

```
10 CLS
20 INPUT Strng$
30 PRINT Strng$
40 PRINT: GOTO 20
```

Enter and run the program. It clears the screen, prints a question mark, displays the cursor, and waits for you to enter a value for *Strng$*, as shown here:

```
? _
```

Enter Laran Stardrake's name.

Type **Laran Stardrake**
and press (ENTER)

The computer accepts Laran's name as the value of *Strng$*, prints the value of *Strng$*, and then loops back to the INPUT statement and waits for a new value of *Strng$*:

```
? Laran Stardrake
Laran Stardrake

? _
```

Now enter Laran's name in reverse order: last name, a comma, and then first name.

Type **Stardrake, Laran**
and press (ENTER)

Oops! Trouble. You see this on the screen:

```
? Stardrake, Laran
?Redo from start

? _
```

If a string contains a comma, you must enclose the entire string in quotation marks. This time enter Laran's name in reverse order, enclosed in quotation marks.

Type **"Stardrake, Laran"**
and press (ENTER)

This time the computer will accept the string containing a comma. The screen looks like this:

```
? "Stardrake, Laran"
Stardrake, Laran

? _
```

Enter more values of *Strng$*. When you are finished, press (CTRL)(BREAK) to stop the program.

Example

Program 6-2, NAME01 (Name Everywhere with Color & Sound INPUT), begins by asking for your name. After you type your name, or any string, the program fills the screen with that string in many colors, accompanied by random "music."

As usual, to find out what a program does, you enter it into memory and run it. First, you see

```
Your name? _
```

```
1 REM ** Name Everywhere with Color & Sound INPUT **
2 ' Teach Yourself GW-BASIC, Chapter 6. Filename: NAME01.BAS

100 REM ** Set up **
110 CLS

200 REM ** Use INPUT to get a value of Name$ **
210 INPUT "Your name"; Naym$

300 REM ** Use a GOTO loop to print name with color & sound **

310 COLOR 31 * RND, 8 * RND              'Top of GOTO loop
320 PRINT Naym$;
330 SOUND 3000 * RND + 1000, .25
340 GOTO 310                             'Bottom of GOTO loop
```

PROGRAM 6-2. Name Everywhere with Color & Sound INPUT

Alice, having recently returned from Wonderland, typed a quotation mark, her name, two spaces, and another quotation mark.

```
Your name? "Alice  "_
```

Then she pressed (ENTER). Quickly the screen filled with her name in many foreground colors on assorted background colors, accompanied by strange music reminiscent of her recent adventure.

Stop the program now, and run it again. Type Alice's name with two trailing spaces, but not enclosed in quotation marks, like this:

```
Your name? Alice
```

—— Type two spaces here

After you press (ENTER), you will again see Alice's name everywhere, but without the two spaces you typed. When you don't enter quotation marks, the computer ignores leading and trailing spaces in a string you enter.

Exercises

1. If a string contains a comma, leading spaces, or trailing spaces, how must you enter it as a value for a variable in an INPUT statement?

2. Consider a message to be printed once on every line, consisting of a person's name (value of *Naym$*) in one random color, followed by a phrase such as "is AOK!" (value of *Phrase$*) in another random color. Write a program that will

    a. Ask for a value of *Naym$*.

    b. Ask for a value of *Phrase$*.

    c. Print the values of *Naym$* and *Phrase$* side by side on one line, with each value in a random color.

    d. Loop back to the statements in c.

USE THE IF STATEMENT FOR DECISION MAKING

6.3

The IF statement tells the computer to make a simple decision. It tells the computer to do a certain operation if a given condition exists (is true). If the condition is not met (is false), the operation is not done. Here is a simple IF statement:

```
420 IF number = 0 THEN PRINT z$
```

This IF statement tells the computer the following:

*   If the value of the numeric variable *number* is equal to zero, then print the value of the string variable z$.

*   If the value of the numeric variable *number* is not equal to zero, then don't print the value of the string variable z$.

Here is another way to think about it:

*   If the value of *number* is equal to zero, execute the statement following the keyword THEN.

- If the value of *number* is not equal to zero, don't execute the statement following the keyword THEN.

And yet another way:

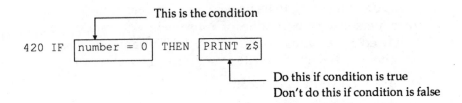

In the foregoing IF statement, the condition is *number = 0*. Here are three possibilities:

- Suppose the value of *number* is 3.14. In this case, the condition is false, and the computer does not print the value of *z$*.

- Suppose the value of *number* is zero. Now the condition is true. The computer prints the value of *z$*.

- Suppose the value of *number* is –7. The condition is false, and the computer does not print the value of *z$*.

The above IF statement is in the general form:

IF *condition* THEN *statement*

In this form, the *statement* can be any GW-BASIC statement. The *condition* is usually a comparison between a variable and a value, between two variables, or between two complicated expressions. Table 6-2 shows some comparison symbols in both math and GW-BASIC notation.

Program 6-3, NZP01 (Negative, Zero, or Positive with IF Statements), tests a number entered from the keyboard to determine whether the number is negative, zero, or positive.

| TABLE 6-2. | Comparison Symbols in Math and GW-BASIC | |

Comparison	Math Symbol	GW-BASIC Symbol
Equal to	=	=
Less than	<	<
Greater than	>	>
Less than or equal to	≤	<=
Greater than or equal to	≥	>=
Not equal to	≠	<>

```
1 REM ** Negative, Zero, or Positive with IF Statements **
2 ' Teach Yourself GW-BASIC, Chapter 6. Filename: NZP01.BAS

100 REM ** Set up **
110 n$ = "negative"
120 z$ = "zero"
130 p$ = "positive"

200 REM ** Tell what to do **
210 CLS
220 PRINT "Enter a number and I will tell you whether"
230 PRINT "your number is negative, zero, or positive."

300 REM ** Ask for a number **
310 PRINT                              'Top of loop
320 INPUT "Enter a number: ", number

400 REM ** Tell about the number **
410 IF number < 0 THEN PRINT n$
420 IF number = 0 THEN PRINT z$
430 IF number > 0 THEN PRINT p$

500 REM ** Go to top of loop **
510 GOTO 310                           'Bottom of loop
```

| PROGRAM 6-3. | Negative, Zero, or Positive with IF Statements |

Blocks 300, 400, and 500 are in a GOTO loop that acquires a number entered from the keyboard and then evaluates whether the number is negative, zero, or positive. These blocks are shown here:

```
300 REM ** Ask for a number **
310 PRINT                                    'Top of loop
320 INPUT "Enter a number: ", number

400 REM ** Tell about the number **
410 IF number < 0 THEN PRINT n$
420 IF number = 0 THEN PRINT z$
430 IF number > 0 THEN PRINT p$

500 REM ** Go to top of loop **
510 GOTO 310                                 'Bottom of loop
```

If you enter a negative number, line 410 causes the value of *n$* ("negative") to be printed. If you enter zero (0), line 420 is activated; the value of *z$* ("zero") is printed. If your number is positive, line 430 prints the value of *p$* ("positive"). Line 510 then sends control back to the beginning of the loop. Use (CTRL)(BREAK) to stop the program. Figure 6-1 shows a sample run.

```
Enter a number and I will tell you whether
your number is negative, zero, or positive.

Enter a number: 0
zero

Enter a number: 3.14
positive

Enter a number: -7
negative

Enter a number: _
```

FIGURE 6-1. | Sample run of Program NZP01

Examples

1. Program 6-4, KWH06 (Cost of Electricity with IF Statement), compares the value of *kwh* that you enter to the baseline *kwh* value of 846. The cost of electricity is then computed in one of two ways, as follows:

    - If the value of *kwh* is less than or equal to 846, then

      ```
      KwhCost = kwh * LoRate
      ```

    - If the value of *kwh* is greater than 846, then

      ```
      KwhCost = 846 * LoRate + (kwh - 846) * HiRate
      ```

```
1 REM ** Cost of Electricity with IF Statement **
2 ' Teach Yourself GW-BASIC, Chapter 6. Filename: KWH06.BAS

100 REM ** Set up **
110 CLS
120 LoRate = .08882
130 HiRate = .13524
140 format$ = "$$###,###.##"

200 REM ** Get number of kilowatt-hours (kwh) **
210 INPUT "Enter number of kilowatt-hours: ", kwh

300 REM ** Compute cost of electricity **
310 IF kwh <= 846 THEN KwhCost = kwh * LoRate
320 IF kwh > 846 THEN KwhCost = 846 * LoRate + (kwh - 846) * HiRate

400 REM ** Print cost of electricity **
410 PRINT
420 PRINT "Total cost of electricity is";
430 PRINT USING format$; KwhCost
```

PROGRAM 6-4. Cost of Electricity with IF Statement

These cost decisions are made by IF statements in lines 310 and 320 of the program. A sample run is shown here for a value of *kwh* less than 846. The cost is computed in line 310.

```
Enter number of kilowatt-hours: 789

Total cost of electricity is       $70.08
```

The next sample run is for a value of *kwh* greater than the baseline value of 846. The cost is computed by line 320.

```
Enter number of kilowatt-hours: 1435

Total cost of electricity is      $154.80
```

For a third run to test the program, try a value of 846. The cost should be computed (in line 310) as $75.14.

2. Block 300 of Program 6-4, KWH06, can be written in several other ways. One is shown here.

```
300 REM ** Compute cost of electricity **
310 IF kwh <= 846 THEN KwhCost = kwh * LoRate: GOTO 410
320 KwhCost = 846 * LoRate + (kwh - 846) * HiRate
```

- If the value of *kwh* is less than or equal to 846, line 310 computes the cost (*KwhCost*), and then sends control to line 410, thus bypassing line 320. Note the colon (:) separating GOTO 410 from the previous statement that computes the value of *KwhCost*.

- If the value of *kwh* is greater than 846, the two statements following THEN in line 310 are not executed. Instead, the computer executes line 320, and continues on to line 410.

Here is yet another way to write block 300.

```
300 REM ** Compute the cost of electricity **
310 IF kwh <= 846 THEN BaseKwh = kwh: XtraKwh = 0
320 IF kwh > 846 THEN BaseKwh = 846: XtraKwh = kwh - 846
330 KwhCost = BaseKwh * LoRate + XtraKwh * HiRate
```

Exercises

1. Write a Program called THERMS01 (Cost of Gas) to compute and
   print the cost of gas measured in therms. Gas is charged at the
   rate of $0.44826 per therm for the first 84 therms, and $0.84849
   per therm for additional therms. Two sample runs of the desired
   program are shown here.
   In sample run #1, the number of therms entered is less than
   the baseline number of 84 therms. Therefore, the cost is computed using the low rate.

   ```
   Enter number of therms of gas: 70

   Total cost of gas is      $31.38
   ```

   In sample run #2, the number of therms entered is greater than
   84. Therefore, 84 therms are charged at the low rate, and the
   therms over 84 are charged at the high rate.

   ```
   Enter number of therms of gas: 97

   Total cost of gas is      $48.68
   ```

2. Write a Program called ENERGY01 (Cost of Energy, Gas &
   Electricity) to compute the total cost of both gas and electricity.
   Use the method shown in Example 1 or 2 to compute the cost of
   electricity, and the method used in your solution to Exercise 1 to
   compute the cost of gas. A sample run is shown here.

   ```
   Enter number of therms of gas:        97
   Enter kilowatt-hours of electricity: 1435

   Cost of gas:             $48.68
   Cost of electricity:     $154.80
   Total utilities cost:    $203.48
   ```

6.4 | LEARN ABOUT WHILE...WEND LOOPS

You have already used GOTO loops to repeat a group of statements. Now learn about another loop structure, called a WHILE...WEND loop. A WHILE...WEND loop repeats a set of statements while a condition is true. A WHILE...WEND loop begins with a WHILE statement (lowest line number), ends with a WEND statement (highest line number), and can have any number of statements in between. The WHILE statement must contain an expression that serves as a condition, which can evaluate to true or false. If the condition is true, the loop continues; if the condition is false, the loop ends, and the program continues with the line that follows the WEND statement (if there is a line).

In the following WHILE...WEND loop, the condition in the WHILE statement is the number one (1). This "condition" is always true. Therefore, the loop continues until you press (CTRL)-(BREAK).

```
10 WHILE 1
20   PRINT "Press CTRL BREAK to stop me"
30 WEND
```

Enter and run the program listed above. The screen quickly fills with the message "Press CTRL BREAK to stop me" as the statement inside the WHILE...WEND loop (line 20) is repeated. Press (CTRL)-(BREAK) to stop the program. The bottom part of the screen displays these lines:

```
Press CTRL BREAK to stop me
Press CTRL BREAK to stop me
Press CTRL BREAK to stop me

Break in 20
```

Any number other than zero (0) serves as a true condition in the WHILE statement. Now change line 10 so that the program looks like this:

```
10 WHILE 0
20   PRINT "Press CTRL BREAK to stop me"
30 WEND
```

Here the condition in the WHILE statement is the number zero (0). This condition is always false. The statement inside the loop (line 20) is not executed, not even once. You can verify this by running the program, as shown here:

```
RUN
Ok
_
```

NOTE: In all the above WHILE...WEND loops, line 20 is indented. This line is *inside* the WHILE...WEND loop, between the beginning of the loop (line 10) and the end of the loop (line 30). Though not a requirement, it is good practice to indent lines inside a WHILE...WEND loop.

Examples

1. The condition in the WHILE statement is usually an expression that evaluates to either true or false. The following program prints the integers from 1 to 10. The condition in the WHILE statement is true when the value of *number* is less than or equal to 10, but false for any value greater than 10.

```
10 CLS
20 number = 1
30 WHILE number <= 10
40   PRINT number,
50   number = number + 1
60 WEND
```

Enter and run the program. The screen will look like this:

```
1        2        3        4        5
6        7        8        9        10
```

2. You can also use a WHILE...WEND loop to count down. Here is a short "Count Down...Blast Off!" program.

```
10 CLS
20 number = 10
```

```
30 WHILE number >= 0
40    PRINT number
50    number = number - 1
60 WEND
70 PRINT "Blastoff!!!"
80 PRINT "Everything is AOK"
```

Line 20 sets the value of *number* to 10. The lines inside the WHILE...WEND loop are repeated as long as the value of *number* is greater than or equal to zero (WHILE *number* >= 0). Since line 50 counts down the value of *number*, eventually it reaches zero, and then goes negative. The loop ends without printing the negative value. Figure 6-2 shows a sample run.

3. Some applications require precise timing of events. For example, suppose you are writing a "flash card" program. You want to put a question on the screen for, say, five seconds, and then show the answer. You can use the TIMER function in a WHILE...WEND loop to construct a time delay, as shown in the following program.

```
10 CLS
20 PRINT "You will hear a beep every second"

30 BEEP                         'Top of GOTO loop
40 start = TIMER
50 WHILE TIMER < start + 1     'One second time delay
60 WEND
70 GOTO 30                      'Bottom of GOTO loop
```

When you run the program, you see the message, "You will hear a beep every second." Indeed, you do hear the computer beep...beep...beep... as the seconds pass. This happens because lines 40 through 60 cause a one-second time delay.

Line 40 sets the value of *start* to the current value of TIMER. TIMER, of course, keeps ticking away, keeping track of the number of seconds since midnight. Therefore, the value of TIMER is increasing. The WHILE...WEND loop goes round and round, as long as TIMER is less than the value of *start* plus one second.

You can shorten the time delay loop by combining lines 40,

```
                    10
                    9
                    8
                    7
                    6
                    5
                    4
                    3
                    2
                    1
                    0
                    Blastoff!!!
                    Everything is AOK
                    Ok
                    _
```

FIGURE 6-2.	Run of CountDown...Blast Off! Program

50, and 60 into a single line. In the next program, line 40 contains three statements separated by colons (:).

```
10 CLS
20 PRINT "You will hear a beep every second"

30 BEEP                                    'Top of loop
40 start = TIMER: WHILE TIMER < start + 1: WEND '1 sec. delay
50 GOTO 30                                 'Bottom of loop
```

You can also easily change the amount of delay. For example, for a 10-second delay, change the WHILE statement as follows:

```
WHILE TIMER < start + 10
```

Program 6-5, DELAY01 (Time Delay Using a WHILE...WEND Loop), illustrates a variable time delay. The amount of delay is entered as the value of a value called, appropriately, *delay*.

```
1 REM ** Time Delay Using a WHILE...WEND Loop **
2 ' Teach Yourself GW-BASIC, Chapter 6. Filename: DELAY01.BAS

10 CLS

20 INPUT "Delay time (seconds)"; delay

30 PRINT
40 PRINT "You will hear a beep every"; delay; "second(s)."

50 WHILE 1
60   BEEP
70   start = TIMER: WHILE TIMER < start + delay: WEND
80 WEND
```

PROGRAM 6-5.   Time Delay Using a WHILE...WEND Loop

Exercises

1. What will be printed when you run the program shown here?

```
10 CLS
20 number = 1
30 WHILE number <= 10
40   PRINT number,
50   number = number + 2
60 WEND
```

2. Write a program to print even numbers, from 2 to a limit you enter in response to an INPUT statement. Here is a sample run.

```
Count by twos to what number? 8

    2           4           6           8
```

USE FOR...NEXT LOOPS FOR EASY COUNTING
6.5

Counting loops occur frequently in programs, so GW-BASIC has a loop structure designed to make counting easy. It is called the FOR...NEXT loop. The following short program contains a FOR...NEXT loop in lines 20 through 40:

```
10 CLS
20 FOR number = 1 TO 10
30   PRINT number,
40 NEXT number
```

The FOR...NEXT loop generates and prints the integers from 1 to 10. Here is a sample run:

```
1         2         3         4         5
6         7         8         9         10
```

The above FOR...NEXT loop tells the computer to count from 1 to 10, as illustrated here:

```
              Count from here to here

        20 FOR number = 1 TO 10
```

As the computer counts from 1 to 10, each value is assigned to the variable *number*. This value is printed by the PRINT statement in line 30, which is inside the FOR...NEXT loop.

A FOR...NEXT loop begins with a FOR statement, ends with a NEXT statement, and can have any number of statements in between. In the FOR statement, a numeric variable must follow the keyword FOR:

```
        20 FOR number = 1 TO 10

                     Numeric variable
```

The same numeric variable follows the keyword NEXT:

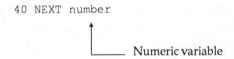

This numeric variable can be used in statements between the FOR and NEXT statements, like this:

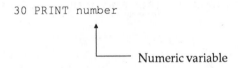

A FOR statement defines a sequence of values for the variable that follows the keyword FOR. Some examples are shown in Table 6-3.

Examples

1. The default screen colors are white letters on a black screen. You can use the COLOR statement to tell the computer to print in any of 16 colors, including black (COLOR 0) and the standard white (COLOR 7). Of course, black on a black screen is invisible.

| TABLE 6-3. | The FOR Statement Defines a Sequence of Values |

FOR Statement	Sequence of Values
FOR number = 1 TO 10	1, 2, 3, 4, 5, 6, 7, 8, 9, 10
FOR k = 1 TO 6	1, 2, 3, 4, 5, 6
FOR x = 0 TO 7	0, 1, 2, 3, 4, 5, 6, 7
FOR n = -1 TO 1	-1, 0, 1

Program 6-6, COLORS01 (A Colorful FOR...NEXT Loop), prints one line in each of the 15 colors and tells you the color number in which it prints. Run the program. If you have a color monitor, you will see 15 vivid colors. Figure 6-3 shows a black and white printout. Most of the work is done by the FOR...NEXT loop shown here:

```
210 FOR kolor = 1 TO 15
220    COLOR kolor
230    PRINT "This is color number"; kolor
240 NEXT kolor
```

Since COLOR is a keyword, a sound-alike word (*kolor*) is used as the numeric variable for the sequence of color numbers, 1 through 15. This variable appears in all four lines of the FOR...NEXT loop.

The statement

```
COLOR kolor
```

```
1 REM ** A Colorful FOR...NEXT Loop **
2 ' Teach Yourself GW-BASIC, Chapter 6. Filename: COLORS01.BAS

100 REM ** Set up **
110 CLS

200 REM ** FOR...NEXT loop to print in 15 foreground colors **
210 FOR kolor = 1 TO 15
220    COLOR kolor
230    PRINT "This is color number"; kolor
240 NEXT kolor

300 REM ** Return screen to white foreground color **
310 COLOR 7
320 PRINT
330 PRINT "This is in the 'normal' screen color"
```

PROGRAM 6-6. A Colorful FOR...NEXT Loop

```
This is color number 1
This is color number 2
This is color number 3
This is color number 4
This is color number 5
This is color number 6
This is color number 7
This is color number 8
This is color number 9
This is color number 10
This is color number 11
This is color number 12
This is color number 13
This is color number 14
This is color number 15

This is in the 'normal' screen color
Ok
—
```

FIGURE 6-3.   Black and white printout of Program 6-6, COLORS01

tells the computer to set the foreground color to the color specified by the value of the numeric variable *kolor*. The information printed by line 230 appears in this color. When it exits from the FOR...NEXT loop, line 310 sets the foreground color to the "normal" color:

```
310 COLOR 7
```

Color numbers from 0 to 15 designate nonblinking colors. Color 0 is black and was not included in the color sequence. Color numbers from 16 to 31 designate blinking colors. To see blinking colors, change the FOR statement to

```
210 FOR kolor = 17 TO 31
```

2. The FOR...NEXT loops you have seen so far count up, from a lower to a higher number. You can also count down, from a higher number to a lower number. To do so, include a STEP clause, as shown in line 20 of the following program.

```
10 CLS
20 FOR number = 10 TO 0 STEP -1
30   PRINT number,
40 NEXT number
```

A sample run is shown below.

```
10          9          8          7          6
5           4          3          2          1
0
```

3. You can put any number in a STEP clause. The number following STEP defines the amount that the variable that follows FOR changes each time. For example, in the following FOR...NEXT loop, the loop variable *k* has this sequence of values: 1, 3, 5, 9.

```
FOR k = 1 TO 9 STEP 2
   PRINT k,
NEXT k
```

The following FOR...NEXT loop uses a noninteger STEP size. The values of *x* are 0, .25, .50, .75, and 1.

```
FOR x = 0 TO 1 STEP .25
   PRINT x,
NEXT x
```

Exercises

1. In each of the following FOR statements, show the sequence of values that will be assigned to the variable following FOR, as shown in Table 6-3.

FOR Statement	Sequence of Values
a. FOR n = 0 TO 5	_____
b. FOR x = .5 TO 2.5	_____
c. FOR y = 1 TO 2.5	_____
d. FOR z = 1 TO 2.5 STEP .5	_____
e. FOR w = 100 TO 200 STEP 10	_____

2. For each sequence of values, write a FOR statement that will generate them.

Sequence of Values	**FOR Statement**
a. 0, 3, 6, 9	_____
b. 10, 8, 6, 4, 2, 0	_____
c. 1000, 2000, 3000	_____
d. 3, 2.5, 2, 1.5, 1	_____

3. Write a program to print a table of values of n and 1.01^n for $n =$ 600, 620, 640, 660, 680, and 700, as shown below. Use a FOR...NEXT loop to generate the sequence of values of n.

```
Value of n      Value of 1.01 ^ n
  600              391.5812
  620              477.8034
  640              583.0108
  660              711.3839
  680              868.0233
  700             1059.153
```

Notice that the value of 1.01^n becomes larger than n somewhere between $n= 640$ and $n = 660$. How can you now modify your program to find the smallest integer value of n for which 1.01^n is equal to or larger than n?

6.6 | MAKE SOUND EFFECTS

Have you ever wondered how they make all those strange sounds in arcade games? Try the following program:

```
10 CLS
30 WHILE 1
40    FOR frequency = 100 TO 300
50       SOUND frequency, .25
60    NEXT frequency
70 WEND
```

The FOR...NEXT loop makes a sequence of very short sounds, starting at 100 Hz and ending at 300 Hz. Thus you hear a rapidly rising pitch. Now change line 40 so that the pitch falls from 300 to 100 Hz:

```
40    FOR frequency = 300 TO 100 STEP -1
```

Run the modified program to hear a familiar arcade game sound. You hear a sound with a rapidly falling pitch. The frequency lowers quickly from 300 Hz to 100 Hz in steps of –1 Hz. The sequence of frequency values is

```
300, 299, 298, ..., 100
```

Now put both ideas together into Program 6-7, SOUND02 (Siren Song). As the name suggests, it makes a sound like a siren. The sound goes up, down, up, down, and so on, until you press (CTRL)-(BREAK).

You can make the pitch rise and fall at different rates by changing lines 120, 220, and 250. For example, to make the pitch rise and fall more quickly, change lines 220 and 250 as shown here:

```
220   FOR frequency = 523 TO 1046 STEP 2     'Rising pitch

250   FOR frequency = 1046 TO 523 STEP -2    'Falling pitch
```

Use Program 6-8, SOUND03 (Sound Effects Experimenter), to experiment with FOR...NEXT loops and find effects to your liking. To get a rising pitch, enter a smaller number for the beginning frequency, a larger number for the ending frequency, and a positive step size, as shown in this sample run:

```
Beginning frequency? 500

Ending frequency   ? 1000

Frequency step size? 10

Duration each sound? .125

Number of times    ? 5
```

The last item entered (Number of times) is the number of times you want the entire sound repeated. When you run the program using

```
1 REM ** Siren Song **
2 ' Teach Yourself GW-BASIC, Chapter 6. Filename: SOUND02.BAS

100 REM ** Set up **
110 CLS
120 duration = .125

200 REM ** Make a rising, then falling sound **
210 WHILE 1

220    FOR frequency = 523 TO 1046          'Rising pitch
230       SOUND frequency, duration
240    NEXT frequency

250    FOR frequency = 1046 TO 523 STEP -1   'Falling pitch
260       SOUND frequency, duration
270    NEXT frequency

280 WEND
```

PROGRAM 6-7.   Siren Song

---

these numbers, you will hear a sound that goes whoop, whoop, whoop, whoop, whoop.

To get a sound with a falling pitch, enter a larger number for the beginning frequency, a smaller number for the ending frequency, and a negative step size, as shown here:

```
Beginning frequency? 3000

Ending frequency   ? 1000

Frequency step size? -100

Duration each sound? .25

Number of times    ? 10
```

The INPUT statements that acquire the above information are in block 200 of the program. Each INPUT statement is preceded by a

```
1 REM ** Sound Effects Experimenter **
2 ' Teach Yourself GW-BASIC, Chapter 6. Filename: SOUND03.BAS

100 REM ** Set up **
110 CLS

200 REM ** Get parameters for experiment **
210 LOCATE 1, 1: INPUT "Beginning frequency"; BeginFreq
220 LOCATE 3, 1: INPUT "Ending frequency   "; FinalFreq
230 LOCATE 5, 1: INPUT "Frequency step size"; StepSize
240 LOCATE 7, 1: INPUT "Duration each sound"; duration
260 LOCATE 9, 1: INPUT "Number of times    "; NmbrTimes

300 REM ** Make the sound **
310 FOR k = 1 TO NmbrTimes
320   FOR frequency = BeginFreq TO FinalFreq STEP StepSize
330     SOUND frequency, duration
340   NEXT frequency
350 NEXT k

400 REM ** Go back for a new set of data **
410 GOTO 110
```

| PROGRAM 6-8. | Sound Effects Experimenter |

LOCATE statement that positions the cursor. For example, this statement in line 240:

```
LOCATE 7, 1
```

puts the cursor at line 7, column 1 of the screen. The string in the INPUT statement ("Duration each sound") is printed at the cursor position. You can use a LOCATE statement to put the cursor anywhere on the screen. For example, LOCATE 12, 40 puts the cursor at line 12, column 40.

Block 300, shown below, features *nested* FOR...NEXT loops, that is a loop within a loop. Lines 320 through 340 comprise the inner loop. This loop is nested inside the outer loop, which begins at line 310 and ends at line 350.

```
300 REM ** Make the sound **
310 FOR k = 1 TO NmbrTimes
320   FOR frequency = BeginFreq TO FinalFreq STEP StepSize
330     SOUND frequency, duration
340   NEXT frequency
350 NEXT k
```

The inner loop makes the rising or falling sound. The outer loop controls the number of times the rising or falling sound is made. Note that the entire inner loop is indented within the outer loop. This is an element of programming style, intended to help you more easily read and understand the program.

Exercises

1. Try each of the following sets of values with Program 6-8, SOUND03. You choose the number of times you want to hear the sound.

Beginning Frequency	Ending Frequency	STEP Size	Duration
1000	10000	1000	0.25
8000	4000	−500	0.125
50	100	5	0.5
440	262	−178	9
200	500	100	6

2. Write another program to experiment with sound effects. Call it SOUND04 (Sound Effects Experimenter #2). Your program should make a sound that goes from a low frequency to a high frequency, and then back down to the low frequency; then repeat the sequence a specified number of times. Begin by acquiring data, as shown here:

```
Low frequency       ? 500
High frequency      ? 1000
Frequency step size? 20
Duration each sound? .25
Number of times     ? 5
```

For variables, consider using *LoFreq, HiFreq, StepSize, duration,* and *NmbrTimes.* After entering the values shown above, you should hear a rapidly rising pitch from 500 Hz to 1000 Hz in steps of 10 Hz, and then a rapidly falling pitch from 1000 Hz to 500 Hz. The sound is heard five times.

EXERCISES

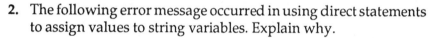

MASTERY
SKILLS
CHECK

1. Here are some numeric and string variables. Circle each string variable.

   pi   PhoneNumber$ x$ Naym   number$

2. The following error message occurred in using direct statements to assign values to string variables. Explain why.

   a. `format = "###,###.##"`
      `Type mismatch`

   b. `Naym$ = Laran Stardrake`
      `Type mismatch`

3. Consider these values assigned to variables:

   `City$ = "Sebastopol"`

   `State$ = "CA"`

   `Zipcode$ = "95472"`

   Use the variables *City$, State$,* and *Zipcode$* in a PRINT statement to print the following:

   `Sebastopol, CA 95472`

4. Write a short program to acquire values for *City$, State$,* and *Zipcode$,* and then print them on one line as in Exercise 3. A sample run is shown here:

   ```
   City    ? Sebastopol
   State   ? CA
   ```

```
Zipcode? 95472

Sebastopol, CA 95472
```

5. A positive integer is even (2, 4, 6, 8, and so on) or odd (1, 3, 5, 7, and so on). Complete the IF statements in the following program so that the computer prints "even" if you enter an even positive integer, or prints "odd" if you enter an odd positive integer:

```
10 CLS
20 INPUT "Enter a positive integer: ", number%

30 IF _____THEN PRINT "even"

40 IF _____THEN PRINT "odd"

50 PRINT
60 GOTO 20
```

Note the use of the integer variable *number%*. This program is designed to work only with positive integers in the range 1 to 32767. However, try zero (0) and negative integers just to see what happens.

6. In preparing for a camping trip, you want to add the weights of items you will carry in your backpack. Item weights are given in pounds and ounces. Here is a REM outline of a program called LBOZ01 (Add Weights Given in Pounds and Ounces).

```
1 REM ** Add Weights Given in Pounds and Ounces **
2 ' Teach Yourself GW-BASIC, Chapter 6. Filename: LBOZ01.BAS

100 REM ** Set up **

200 REM ** Get weight in pounds & ounces, exit if pounds < 0 **

300 REM ** Add to previous totals and go back for more data **

400 REM ** Convert ounces to pounds & ounces, compute totals **

500 REM ** Print totals **
```

In block 200, use an IF statement to exit from the block if the value of pounds is less than zero. In this case, exit to line 410 in block 400, compute the final totals so that the number of ounces is less than 16 (convert ounces to pounds and ounces), and then print the totals (block 500). A sample run is shown here.

```
Pounds? 0
Ounces? 13

Pounds? 2
Ounces? 0

Pounds? 7
Ounces? 12

Pounds? -1

Total weight: 10 pounds, 9 ounces
```

7. The following program uses a GOTO loop to repeatedly sound three tones. Rewrite the program using a WHILE...WEND loop instead of a GOTO loop.

```
10 CLS
20 SOUND 262, 9
30 SOUND 440, 9
40 SOUND 523, 9
50 GOTO 20
```

8. Rewrite the program in Exercise 7 so that the three tones are sounded exactly five times. Write the program in two ways.

    a. Use a WHILE...WEND loop.

    b. Use a FOR...NEXT loop.

9. Write a program to display an empty screen in each background screen color (0 through 7) for two seconds. Use a WHILE...WEND loop for the two-second time delay, as shown in Section 6.4.

10. In Chapter 5, you saw programs by Zappy Artist to plot random pixels, and to draw random lines, boxes, and circles. Rewrite Program 5-11, ZAPPY03 (Zappy Artist Plots Pixels Pixilatedly), in two ways.

a. Use a WHILE...WEND loop instead of a GOTO loop.

b. Use a FOR...NEXT loop to plot a specific number of pixels. Use an INPUT statement to acquire the number of pixels to plot.

Function Junction

►7◄

CHAPTER OBJECTIVES

▶ Learn about functions without arguments   7.1

▶ Learn about numeric functions that require
arguments   7.2

▶ Learn about string functions that require
arguments   7.3

▶ Understand ASCII codes and characters   7.4

▶ Sample a flock of numeric functions   7.5

▶ Explore wiggly functions with Zappy Artist   7.6

GW-BASIC has a rich repertoire of built-in *functions*. A function is a keyword that, when used, returns a *value*; this value is the result computed by the function. GW-BASIC has *numeric functions* and *string functions*. The value of a numeric function is a number; the value of a string function is a string. String function names, like string variable names, end with a dollar sign ($).

Some functions require *arguments*; others do not. An argument is a number or string on which the function operates to produce the value of the function.

NOTE: Some activities in this chapter require the use of double precision numbers, variables, and numeric functions. Therefore, load GW-BASIC with the /D option. At the DOS A prompt (A>) or C prompt (C>), type **GWBASIC /D** and press »ENTER...

SKILLS
CHECK

EXERCISES

You now know quite a bit about GW-BASIC. In particular, you can

- Understand the use of the following GW-BASIC keywords:

BEEP	INPUT	NEXT	RUN	TIMER
CIRCLE	KEY	OFF	SCREEN	TO
CLS	LINE	ON	SOUND	USING
COLOR	LIST	PRINT	STEP	WEND
DATE$	LLIST	PSET	SYSTEM	WHILE
FOR	LOCATE	RANDOMIZE	TAB	WIDTH
GOTO	LPRINT	REM	THEN	
IF	NEW	RND	TIME$	

- Read and understand programs that use the above keywords, along with numbers, strings, numeric variables, and string variables

- Understand the use of decision structures using IF...THEN

- Understand the use of these loop structures: GOTO, WHILE...WEND, and FOR...NEXT...STEP

- Write programs using the above keywords and structures

LEARN ABOUT FUNCTIONS WITHOUT ARGUMENTS

The simplest type of function is one that does not require an argument. For example, RND and TIMER are numeric functions that do not require an argument. In this section, you will learn how to use INKEY$, a string function that does not require an argument.

Examples

1. **TIMER numeric function**   This function returns the number of elapsed seconds since midnight, according to the computer's clock. At midnight, the value of TIMER is zero (0). At high noon, the value of TIMER is 43200. At one minute before midnight, the value of TIMER is 86340. At one second before midnight, the value of TIMER is 86399. Use a direct PRINT statement to print values of TIME$ and TIMER:

```
PRINT TIME$, TIMER
12:11:04       43864.15
```

The time shown (12:11:04) is about 43864 seconds after midnight. Because the value of TIMER is precise to one clock tick, or about 1/18 second, you will usually see the value of TIMER printed with two places after the decimal point.

2. **INKEY$ string function**   INKEY$ scans the keyboard for a keypress. If a key or combination of keys has been pressed, the value of INKEY$ is a one- or two-byte string that corresponds to the key or key combination. If no key has been pressed, the value of INKEY$ is the null, or empty, string (""). INKEY$ does not wait for a keypress, as does the INPUT$ function, described later in this chapter.

    Try the following program. It continues while the value of INKEY$ is the empty string (""). That is, it continues as long as you *don't* press a key.

```
10 WHILE INKEY$ = ""
20    PRINT "Press a key to stop me"
30 WEND
```

Enter and run the program. The screen quickly fills with the message "Press a key to stop me." If you don't press a key, the condition INKEY$ = "" is true, and the WHILE...WEND loop continues. Press a key, and the condition becomes false; the loop ends.

Use Program 7-1, INKEY01 (INKEY$ Demonstrator), to learn more about INKEY$. Run this program several times. Each time, use a different key or key combination to stop the program. In the rest of this book, you will frequently see the (ESC) key used as a means of "escaping" from a program. Run the program INKEY01 and press (ESC). This keypress is displayed as a small left-pointing arrow, as shown here:

```
Press a key to stop me
Press a key to stop me
Press a key to stop me

You pressed ←
Ok

_
```

```
1 REM ** INKEY$ Demonstrator **
2 ' Teach Yourself GW-BASIC, Chapter 7. Filename: INKEY01.BAS

10 CLS

20 anykey$ = ""                      'anykey$ = empty string

30 WHILE anykey$ = ""                'Loop while no key press
40   PRINT "Press a key to stop me"
50   anykey$ = INKEY$                'anykey$ "remembers" keypress
60 WEND

70 PRINT
80 PRINT "You pressed "; anykey$     'Some keys don't print
```

PROGRAM 7-1.   INKEY$ Demonstrator

3. You can write a WHILE...WEND loop that requires a designated keypress as the interrupt key. For example, to end the following WHILE...WEND loop, press the (ESC) key:

```
10 WHILE INKEY$ <> CHR$(27)
20   PRINT "Press the Esc key to stop me"
30 WEND
```

Run this program. Press several keys other than (ESC)—the program continues to run. You must press the (ESC) key to stop the program.

The statement

```
WHILE INKEY$ <> CHR$(27)
```

tells the computer to continue the WHILE...WEND loop while the value of INKEY$ is not equal to the character whose ASCII code is 27. CHR$ is a string function. Its value is the character whose ASCII code number is enclosed in parentheses. For example, CHR$(32) is a space; CHR$(65) is the uppercase letter A; CHR$(1) is a tiny face. You will learn about ASCII codes and the CHR$ function later in this chapter.

4. Program 7-2, INKEY02 (Demonstrate INKEY$ and TIMER Functions), uses both the INKEY$ string function and the TIMER

```
1 REM ** Demonstrate INKEY$ and TIMER Functions **
2 ' Teach Yourself GW-BASIC, Chapter 7. Filename: INKEY02.BAS

10 CLS

20 TIME$ = "23:59:50"        '10 seconds before midnight

30 WHILE INKEY$ = ""         'Loop while no key press
40   PRINT TIMER,
50 WEND
```

PROGRAM 7-2.   Demonstrate INKEY$ and TIMER Functions

numeric function. This program sets the time to 10 seconds before midnight, then starts printing the value of TIMER. Press any key (the spacebar is a good choice) to stop the program. Check your reaction time—how soon after midnight (TIMER = 0) can you stop the program? Part of a run is shown below, where the program was stopped a fraction of a second after the value of TIMER became zero.

```
86399.88      86399.88      86399.94      86399.94      86399.94
86399.94       0 ·          0             0             0
.05           .05           .05           9.999999E-02
9.999999E-02                9.999999E-02                .167
.16           .16           .21           .21
Ok
_
```

Exercises

1. How long does it take your computer to multiply two numbers? Use the following program to find out. It prints the value of TIMER, multiplies two numbers 10,000 times, prints the value of TIMER, and stops.

```
10 CLS
20 PRINT "Start:  TIMER ="; TIMER
30 FOR k = 1 TO 10000
40    product = 1.23 * 4.56
50 NEXT k
60 PRINT "Finish: TIMER ="; TIMER
```

   The results of a run are shown below. What is the average time for one multiplication?

```
Start:  TIMER = 51574.65
Finish: TIMER = 51587.06
```

2. In Exercise 1, the elapsed time includes some "overhead" because of the way the FOR...NEXT loop is done. To minimize this effect, you can put, say, 10 lines inside the loop, each with one multiplication. Modify the program to do this. While you are at it, also

compute and print the average time for one multiplication, as shown here:

```
Start:  TIMER = 52116.93
Finish: TIMER = 52124.95
Elapsed time:   8.019531
Average time:   8.019532E-04
```

3. Use INKEY$ in a WHILE...WEND loop to print "Press the space-bar to stop me" repeatedly until someone presses the spacebar.

LEARN ABOUT NUMERIC FUNCTIONS THAT REQUIRE ARGUMENTS

7.2

Many GW-BASIC functions operate on arguments to compute the value of the function. The value of the function thus depends on the value of the argument. The argument is enclosed in parentheses, and follows the name of the function.

Examples

1. **FIX numeric function** FIX is a numeric function of a numeric argument. It returns the integer part of its numeric argument. For example:

```
PRINT FIX(3.14), FIX(-3.14), FIX(.99), FIX(-.99)
  3            -3            0            0
```

2. **INT numeric function** The INT function is a numeric function of a numeric argument. It returns the greatest integer value of the argument enclosed in parentheses. INT(*number*) is the greatest integer that is less than or equal to the value of *number*. Some examples of the INT function are

Non-negative numbers	**Negative numbers**
INT(0) = 0	INT(-1) = -1
INT(3.14) = 3	INT(-3.14) = -4
INT(.99) = 0	INT(-.99) = -1

Use Program 7-3, FIXINT (Demonstrate FIX and INT Numeric Functions), to learn more about FIX and INT. For integer arguments, FIX and INT return the same results. The results are also the same for positive noninteger arguments. For negative noninteger arguments, however, the values differ by one, as shown in the following sample run:

```
Argument, please? .123
FIX(argument) is  0
INT(argument) is  0

Argument, please? -.123
FIX(argument) is  0
INT(argument) is  -1
```

Exercises

1. The integer division operation (\) is used only for integers in the range –32768 to 32767. Use a FIX or INT program to compute the integer quotient for integer values entered as values of double precision variables *dividend#* and *divisor#*. Here is a sample run:

```
Dividend? 23456789
Divisor ? 37

Integer quotient: 633967

Dividend? 23456789
Divisor ? -13

Integer quotient: -1804368
```

2. The integer remainder operation (MOD) is used only for integers in the range –32768 to 32767. Modify the program in Exercise 1 so that the computer computes and prints the integer quotient and integer remainder for integer values *dividend#* and *divisor#*. Here is a sample run:

```
Dividend? 23456789
Divisor ? 37

Integer quotient:  633967
Integer remainder: 10

Dividend? 23456789
Divisor ? -13

Integer quotient: -1804368
Integer remainder: 5
```

3. The possible values of INT(2 * RND) are 0 and 1. No other values are possible. For each expression below, show or describe the set of possible values.

   a. INT(10 * RND)
   b. 10 * INT(RND)
   c. INT(101 * RND)
   d. INT(3 * RND) – 1
   e. 2 * INT(5 * RND) + 1
   f. INT(10 * RND) / 10

```
1 REM ** Demonstrate FIX and INT Numeric Functions **
2 ' Teach Yourself GW-BASIC, Chapter 7. Filename: FIXINT.BAS

10 CLS

20 WHILE 1
30   INPUT "Argument, please"; argument
40   PRINT "FIX(argument) is "; FIX(argument)
50   PRINT "INT(argument) is "; INT(argument)
60   PRINT
70 WEND
```

PROGRAM 7-3.   Demonstrate FIX and INT Numeric Functions

4. Write a program to simulate the rolling of one six-sided die. The possible values are 1, 2, 3, 4, 5, and 6. A sample run might go like this:

```
How many rolls? 10
   3            4            5            6            2
   1            6            2            1            4
```

5. Write a program to simulate the flipping of a coin. A sample run is shown here:

```
How many flips? 10
Head         Tail         Tail         Tail         Tail
Head         Head         Tail         Head         Tail
```

7.3 LEARN ABOUT STRING FUNCTIONS THAT REQUIRE ARGUMENTS

A string function name, like a string variable name, ends in a dollar sign ($). The value of a string function is a string. Earlier in this chapter, you learned how to use INKEY$, a string function that does not require an argument. Now learn how to use some string functions that do require arguments.

Examples

1. **INPUT$ string function**   INPUT$(*n*) is a string function with a numeric argument. INPUT$(*n*) tells the computer to wait for a string of *n* characters to be entered from the keyboard. For example, INPUT$(1) tells the computer to wait for one character to be entered from the keyboard. You can press a letter key, a number key, or a punctuation key. (SHIFT) plus another key counts as one key.

   Use Program 7-4, INPUT$01 (Demonstrate INPUT$ String Function), to learn more about INPUT$. Press the (ESC) key to end the program. Note the use of a dollar sign ($) in the filename INPUT$01. Certain characters other than letters and numbers

```
1 REM ** Demonstrate INPUT$ String Function **
2 ' Teach Yourself GW-BASIC, Chapter 7. Filename: INPUT$01.BAS

10 CLS

20 WHILE anykey$ <> CHR$(27)        'Loop while Esc not pressed
30    PRINT "Press a key"
40    anykey$ = INPUT$(1)
50    PRINT "You pressed "; anykey$
60    PRINT
70 WEND

80 PRINT "You pressed the Esc key, which ends the program."
```

PROGRAM 7-4. Demonstrate INPUT$ String Function

may be used in filenames. Consult your DOS Reference Manual for information about this.

Figure 7-1 shows an annotated run of Program 7-4, INPUT$01. Note that some keys, such as ⟨ENTER⟩ or the cursor control keys (arrow keys), are nonprinting keys. Try pressing these keys when you run the program, and see what happens.

The program line

```
40 anykey$ = INPUT$(1)
```

tells the computer to wait for someone to enter one character by pressing one key, or a key combination such as ⟨SHIFT⟩ plus another key. The character entered is assigned as the value of the string variable *anykey$*.

2. **MID$ string function** MID$ is a string function of three arguments: one string argument and two numeric arguments. When a function has more than one argument, the arguments are separated by commas. You use MID$ to select a portion of a string (a substring) from within a string. For example, the word "proverb" contains these shorter words:

pro   prove   prover   rove   rover   over   verb

```
Press a key
You pressed a

Press a key
You pressed A    ((SHIFT) + A counts as one key)

Press a key
You pressed 8

Press a key
You pressed *    ((SHIFT) + 8 counts as one key)

Press a key
You pressed     (Some keys are nonprinting)

Press a key
You pressed ←   (Press (ESC) to end the program)

You pressed the Esc key, which ends the program.
Ok
_
```

FIGURE 7-1.   An annotated run of Program INPUT$01

You can use MID$ to select these words within "proverb," or to select the entire word "proverb." Here are direct PRINT statements that use MID$ to print two substrings of "proverb."

```
PRINT MID$("proverb", 1, 3)
pro

PRINT MID$("proverb", 2, 5)
rover
```

The value of the MID$ function is a substring of the function's first argument. The second argument is numeric; it specifies the position within the string at which to begin. The third argument is also numeric; it specifies how many characters to select, counting from where the substring begins.

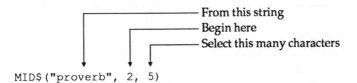

```
MID$("proverb", 2, 5)
```

3. **Word Maker program** Suppose you want to name a new product, or even a new company. Perhaps you are writing a novel and want to create unusual names for characters or places. Why not use your computer to help you invent names? How would you write a program to print names that are pronounceable, but seem exotic, or even fantastic?

Program 7-5, WRDMKR01 (Word Maker), generates random five-letter words in this format: consonant, vowel, consonant, vowel, consonant (*cvcvc*). In this program, the letter *y* can appear as either a consonant or vowel. Here are some possible random words:

kobar nigom conan zyyox dufet

The Word Maker program uses MID$ to select random consonants from the value of *consonant$*, and random vowels from the value of *vowel$*. The string variables *consonant$* and *vowel$* are assigned values during the setup block of the program, in lines 120 and 130.

In line 240, the statement

```
word$ = ""
```

tells the computer to assign the null string as the value of *word$*. Each time the WHILE...WEND loop is repeated, *word$* is reset to the empty string, thus erasing any previous value.

In lines 260, 280, and 300, the statement

```
word$ = word$ + MID$(consonant$, INT(21 * RND) + 1, 1)
```

tells the computer to select one random letter from the value of *consonant$*, and catenate (join) it to the value of *word$*. When used with strings, the plus sign (+) means catenate, or put together

```
1 REM ** Word Maker **
2 ' Teach Yourself GW-BASIC, Chapter 7. Filename: WRDMKR01.BAS

100 REM ** Set up **
110 RANDOMIZE TIMER
120 consonant$ = "bcdfghjklmnpqrstvwxyz"        '21 consonants
130 vowel$ = "aeiouy"                            '6 vowels
140 CLS

200 REM ** WHILE...WEND loop to make random words **
210 WHILE 1

220    BEEP: PRINT "Press a key for a word, Esc to quit"
230    akey$ = INPUT$(1): IF akey$ = CHR$(27) THEN END

240    word$ = ""             'Start with the empty string ("")

250    ' Add a consonant, vowel, consonant, vowel, consonant
260    word$ = word$ + MID$(consonant$, INT(21 * RND) + 1, 1)
270    word$ = word$ + MID$(vowel$, INT(6 * RND) + 1, 1)
280    word$ = word$ + MID$(consonant$, INT(21 * RND) + 1, 1)
290    word$ = word$ + MID$(vowel$, INT(6 * RND) + 1, 1)
300    word$ = word$ + MID$(consonant$, INT(21 * RND) + 1, 1)

310    ' Print the word
320    PRINT "Your random 'cvcvc' word is: "; word$
330    PRINT

340 WEND
```

PROGRAM 7-5. | Word Maker

with, or attach to. The following MID$ function illustrates how this single letter is selected from *consonant$*.

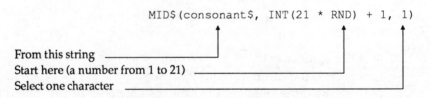

MID$(consonant$, INT(21 * RND) + 1, 1)

From this string
Start here (a number from 1 to 21)
Select one character

Lines 270 and 290 work in similar fashion to select a random vowel from *vowel$* and catenate it to the value of *word$*.

A sample run is shown below. When you run this program, the words generated will probably be different, since the letters in the words are randomly selected. Press (ESC) to end the program.

```
Press a key for a word, Esc to quit
Your random 'cvcvc' word is: rudob

Press a key for a word, Esc to quit
Your random 'cvcvc' word is: cunan

Press a key for a word, Esc to quit
Your random 'cvcvc' word is: lyfar
```

You can easily modify the progam to generate words that have a different consonant-vowel structure.

REMEMBER: Modifying a program is a good way for you to make sure you understand how the program works. The best way to learn how to program is to write programs and make them work. In programming, you can usually do things in more than one way. Try writing your own versions of programs you see in this book.

Exercises

1. Complete the following program so that the computer waits for entry of a three-character string and assigns it to *ThreeKey$*:

```
10 CLS
20 WHILE 1
30   PRINT "Enter three characters"

40   ThreeKey$ = _____

50   PRINT "You entered: "; ThreeKey$
60   PRINT
70 WEND
```

2. Write a program to acquire a three-letter word (or any three-letter string), and then print it with the letters (or characters) in reverse order. For example:

```
Enter a 3-letter word: dam
The reverse word is:    mad

Enter a 3-letter word: mom
The reverse word is:    mom
```

Note that "mom" is a *palindrome*—the word and its reverse order are the same. Lewis Carroll had a word for words like "dam" that, in reverse, spell another word. He called them *semordnilaps*. What is the reverse of semordnilap?

3. Modify Program 7-5, WRDMKR01, so that the new version prints random words in the form *vccvcv*. Examples of such words are Athena, Ursula, and Othelo—although you probably won't see these when you run your program.

7.4 UNDERSTAND ASCII CODES AND CHARACTERS

You can print many different characters on the screen. Some of these characters are visible on the keyboard, and you can use the keyboard to enter them. For example:

Uppercase letters:	A	B	C	D
Lowercase letters:	a	b	c	d
Digits:	1	2	3	4
Punctuation:	.	,	;	:
Special characters:	@	#	$	*

There are also characters you don't see on the keyboard. Some are shown here:

Card characters:	♥	♦	♣	♠	
Greek letters:	α	β	ε	π	Σ
Math symbols:	√	±	≤	≡	≈
Graphics characters:	╝	╨	╫	■	

Every computer character has an *ASCII code*. An ASCII code is an integer in the range 0 to 255. ASCII stands for American Standard Code for Information Interchange. Here are some examples.

The ASCII code for A is 65
The ASCII code for B is 66
The ASCII code for a is 97
The ASCII code for b is 98
The ASCII code for * is 42
The ASCII code for ♥ is 3

You have probably guessed that the ASCII code for C is 67. For the uppercase letters A to Z, the ASCII codes are 65 to 90. For the lowercase letters a to z, the ASCII codes are 97 to 122. Digits also have ASCII codes; the codes for the digits 0 to 9 are 48 to 57. ASCII codes from 128 to 255 are codes for special characters, such as foreign alphabets, graphics characters, and math symbols.

Examples

1. **CHR$ string function** CHR$ is a string function of a numeric argument. The argument must be an ASCII code, an integer in the range 0 to 255. The value of CHR$ is the one-character string that corresponds to the ASCII code. You can use CHR$ in a direct PRINT statement to print an ASCII character. Here are some examples.

```
PRINT CHR$(65)
A

PRINT "JACK " + CHR$(3) + " Jill"
Jack ♥ Jill
```

Use the following short program to see ASCII characters of your choice. To print a character on the screen, type its ASCII code (0 to 255) and press (ENTER). Figure 7-2 is an annotated run of this program.

```
10 CLS : WIDTH 40          (Do it in big letters)
20 WHILE 1
30   INPUT "ASCII code (0 to 255)"; ascii
40   PRINT "Thanks for calling my number! "; CHR$(ascii)
50   PRINT
60 WEND
```

```
ASCII code (0 to 255)? 65
Thanks for calling my number! A        (CHR$(65) is uppercase A)

ASCII code (0 to 255)? 42
Thanks for calling my number! *        (CHR$(42) is an asterisk)

ASCII code (0 TO 255)? 1
Thanks for calling my number! ☺        (CHR$(1) is a tiny face)

ASCII code (0 to 255)? 206
Thanks for calling my number! ╬        (CHR$(206) is a graphics character)

ASCII code (0 to 255)? 227
Thanks for calling my number! π        (CHR$(227) is the Greek letter pi)

ASCII code (0 to 255)? _
```

FIGURE 7-2. ASCII codes and characters

You can use Program 7-6, ASCII01 (ASCII Codes and Characters), to print many ASCII codes and characters on the screen. You enter the first and last ASCII codes you want to see. The program then prints all the ASCII codes in between, and corresponding characters, from your first entered code to your last entered code. Code and character pairs are printed ten to a line, and the lines are double-spaced. Figure 7-3 is a sample run showing 100 codes and characters, from ASCII code 128 to ASCII code 227.

In line 60, the statement

```
PRINT ascii; CHR$(ascii); SPACE$(2);
```

prints the ASCII code (value of *ascii*), the ASCII character (value of CHR$(*ascii*)), and two spaces. The value of *ascii* is printed with a leading and a trailing space. SPACE$ is a string function of a numeric argument. SPACE$(2) creates two spaces, which are then printed.

In line 70, the statement

```
IF (ascii - FirstCode + 1) MOD 10 = 0 THEN PRINT: PRINT
```

```
1 REM ** ASCII Codes and Characters with CHR$ String Function **
2 ' Teach Yourself GW-BASIC, Chapter 7. Filename: ASCII01.BAS

10 CLS : KEY OFF

20 INPUT "First ASCII code"; FirstCode
30 INPUT "Last ASCII code "; LastCode

40 CLS

50 FOR ascii = FirstCode TO LastCode
60    PRINT ascii; CHR$(ascii); SPACE$(2);
70    IF (ascii - FirstCode + 1) MOD 10 = 0 THEN PRINT : PRINT
80 NEXT ascii

90 akey$ = INPUT$(1): GOTO 10    'Wait for keypress, then go back
```

PROGRAM 7-6. ASCII Codes and Characters with CHR$ String Function

128 Ç	129 ü	130 é	131 â	132 ä	133 à	134 å	135 ç	136 ê	137 ë
138 è	139 ï	140 î	141 ì	142 Ä	143 Å	144 É	145 æ	146 Æ	147 ô
148 ö	149 ò	150 û	151 ù	152 ÿ	153 Ö	154 Ü	155 ¢	156 £	157 ¥
158 ₨	159 ƒ	160 á	161 í	162 ó	163 ú	164 ñ	165 Ñ	166 ª	167 º
168 ¿	169 ⌐	170 ¬	171 ½	172 ¼	173 ¡	174 «	175 »	176 ░	177 ▒
178 ▓	179 │	180 ┤	181 ╡	182 ╢	183 ╖	184 ╕	185 ╣	186 ║	187 ╗
188 ╝	189 ╜	190 ╛	191 ┐	192 └	193 ┴	194 ┬	195 ├	196 ─	197 ┼
198 ╞	199 ╟	200 ╚	201 ╔	202 ╩	203 ╦	204 ╠	205 ═	206 ╬	207 ╧
208 ╨	209 ╤	210 ╥	211 ╙	212 ╘	213 ╒	214 ╓	215 ╫	216 ╪	217 ┘
218 ┌	219 █	220 ▄	221 ▌	222 ▐	223 ▀	224 α	225 ß	226 Γ	227 π

FIGURE 7-3. ASCII codes and characters printed by Program ASCII01

causes two empty PRINT statements to occur after every ten pairs of codes and characters. This causes the lines to be double-spaced so you can read them more easily. For the run shown in Figure 7-3, the value of *FirstCode* is 128 and the value of *ascii* runs from 128 to 227. The condition, (*ascii* – *FirstCode* + 1) MOD 10 = 0, is true for *ascii* = 137, 147, 157, and so on, up to 227.

In line 90, the statement

```
akey$ = INPUT$(1): GOTO 10
```

tells the computer to wait for one keypress. Press a key, and the program begins again at line 10, so you can look at another group of ASCII codes and characters.

2. **ASC numeric function** The ASC function is just the opposite of the CHR$ function. ASC is a numeric function of a string argument. ASC returns the ASCII code of a character. For example, ASC("A") is 65, and ASC("*") is 42. If the argument consists of two or more characters, the ASC function returns the ASCII code of the first character. For example, ASC("ABC") is 65, and ASC("abc") is 97. Note that ASC("") is illegal and causes an error. There is no ASCII code for the null string.

Use the short program shown below to print on the screen the ASCII codes of characters you type on the keyboard.

```
10 CLS : WIDTH 40                (Do it in big letters)
20 WHILE 1
30   INPUT "Enter a character: ", character$
40   PRINT "The ASCII code is: "; ASC(character$)
50   PRINT
60 WEND
```

Figure 7-4 shows an annotated run of the foregoing program. Entering the first two characters (a and A) is easy. However, it is a little more difficult to enter the tiny face (☺), the graphics character (╬), and the Greek letter pi (π). To type these characters, you use the (ALT) key and the numeric keypad on the right side of the keyboard.

- To enter the tiny face (☺), hold down the (ALT) key, type **1** on the numeric keypad, and then release the (ALT) key. You should see the tiny face on the screen. If not, use (BACKSPACE) to erase the incorrect character and try again. When you see the tiny face, press (ENTER).

- To enter the graphics character (╬), hold down the (ALT) key, type **206** on the numeric keypad, and then release the (ALT) key. Press (ENTER).

- To enter the Greek letter pi (π), hold down the (ALT) key, type **227** on the numeric keypad, and then release the (ALT) key. Press (ENTER).

- In general, to type any ASCII character on the screen, hold down the (ALT) key, type the character's ASCII code on the numeric keypad, and then release the (ALT) key. Try this with some ASCII codes in the range 128 to 255, and then with codes in the range 0 to 31. Some of the codes in the range 0 to 31 may cause an "Illegal function call" error message.

```
Enter a character: a
The ASCII code is: 97

Enter a character: A        ((SHIFT) + A)
The ASCII code is: 65

Enter a character: ☺        ((ALT) + 1)
The ASCII code is: 1

Enter a character: ╬        ((ALT) + 206)
The ASCII code is: 206

Enter a character: π        ((ALT) + 227)
The ASCII code is: 227

Enter a character: _
```

FIGURE 7-4. ASCII codes for characters entered from the keyboard

7.5 | SAMPLE A FLOCK OF NUMERIC FUNCTIONS

GW-BASIC provides many of the functions commonly used in math, science, and engineering. In this section, you will sample the functions shown in Table 7-1. For each function shown in this section, it is assumed that you are familiar with the mathematical definition and usage of the function.

Examples

1. **Absolute value function (ABS)** The ABS function returns the absolute value of any numeric argument. Here are examples.

```
PRINT ABS(-7), ABS(7), ABS(0)
 7            7            0
```

Use this short program to learn more about the ABS function:

```
10 CLS
20 WHILE 1
30    INPUT "Number, please   "; x
40    PRINT "Absolute value is "; ABS(x)
50    PRINT
60 WEND
```

TABLE 7-1. | Some GW-BASIC Math Functions

Function	Keyword	Example
Absolute value	ABS	ABS($x - g$)
Square root	SQR	SQR(2)
Exponential, base e	EXP	EXP($-x$)
Logarithm, base e	LOG	LOG(10)
Sine	SIN	SIN(angle)
Cosine	COS	COS(3.14159 / 6)
Tangent	TAN	TAN(degrees * 3.14159 / 180)
Inverse tangent	ATN	ATN(a / b)

2. **Square root function (SQR)**   Use the SQR function to compute the square root of a non-negative argument. (A negative argument causes an "Illegal function call" error message.) Here are some examples.

```
PRINT SQR(0), SQR(2), SQR(16)
 0              1.414214      4

PRINT SQR(-16)
Illegal function call
```

Use the following program to learn more about the SQR function.

```
10 CLS
20 WHILE 1
30    INPUT "Number, please "; x
40    PRINT "Square root is "; SQR(x)
50    PRINT
60 WEND
```

3. **Logarithm, base *e*, function (LOG)**   Use the LOG function to compute the logarithm, base *e*, of a numeric argument. The value of *e* is approximately 2.718282. This is the *natural logarithm* function, usually shown in math books as *ln* or log_e. The LOG function is used for positive values of its argument. A zero or negative argument causes an "Illegal function call" error message. Here are some examples.

```
PRINT LOG(1), LOG(2.718282), LOG(10)
 0            1                2.302585

PRINT LOG(0)
Illegal function call

PRINT LOG(-1)
Illegal function call
```

Use the following program to learn more about the LOG function. Try some values of *x* between 0 and 1.

```
10 CLS
20 WHILE 1
30    INPUT "Number, please "; x
40    PRINT "Log, base e, is "; LOG(x)
```

```
50   PRINT
60 WEND
```

4. **Exponential, base *e*, function (EXP)** The EXP function is the inverse of the LOG function. Use it to compute a power of *e*, where *e* is approximately equal to 2.718282. Examples are shown below, including an overflow for a too-large value, and a replacement by zero for a too-small value.

```
PRINT EXP(0), EXP(1), EXP(-1)
 1              2.718282      .3678795

PRINT EXP(100)
Overflow
 1.701412E+38

PRINT EXP(-100)        (Too-small value replaced by zero)
 0
```

Use the following program to learn more about the EXP function. What is the largest integer argument that does not cause an overflow? What is the most negative argument that does not cause the value to be replaced by zero?

```
10 CLS
20 WHILE 1
30   INPUT "Number, please "; x
40   PRINT "EXP(number) is "; EXP(x)
50   PRINT
60 WEND
```

5. **Trigonometric functions (SIN, COS, TAN, ATN)** The sine (SIN), cosine (COS), and tangent (TAN) functions operate on arguments expressed in *radians*, where 2π radians = 360 degrees. Examples of these three functions are

```
angle = 3.141593 / 3          (Equivalent to 60 degrees)

PRINT SIN(angle), COS(angle), TAN(angle)
 .8660256      .4999999      1.732052
```

The following program accepts an angle measured in degrees (line 30), then converts it to radians (line 40). You can use this program to learn more about the SIN, COS, and TAN functions.

```
10 CLS
20 WHILE 1
30    INPUT "Angle in degrees"; degrees
40    radians = 3.141593 * degrees / 180
50    PRINT "The sine is     "; SIN(radians)
60    PRINT "The cosine is   "; COS(radians)
70    PRINT "The tangent is "; TAN(radians)
80    PRINT
90 WEND
```

Use ATN to compute the inverse tangent. You can think of it as an angle expressed in radians. Here are some examples.

```
PRINT ATN(0), ATN(1), ATN(-1)
 0              .7853983     -.7853983

PRINT ATN(1.7E38), ATN(-1.7E38)
 1.570796      -1.570796
```

You can use the following program to learn more about the ATN function. Results are given in both radians and degrees.

```
10 CLS
20 WHILE 1
30    INPUT "Number, please "; x
40    PRINT "ATN in radians is "; ATN(x)
50    PRINT "ATN in degrees is "; ATN(x) * 180 / 3.141593
60    PRINT
70 WEND
```

Exercises

1. In a right triangle, the length of the hypotenuse (c) can be computed from the lengths of the other two sides (a and b), as shown here:

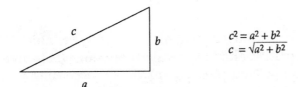

$$c^2 = a^2 + b^2$$
$$c = \sqrt{a^2 + b^2}$$

Write a program to compute the value of c for values of a and b entered in response to INPUT statements. Here is a sample run.

```
Length of side a? 3
Length of side b? 4

Length of hypotenuse: 5
```

2. GW-BASIC's LOG function computes the logarithm, base e, of its argument. This type of logarithm is also called the *natural logarithm*, or Naperian logarithm. You can also compute the logarithm, base 10 (also called the *common logarithm*, or Briggs' logarithm). Use the following formula to compute the base 10 logarithm:

$$\log_{10} x = (\log_{10} e)(\log_e x)$$
$$= 0.4342945 \log_e x$$

Write a program to compute the logarithm, base 10, of a number entered from the keyboard. A sample run might look like this:

```
Number, please ? 10
Log base 10 is    1

Number, please ? .1
Log base 10 is   -1

Number, please ? 2.718282
Log base 10 is    .4342946
```

NOTE: If you want to use double precision, use a more precise value for $\log_{10} e$, as follows: 0.4342944819032518. Remember, though, to obtain double precision results, you must load GW-BASIC with the /D option (**GWBASIC /D**).

3. When you pluck a string on a guitar, the sound rises quickly to a maximum intensity, and then decays more slowly. The intensity, expressed in sound pressure (p), decays according to the following formula:

$$\frac{p}{p_0} = e^{-kt}$$

where p = sound intensity at time t
       p_0 = maximum intensity at $t = 0$
       k = constant that depends on the instrument

Suppose that, for the guitar string, the value of k is 3.5. Then the value of p / p_0 is $e^{-3.5t}$. Write a program to compute the value of p / p_0 (call it *ratio*) for a value of t entered from the keyboard. Here is a sample run.

```
Value of time ? .01
P / P0 ratio is .9656054

Value of time ? .1
P / P0 ratio is .7046881

Value of time ? 1
P / P0 ratio is 3.019738E-02
```

4. Rewrite the two programs shown in Example 5 so that all calculations are done in double precision. You must load GW-BASIC using the /D option (**GWBASIC /D**). You must also use this more precise approximation for π:

$\pi = 3.141592653589793$ (*approximately*)

Here are sample runs of both progams. The first program computes SIN, COS, and TAN.

```
Angle in degrees? 30
The sine is     .5
The cosine is   1
The tangent is  .5773502691896257
```

The second program computes ATN in radians and degrees.

```
Number, please ?  1
ATN in radians is  .7853981633974483
ATN in degrees is  45
```

7.6   EXPLORE WIGGLY FUNCTIONS WITH ZAPPY ARTIST

"Look, it wiggles," said Zappy squirmingly. Sure enough, there on the screen are a bunch of tiny faces wiggling back and forth. "You use wiggly functions like SIN and COS."

Program 7-7, ZAPPY07 (Zappy Artist Explores Wiggly Functions), uses the SIN function to make tiny faces (ASCII code 1) appear to wiggle back and forth on the screen. Figure 7-5 shows a "snapshot" of the screen while Program ZAPPY07 is running.

```
1 REM ** Zappy Artist Explores Wiggly Functions **
2 ' Teach Yourself GW-BASIC, Chapter 7. Filename: ZAPPY07.BAS

100 REM ** Set up **
110 RANDOMIZE TIMER
120 KEY OFF: CLS

200 REM ** Assign an ASCII character to wiggler$ **
210 wiggler$ = CHR$(1)              'Tiny face

300 REM ** Make wiggler wiggle while Esc not pressed **
310 x = 0
320 WHILE INKEY$ <> CHR$(27)
330   col = 40 + FIX(39 * SIN(x)) 'Column for next appearance
340   COLOR INT(15 * RND) + 1
350   PRINT TAB(col); wiggler$     'Tab to column, print wiggler
360   delay = .125
370   start = TIMER: WHILE TIMER < start + delay: WEND
380   x = x + .25
390 WEND

400 REM ** You get here if someone pressed Esc **
410 LOCATE 25, 1: PRINT "Press a key to end program";
420 akey$ = INPUT$(1): COLOR 7: KEY ON: CLS : END
```

PROGRAM 7-7.   Zappy Artist Explores Wiggly Functions

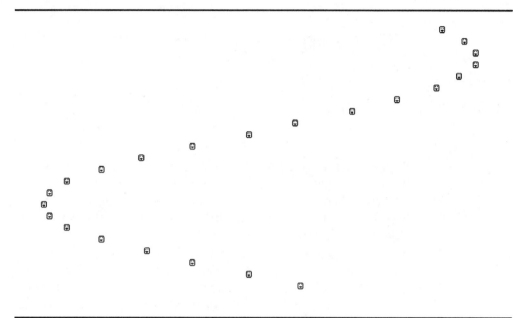

FIGURE 7-5. | A snapshot of Program ZAPPY07 in action

Run the program, and you will see a "sine wave" of tiny faces in random colors. Press (ESC) to stop the program—the message "Press a key to end program" appears at the bottom of the screen. Press a key, and the screen returns to its "normal" state. Note that the key line is turned off at the beginning of the program (line 120) and turned on when you end the program (line 420).

Make the program run more slowly. Change the value of *delay* in line 360 to at least one second (*delay* = 1), and then run the program. Now you can more easily watch the faces printed in columns determined by line 330, shown here:

```
330 col = 40 + FIX(39 * SIN(x)) 'Column for next appearance
```

The value of *x* is set to zero in line 310 and increased by .25 in line 380. Run the following program to see the first 20 values of *x*, SIN(*x*), FIX(39 * SIN(*x*)), and *col*.

```
10 CLS
20 PRINT "x", "SIN(x)", "FIX(39*SIN(x)) "; "col"
30 x = 0
40 FOR k = 1 TO 20
50   col = 40 + FIX(39 * SIN(x))
60   PRINT x, SIN(x), FIX(39 * SIN(x)), col
70   x = x + .25
80 NEXT k
```

"Here is another program," noted Zappy audibly. "Note that it is similar to the first one. So edit the first program to get the second one." With that advice, he wiggled out the door and down the street, waving one hand in sine-like undulations and the other in cosine-like crests and troughs.

Program 7-8, ZAPPY08 (Zappy Artist Explores Wiggly Functions #2), uses both the SIN and the COS functions to produce a more complex wiggle. The essential change is in line 330. Also, the time delay from Program ZAPPY07 is replaced here by a SOUND statement (line 360). The frequency of the sound is a function of the value of *col*, computed in line 330.

Exercises

1. Modify block 200 of Program 7-7, ZAPPY07, to acquire two values by means of INPUT statements. The first value is the ASCII code of the character to be assigned to *wiggler$*. The second value is the value of *delay*. Also, delete line 360 of the program so that it doesn't preempt the delay you enter. A sample run might begin with these values:

   ```
   ASCII code ? 176
   Delay (sec)? 1
   ```

2. In both programs, the argument *x* used in the SIN and COS functions is in radians. Complete a modified block 300 of Program ZAPPY07 so that a variable called *degrees* is increased each time through the WHILE...WEND loop, then converted to radians and assigned to *x*. Complete line 325 in the next listing.

```
300 REM ** Make wiggler wiggle while Esc not pressed **
310 degrees = 0
320 WHILE INKEY$ <> CHR$(27)

325   x = _____

330   col = 40 + FIX(39 * SIN(x)) 'Column for next appearance
340   COLOR INT(15 * RND) + 1
350   PRINT TAB(col); wiggler$ 'Tab to column, print wiggler
360   delay = .125
370   start = TIMER: WHILE TIMER < start + delay: WEND
380   degrees = degrees + 20
390 WEND
```

```
1 REM ** Zappy Artist Explores Wiggly Functions #2 **
2 ' Teach Yourself GW-BASIC, Chapter 7. Filename: ZAPPY08.BAS

100 REM ** Set up **
110 RANDOMIZE TIMER
120 KEY OFF: CLS

200 REM ** Assign an ASCII character to wiggler$ **
210 wiggler$ = CHR$(15)    'ASCII character 15

300 REM ** Make wiggler wiggle while Esc not pressed **
310 x = 0
320 WHILE INKEY$ <> CHR$(27)
330   col = 40 + FIX(20 * SIN(x) + 19 * COS(2 * x)) 'More wiggly!
340   COLOR INT(15 * RND) + 1
350   PRINT TAB(col); wiggler$
360   SOUND 100 + 20 * col, 1
370   x = x + .25
380 WEND

400 REM ** You get here if someone pressed Esc **
410 LOCATE 25, 1: PRINT "Press a key to end program";
420 akey$ = INPUT$(1): COLOR 7: KEY ON: CLS : END
```

PROGRAM 7-8.   Zappy Artist Explores Wiggly Functions #2

MASTERY
SKILLS
CHECK

EXERCISES

1. In the space provided, write the letter of the item from the right column that describes the item in the left column.

    function _____   a. Value is a number
    argument _____   b. Value is between 0 and 1
    numeric function _____   c. Requires three arguments
    string function _____   d. Returns a value
    ASC _____   e. Must be enclosed in parentheses
    EXP(1)_____   f. Does not require an argument
    INKEY$ _____   g. Value is a string
    LOG _____   h. Numeric function of string argument
    MID$ _____   i. Natural logarithm
    RND _____   j. Approximately 2.718282

2. Complete the following program. It prints the value of TIMER, and also computes and prints the value expressed in hours, minutes, and seconds.

    ```
    10 CLS
    20 tmr = TIMER
    30 minutes = INT(tmr / 60)
    40 seconds = tmr - 60 * minutes

    50 hours = _____

    60 minutes = _____

    70 PRINT "TIMER: "; tmr
    80 PRINT hours; "hours,"; minutes; "minutes,"; seconds; "seconds"
    ```

    The following sample run uses values that appeared in Section 7.1, Example 1.

    ```
    TIMER: 43864.15
     12 hours, 11 minutes, 4.148438 seconds
    ```

3. The following program rounds a number to the nearest integer, assigns the rounded value to *rounded*, then prints the value of *rounded*.

```
10 CLS
20 WHILE 1
30   INPUT "Number, please"; number
40   rounded = FIX(number + .5)
50   PRINT "Rounded to nearest integer: "; rounded
60   PRINT
70 WEND
```

A test run is shown here:

```
Number, please? 3.14
Rounded to nearest integer: 3

Number, please? 2.718
Rounded to nearest integer: 3

Number, please? 7.5
Rounded to nearest integer: 8
```

The program seems to work for positive numbers. Test it for negative numbers, including –3.14, –2.718, and –7.5. The results should be –3, –3, and –8, respectively. If the program fails, explain why, and then fix it.

4. Write a program to simulate rolling two six-sided dice. The possible values are 2 through 12, but are not equally probable. Therefore, you cannot do this with a single random number. Instead, you must simulate rolling each die (1 to 6), and then add the results. A sample run of the desired program is shown here.

```
How many rolls? 10

9            12          5           9           9
7            6           3           8           4
```

5. Write a program to simulate flipping two coins. For each event, print the outcome as HH (two heads), HT (head and tail), TH (tail and head), or TT (two heads), as shown in this sample run:

```
How many flips? 10

HH           TH          TH          HT          HH
TH           TH          HT          TT          HH
```

6. The next program "paints" SCREEN 1 from the left edge to the right edge with 320 vertical lines. The lines are drawn in this color pattern: 1, 2, 3, 1, 2, 3, 1, 2, 3, and so on, as determined in line 60 of the program. Run the program to see how it works. When it finishes painting the screen, it waits for a keypress, and then returns to SCREEN 0.

```
10 SCREEN 1: KEY OFF: CLS
20 kolor = 1
30 FOR k = 0 TO 319
40    col = k
50    LINE (col, 0)-(col, 199), kolor
60    kolor = kolor + 1: IF kolor = 4 THEN kolor = 1
70 NEXT k
80 akey$ = INPUT$(1): SCREEN 0: WIDTH 80: KEY ON: END
```

Run this program and watch what happens. Then change lines 30 and 40, as follows:

```
30 FOR k = 0 TO 46
40    col = EXP(.125 * k)
```

Describe what will happen if you run the modified program. What will the screen look like? Once you have predicted the appearance of the screen, run the program to verify your conjecture.

7. Write a program to draw one sine wave across SCREEN 1, as shown in the following diagram:

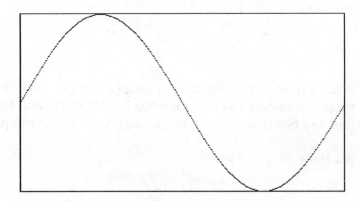

Building Blocks: User-Defined Functions and Subroutines

CHAPTER OBJECTIVES

You can design your own functions in GW-BASIC, and use them in the same ways you use the built-in functions. In Chapter 8, you will learn how to name, define, and use the functions that **you** design.

You will also explore *subroutines.* A subroutine is a self-contained set of program lines that can be called (used) from anywhere in a program. The subroutine performs its task, then returns control to the part of the program that called the subroutine.

EXERCISES

Your knowledge of GW-BASIC is increasing rapidly. Your repertoire now includes the following skills:

1. You understand and can use these keywords:

ABS	FIX	LLIST	RANDOMIZE	TAN
ASC	FOR	LOCATE	REM	THEN
ATN	GOTO	LOG	RND	TIME$
BEEP	IF	LPRINT	RUN	TIMER
CHR$	INKEY$	MID$	SCREEN	TO
CIRCLE	INPUT	NEW	SIN	USING
CLS	INPUT$	NEXT	SOUND	WEND
COLOR	INT	OFF	SPACE$	WHILE
COS	KEY	ON	SQR	WIDTH
DATE$	LINE	PRINT	STEP	
EXP	LIST	PSET	TAB	

2. You can read and understand programs that include the above keywords, along with numbers, strings, variables, and functions.

3. You understand these decision and loop control structures: IF...THEN, GOTO, WHILE...WEND, and FOR...NEXT...STEP.

4. You can write programs using all of the foregoing GW-BASIC elements. Furthermore, you can write them in good style, so that other people can read and understand your programs—and so that **you** can read and understand your programs a year from now.

DEFINE NUMERIC FUNCTIONS WITHOUT ARGUMENTS

8.1

To define and name your own function, use the DEF FN statement. Here is a user-defined function to "roll" one six-sided die (D6). This function, which does not have an argument, returns a random integer in the range 1 to 6.

```
DEF FNrollD6 = INT(6 * RND) + 1
```

The name of this function is FNrollD6. The name of a user-defined function always begins with FN. You may compose the part of the name following FN. In the DEF FN statement, the function name (FNrollD6) is followed by an equal sign (=) and a numeric expression (INT(6 * RND) + 1) that defines the function. The elements of this function definition are illustrated here:

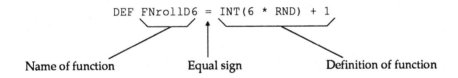

In Program 8-1, DICE02 (Roll Two Six-Sided Dice (2D6)), the function FNrollD6 is used twice. Because the function must be defined before it can be used, the function definition appears near the beginning of the program, in block 100.

In the sample run shown next, a key other than (ESC) was pressed twice to get two simulated rolls of two dice. The computer is waiting for another keypress. Press (ESC) to end the program.

```
Press a key to roll, or ESC to quit
The roll is 6

Press a key to roll, or ESC to quit
The roll is 11

Press a key to roll, or ESC to quit
```

The program line

```
330   akey$ = INPUT$(1): IF akey$ = CHR$(27)THEN END
```

tells the computer to wait for one keypress. If the key pressed is the
(ESC) key, the condition *akey$* = CHR$(27) is true, and the program
ends. For any other key, the condition is false and the program
continues.

Examples

1. **Roll 2D6** The user-defined function FNroll2D6, shown here,
   simulates rolling two six-sided dice (2D6).

   ```
   DEF FNroll2D6 = INT(6 * RND)+ INT(6 * RND) + 2
   ```

2. **Roll a fantasy game character** Roll a character?! Relax— no
   mugging intended. Millions of game players know that "rolling

---

```
1 REM ** Roll Two Six-Sided Dice (2D6) **
2 ' Teach Yourself GW-BASIC, Chapter 8. File: DICE02.BAS

100 REM ** Define FNrollD6, a function to 'roll' one die **
105 ' Returns an integer, 1 to 6
110 DEF FNrollD6 = INT(6 * RND) + 1

200 REM ** Set up **
210 RANDOMIZE TIMER
220 CLS

300 REM ** WHILE...WEND loop to roll dice. Press ESC to quit **
310 WHILE 1
320   BEEP: PRINT "Press a key to roll, or ESC to quit"
330   akey$ = INPUT$(1): IF akey$ = CHR$(27) THEN END
340   PRINT "The roll is"; FNrollD6 + FNrollD6
350   PRINT
360 WEND
```

PROGRAM 8-1.   Roll Two Six-Sided Dice (2D6)

a character" means creating a character in a fantasy role-playing game such as Dungeons & Dragons, Land of Ninja, or Rune-Quest. A character is defined by a set of basic characteristics. For example, in one game system, a character has these seven characteristics: Strength, Constitution, Size, Intelligence, Intuition, Dexterity, and Appearance.

One way to create a character is by the "trust-to-luck" method used in Program 8-2, RPGAME01 (Roll a Fantasy Game Charac-

```
1 REM ** Roll a Fantasy Game Character **
2 ' Teach Yourself GW-BASIC, Chapter 8. File: RPGAME01.BAS

100 REM ** Define a function to 'roll' 3D6 **
110 DEF FNroll3D6 = INT(6 * RND) + INT(6 * RND) + INT(6 * RND) + 3

200 REM ** Set up **
210 RANDOMIZE TIMER

300 REM ** Get name of character and print it **
310 CLS
320 INPUT "Name of character"; Naym$
330 CLS : PRINT Naym$
340 PRINT

400 REM ** Roll 3D6 for each characteristic -- print it **
410 PRINT "Strength", FNroll3D6
420 PRINT "Constitution", FNroll3D6
430 PRINT "Size", FNroll3D6
440 PRINT "Intelligence", FNroll3D6
450 PRINT "Intuition", FNroll3D6
460 PRINT "Dexterity", FNroll3D6
470 PRINT "Appearance", FNroll3D6

500 REM ** Tell how to do again **
510 PRINT
520 PRINT "Press a key for another, or ESC to quit"
530 akey$ = INPUT$(1)
540 IF akey$ <> CHR$(27) THEN GOTO 310 ELSE END
```

PROGRAM 8-2. Roll a Fantasy Game Character

ter). You roll 3D6 (three dice with six sides each) for each characteristic. Therefore, each characteristic has a value from 3 to 18, the higher the better. The function FNroll3D6 defined in line 110 simulates rolling three six-sided dice. It is used seven times in block 400 to obtain values for the seven characteristics. A roll is a number from 3 to 18, with 10 or 11 being an average roll.

The program lines

```
530 akey$ = INPUT$(1)
540 IF akey$ <> CHR$(27)THEN GOTO 310 ELSE END
```

cause a GOTO 310 if a key other than (ESC) is pressed. If (ESC) is pressed, the program ends.

Line 540 is an example of an IF...THEN...ELSE statement. If the condition is true, the statement following THEN is executed. If the condition is false, the statement following ELSE is executed.

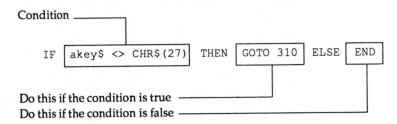

Figure 8-1 shows annotated results from three sample runs of Program RPGAME01. These were selected from several runs made in search of interesting characters for a role-playing game. Each character is named and given a rudimentary "personality." The personality will be refined during game play.

Exercises

1. Suppose you are writing a math drill program that teaches the addition table.

   a. Write a statement to define the function FNdigit that returns a random decimal digit, 0 to 9.

b. Test your function (FNdigit) by using it in a short program to print 20 random decimal digits (or however many you want to print). A sample run is shown here:

4	4	5	3	0
2	8	9	1	3
2	2	9	0	6
5	5	2	0	1

Sample run #1:

Barostan

Strength	17
Constitution	16
Size	14
Intelligence	8
Intuition	10
Dexterity	16
Appearance	10

Barostan is big, strong, rugged, and agile, but not too bright. He is good to have on your side in a fight, if someone will tell him who to attack. He acts first, then thinks later, if at all.

Sample run #2:

Joleeen

Strength	13
Consitution	11
Size	7
Intelligence	13
Intuition	11
Dexterity	18
Appearance	13

Joleen is a clown, mime, acrobat, dancer, or whatever else might entertain an audience. She wants to travel with a troupe of wandering entertainers, and perform at faires and festivals. She will charm you.

Sample run #3:

Rokana

Strength	10
Constitution	9
Size	11
Intelligence	17
Intuition	18
Dexterity	10
Appearance	11

Rokana is quiet and introspective. She wants to study and become a sage, healer, and magic user. Her high intelligence and intuition make her well suited to achieve her goal.

FIGURE 8-1. Fantasy role-playing game characters, Program RPGAME01

2. Modify Program 8-2, RPGAME01, so that it rolls a D&D character. A D&D character has these six characteristics: Strength, Intelligence, Wisdom, Dexterity, Constitution, and Charisma.

8.2 DEFINE STRING FUNCTIONS WITHOUT ARGUMENTS

You can define a string function in much the same way that you define a numeric function. In a DEF FN statement, you write the name of the function, followed by an equal sign (=), followed by a string expression. The name of a string function must end in a dollar sign ($).

The function FNflip$, defined below, returns the values *H* or *T*, randomly selected. You can use it to simulate flipping a coin.

```
DEF FNflip$ = MID$("HT", INT(2 * RND)+ 1, 1)
```

The FNflip$ function appears in Program 8-3, COIN02 (Flip a Fair Coin). Press a key other than (ESC) to simulate flipping a coin, or press (ESC) to quit. A sample run of Program COIN02 is shown here:

```
Press a key to flip, or ESC to quit
The flip is T

Press a key to flip, or ESC to quit
The flip is H

Press a key to flip, or ESC to quit
The flip is H
```

Examples

1. **FNc$ and FNv$** These two functions are defined below. Function FNc$ returns a random consonant; function FNv$ returns a random vowel. The letter *y* is included as both a consonant and a vowel.

```
DEF FNc$ = MID$("bcdfghjklmnpqrstvwxyz", INT(21 * RND)+ 1, 1)

DEF FNv$ = MID$("aeiouy", INT(6 * RND) + 1, 1)
```

```
1 REM ** Flip a Fair Coin **
2 ' Teach Yourself GW-BASIC, Chapter 8. File: COIN02.BAS

100 REM ** Define FNflip$, a string function to 'flip' one coin **
105 ' Returns a string, "H" or "T", equally probable
110 DEF FNflip$ = MID$("HT", INT(2 * RND) + 1, 1)

200 REM ** Set up **
210 RANDOMIZE TIMER
220 CLS

300 REM ** WHILE...WEND loop to flip coin. Press ESC to quit **
310 WHILE 1
320   BEEP: PRINT "Press a key to flip, or ESC to quit"
330   akey$ = INPUT$(1): IF akey$ = CHR$(27) THEN END
340   PRINT "The flip is "; FNflip$
350   PRINT
360 WEND
```

PROGRAM 8-3.   Flip a Fair Coin

Both of these functions are used in Program 8-4, WRDMKR02 (Word Maker with Consonant & Vowel Functions). This program is a revision of Program 7-5, WRDMKR01, which appeared in Chapter 7. Note that it is now much shorter. Here are two words produced by Program WRDMKR02.

```
Press a key for a word, Esc to quit
Your random 'cvcvc' word is: zenoz

Press a key for a word, Esc to quit
Your random 'cvcvc' word is: dajas
```

2. **FNLttr$** The function FNLttr$, defined below, returns a random letter. The function depends, however, on a string variable, *alphabet$*, that must be assigned a value before the function is used. This value does not have to be assigned before the function is defined in a program.

```
DEF FNLttr$ = MID$(alphabet$, INT(26 * RND)+ 1, 1)
```

```
1 REM ** Word Maker with Consonant & Vowel Functions **
2 ' Teach Yourself GW-BASIC, Chapter 8. Filename: WRDMKR02.BAS

100 REM ** Define random consonant & vowel functions **
110 DEF FNc$ = MID$("bcdfghjklmnpqrstvwxyz", INT(21 * RND) + 1, 1)
120 DEF FNv$ = MID$("aeiouy", INT(6 * RND) + 1, 1)

200 REM ** Set up **
210 RANDOMIZE TIMER
220 CLS

300 REM ** WHILE...WEND loop to make random words **
310 WHILE 1

320    BEEP: PRINT "Press a key for a word, Esc to quit"
330    akey$ = INPUT$(1): IF akey$ = CHR$(27) THEN END

340    word$ = FNc$ + FNv$ + FNc$ + FNv$ + FNc$    'Here's the word

350    PRINT "Your random 'cvcvc' word is "; word$
360    PRINT

370 WEND
```

| PROGRAM 8-4. | Word Maker with Consonant & Vowel Functions |

Program 8-5, ALPHA01 (Alphabet Soup with FNLttr$ Function), puts random letters in random places on the screen. The string variable *alphabet$* is assigned a string consisting of the 26 letters of the alphabet, in uppercase. If you prefer seeing lowercase letters in your alphabet soup, change this assignment to suit your tastes.

Line 110 defines the FNLttr$ function. Line 220 assigns a value to *alphabet$*, the string variable used in the function. This assignment must occur before the function is used. Line 360 uses the function to print random letters selected from the string assigned to *alphabet$*. You can assign a string consisting of any 26 characters to *alphabet$* and see them in your alphabet soup. Just rewrite line 220.

3. You can define the FNLttr$ function in an entirely different way. The definition shown below returns a random uppercase letter, any letter from *A* to *Z*.

```
DEF FNLttr$ = CHR$(INT(26 * RND) + 65) 'Uppercase letters
```

This function is completely self-contained. It does not require a string variable, such as *alphabet$*. Try this function in line 110 of Program ALPHA01. Also, delete line 220 from the program—it is not needed. Run the modified program to test this new definition of the FNLttr$ function.

```
1 REM ** Alphabet Soup with FNLttr$ Function **
2 ' Teach Yourself GW-BASIC, Chapter 8. Filename: ALPHA01.BAS

100 REM ** Define FNLttr$, a random letter function **
110 DEF FNLttr$ = MID$(alphabet$, INT(26 * RND) + 1, 1)

200 REM ** Set up **
210 RANDOMIZE TIMER
220 alphabet$ = "ABCDEFGHIJKLMNOPQRSTUVWXYZ"
230 WIDTH 40: KEY OFF: CLS

300 REM ** Random letters in random places & colors **

310 WHILE INKEY$ <> CHR$(27)          'Loop while ESC not pressed
320    row = INT(25 * RND) + 1
330    col = INT(40 * RND) + 1
340    kolor = INT(15 * RND) + 1
350    COLOR kolor
360    LOCATE row, col: PRINT FNLttr$;
370 WEND

400 REM ** Return to normal SCREEN 0 and end program **
410 SCREEN 0: COLOR 7: WIDTH 80: KEY ON: END
```

PROGRAM 8-5. Alphabet Soup with FNLttr$ Function

Exercises

1. Use the method shown in Example 3 to define FNLttr$ so that it returns a random lowercase letter.

2. Use the method shown in Example 3 to define a random character function called FNchar$. This function should return random characters whose ASCII codes are in the range 123 to 254, inclusive. Appendix C, "ASCII Codes and Characters," shows you what these characters look like.

| 8.3 | ## DEFINE NUMERIC FUNCTIONS WITH ARGUMENTS |

The user-defined functions you have seen so far do not require arguments. You can also define functions that have arguments. As with built-in functions, the argument is enclosed in parentheses following the name of the function. The function FNran, shown next, is a function of one numeric argument, n. The value of FNran(n) is a random integer in the range 1 to n.

```
DEF FNran(n)= INT(n * RND) + 1
```

The argument n is a *local variable;* that is, the value of n has no meaning outside of the function definition. You may use n as a variable name elsewhere in the program without affecting its use as an argument name in the definition of FNran. You can also replace the arbitrary n on both sides of the equal sign with any name. For example:

```
DEF FNran(range)= INT(range * RND) + 1
```

A simple multiplication drill program is shown next. It presents single-digit multiplication problems. The FNran function is defined in line 20 and used in lines 30 and 40 to obtain values of a and b. Each value is a random integer in the range 1 to 9.

```
10 DEF FNran(n)= INT(n * RND) + 1
20 RANDOMIZE TIMER: CLS
```

```
30 a = FNran(9)
40 b = FNran(9)
50 PRINT a; "x"; b; "= "; : INPUT answer
60 IF answer = a * b THEN PRINT "Correct. Good work!"
70 IF answer <> a * b THEN PRINT "Oops. The answer is "; a * b
80 PRINT : GOTO 30
```

In the sample run shown below, the first answer is correct and produces the string printed by line 60. The second answer is incorrect and produces the string and correct answer printed by line 70.

```
 7 x 3 = ? 21
Correct. Good work!

 3 x 9 = ? 28
Oops. The answer is 27
```

Examples

1. **FNsind function** The FNsind function, defined here, computes the sine of an angle expressed in degrees.

```
DEF FNsind(x)= SIN(3.141593 * x / 180)
```

Use the following short program to try out the FNsind function.

```
10 DEF FNsind(x)= SIN(3.141593 * x / 180)
20 CLS
30 INPUT "Angle in degrees"; degrees
40 PRINT "The sine is: "; FNsind(degrees)
50 PRINT : GOTO 30
```

Note that the angle is entered as the value of *degrees*. The variable named *degrees* is used as the argument of FNsind in line 40. The value of *degrees* is used in place of *x* in computing the value of FNsind, as defined in line 10.

2. **FNsind# double precision function** FNsind, as defined in Example 1, is a single precision function. You can also define a double precision version, called FNsind#, as shown next.

```
DEF FNsind#(x#)= SIN(3.141592653589793 * x# / 180)
```

Note the following things about this function definition:

- The name of the function, FNsind#, ends in the number symbol (#), which designates double precision.

- The local variable (x#) used in the definition is a double precision variable.

- The value of pi (3.141592653589793) has more than seven digits; therefore, it is recognized as double precision.

- The number 180 is an exact integer, not an approximation, so it doesn't have to be designated as double precision. However, it is all right to write it as 180#.

3. **FNhyp function**   A user-defined function can have more than one argument. The FNhyp function, defined here, computes the length of the hypotenuse of a right triangle, given the lengths of the other two sides, *a* and *b*, as arguments.

```
DEF FNhyp(a, b)= SQR(a ^ 2 + b ^ 2)
```

When a function has more than one argument, the arguments are separated by commas, as shown above. Now use the following short program to try out the FNhyp function.

```
10 DEF FNhyp(a, b)= SQR(a ^ 2 + b ^ 2)
20 CLS
30 INPUT "Length of side a      "; a
40 INPUT "Length of side b      "; b
50 PRINT "Length of hypotenuse:"; FNhyp(a, b)
60 PRINT : GOTO 30
```

4. **FNran% function**   The FNran% function, defined here, is an integer function of two integer arguments. It returns random integers in the range specified by its two arguments.

```
DEF FNran%(Lo%, Hi%)= INT((Hi% - Lo% + 1) * RND) + Lo%
```

You can use the following program to get ten random integers, from 5 to 8 or from 3 to 10, or any range appropriate for GW-BASIC integers.

```
10 DEF FNran%(Lo%, Hi%)= INT((Hi% - Lo% + 1) * RND) + Lo%
20 RANDOMIZE TIMER: CLS
30 INPUT "Enter Lo% & Hi%, separated by a comma: ", Lo%, Hi%
40 PRINT : PRINT "Here are 10 random numbers:"
50 PRINT
60 FOR k = 1 TO 10
70   PRINT FNran%(Lo%, Hi%)
80 NEXT k
```

The program line

```
30 INPUT "Enter Lo% & Hi%, separated by a comma: ", Lo%, Hi%
```

allows you to enter the values of both *Lo%* and *Hi%*. Use a comma to separate these values, as shown in the following sample run:

```
Enter Lo% & Hi%, separated by a comma: -9, 9

Here are 10 random numbers:

4            1            2           -4          -4
5           -9           -5            6           7
```

Exercises

1. A short multiplication practice program appeared near the beginning of this section. Lines 20, 30, and 40 of that program are shown here:

```
20 DEF FNran(n)= INT(n * RND) + 1
30 a = FNran(9)
40 b = FNran(9)
```

a. Modify the program so that each problem ($a \times b$) consists of a number from 1 to 12 (value of a) multiplied by a number from 1 to 12 (value of b).

b. Modify the program so that each problem ($a \times b$) consists of a number from 0 to 9 (value of a) multiplied by a number from 0 to 19 (value of b).

2. Complete the following program to compute the projected population (P_n) in n years based on a current population (P_o) that is growing at the rate of r percent per year.

$$P_n = P_o (1 + r/100)^n$$

where: P_n is the population in n years
P_o is the current population
r is the percent growth per year
n is the number of years

Define a function called FNpop in line 20, below, and use it in line 40.

```
10 CLS
20 DEF _____
30 INPUT "Enter p0, r, n, separated by commas: ", p0, r, n
40 PRINT "The projected population is: "; _____
50 PRINT : GOTO 30
```

8.4 DEFINE STRING FUNCTIONS WITH ARGUMENTS

In programming, you can usually do things in more than one way. Program 8-6, WRDMKR03 (Word Maker with Random Character Function), uses a defined string function called FNranchr$ to generate random consonants and vowels. The value of FNranchr$ is a single character selected at random from a string argument. If you run this program, you will see results similar to those of Programs 7-5, WRDMKR01, and 8-4, WRDMKR02.

```
1 REM ** Word Maker with Random Character Function **
2 ' Teach Yourself GW-BASIC, Chapter 8. Filename: WRDMKR03.BAS

100 REM ** Define FNranchr$, a random character function **
105 ' Returns one random character from a string argument
110 DEF FNranchr$(s$) = MID$(s$, INT(LEN(s$) * RND) + 1, 1)

200 REM ** Set up **
210 RANDOMIZE TIMER
220 consonant$ = "bcdfghjklmnpqrstvwxyz"          '21 consonants
230 vowel$ = "aeiouy"                             '6 vowels
240 CLS

300 REM ** WHILE...WEND loop to make random words **
310 WHILE 1

320    BEEP: PRINT "Press a key for a word, Esc to quit"
330    akey$ = INPUT$(1): IF akey$ = CHR$(27) THEN END

340    word$ = ""              'Start with the empty string ("")

350    ' Add a consonant, vowel, consonant, vowel, consonant
360    word$ = word$ + FNranchr$(consonant$)
370    word$ = word$ + FNranchr$(vowel$)
380    word$ = word$ + FNranchr$(consonant$)
390    word$ = word$ + FNranchr$(vowel$)
400    word$ = word$ + FNranchr$(consonant$)

410    ' Print the word
420    PRINT "Your random 'cvcvc' word is: "; word$
430    PRINT

440 WEND
```

| PROGRAM 8-6. | Word Maker with Random Character Function |

The FNranchr$ function is defined in block 100.

```
100 REM ** Define FNranchr$, a random character function **
105 ' Returns one random character from a string argument
110 DEF FNranchr$(s$)= MID$(s$, INT(LEN(s$) * RND) + 1, 1)
```

Line 110 introduces a new function called LEN. LEN is a numeric function of a string argument. Its value is the number of characters, including spaces (if any), in a string argument. For example, LEN("abc") is 3, and LEN("a b c") is 5.

In Program WRDMKR03, lines 360 through 400 use the FNranchr$ function.

```
360    word$ = word$ + FNranchr$(consonant$)
370    word$ = word$ + FNranchr$(vowel$)
380    word$ = word$ + FNranchr$(consonant$)
390    word$ = word$ + FNranchr$(vowel$)
400    word$ = word$ + FNranchr$(consonant$)
```

In line 360, the argument of the FNranchr$ function is *consonant$*. So the value of *consonant$* is used in place of *s$* in the definition of the FNranchr$ function (see line 110), like this:

```
MID$(consonant$, INT(LEN(consonant$) * RND) + 1, 1)
```

The value of *consonant$* is a string with 21 letters. Therefore:

LEN(*consonant$*) is 21.

INT(LEN(*consonant$*) * RND) + 1 is a random integer from 1 to 21.

MID$(*consonant$*, INT(LEN(*consonant$*) * RND + 1, 1) is a random letter selected from the value of *consonant$*.

In line 370, a similar process selects a random vowel from the value of *vowel$*.

Note that you can use FNranchr$ to select a random character from any string. Just use the string as the argument of FNranchr$. For example, perhaps this next program can write the great American novel, if you run it billions of times and do a great job of editing.

```
10 DEF FNranchr$(s$)= MID$(s$, INT(LEN(s$) * RND) + 1, 1)
20 RANDOMIZE TIMER: CLS
30 alphabet$ = "             aaabcdeeefghiiijklmnooopqrstuuuvwxyz"
40 FOR k = 1 TO 1000
50   PRINT FNranchr$(alphabet$);
60 NEXT k
```

Line 30 assigns to *alphabet$* a string consisting of 12 spaces and the 26 letters of the alphabet. Each consonant appears once; each vowel appears three times. Try this program with **your** alphabet.

Examples

1. **FNLower$ function** The FNLower$ function, defined below, plays a very specific role. It converts an uppercase letter to the corresponding lowercase letter. Therefore, when you use FNLower$, you must supply as an argument the uppercase letter for which you want the corresponding lowercase letter as the result.

```
20 DEF FNLower$(upper$)= CHR$(ASC(upper$) + 32)
```

This function depends on the fact that the ASCII code for a lowercase letter is exactly 32 greater than the ASCII code for the corresponding uppercase letter. For example, the ASCII code for *a* is 97, and the ASCII code for *A* is 65; the ASCII code for *z* is 122, and the ASCII code for *Z* is 90.

   Use the following short program to try out the FNLower$ function:

```
10 DEF FNLower$(upper$)= CHR$(ASC(upper$) + 32)
20 CLS
30 WHILE 1
40   INPUT "Enter an uppercase letter: ", Letter$
50   PRINT "Lowercase equivalent is:   "; FNLower$(Letter$)
60   PRINT
70 WEND
```

2. **Yet another FNranchr$ function** The FNranchr$ function defined here returns a random character defined by two numeric arguments. The two arguments are ASCII codes for the lowest and highest possible characters.

```
DEF FNranchr$(Lo%, Hi%)= CHR$(INT((Hi% - Lo% + 1) * RND) + Lo%)
```

This defines FNranchr$ as a string function of two integer arguments, *Lo%* and *Hi%*. The first argument must be less than or equal to the second argument, and both arguments must be in the range for ASCII codes (0 to 255). Use the following program to check out this new FNranchr$ function.

```
10 DEF FNranchr$(Lo%, Hi%)= CHR$(INT((Hi% - Lo% + 1) * RND) + Lo%)
20 RANDOMIZE TIMER: CLS
30 INPUT "ASCII limits (low, high)"; Lo%, Hi%
40 PRINT
50 FOR k = 1 TO 20
60   PRINT FNranchr$(Lo%, Hi%),
70 NEXT k
80 PRINT : GOTO 30
```

Exercises

1. Write a DEF FN statement that defines the FNUpper$ string function to convert a lowercase letter (*a* to *z*) to the corresponding uppercase letter (*A* to *Z*). FNUpper$ is a function of one string argument. Use *Lower$* as the argument in your definition.

2. Write a DEF FN statement to define the FNmonth$ string function, as follows:

   a. FNmonth$ is a function of one numeric argument called *m*.

   b. The value of FNmonth$ is a three-character string selected from this string:

   ```
   "JanFebMarAprMayJunJulAugSepOctNovDec"
   ```

   c. FNmonth$ is defined for integer values of *m* from 1 to 12, as follows: FNmonth$(1) is Jan, FNmonth$(2) is Feb, FNmonth$(3) is Mar, and so on. FNmonth$(12) is Dec.

LEARN HOW TO USE SUBROUTINES

A subroutine is a piece of a program designed to be called (used) from anywhere in the program, except from the subroutine itself. You use a GOSUB statement in the main program to call a subroutine. When the subroutine completes its task, it executes a RETURN statement, which returns control to the part of the program that called the subroutine.

Program 8-7, DELAY02 (Beep with Time Delay Subroutine), has a main program in lines 10 through 70, and a time delay subroutine in line 110. The program executes lines 10 and 20, then enters the WHILE...WEND loop in lines 30 through 60. Each time through the loop, the computer beeps (line 40), goes to the subroutine (from line 50), executes the subroutine (line 110), returns to line 60 (via RETURN in line 110), and repeats the loop—unless someone has pressed the (ESC) key.

When you run the program, you will see the message "You will hear a beep every second" near the top of the screen, and hear a beep

```
1 REM ** Beep with Time Delay Subroutine **
2 ' Teach Yourself GW-BASIC, Chapter 8. Filename: DELAY02.BAS

10 CLS
20 PRINT "You'll hear a beep every second (Press ESC to quit)"

30 WHILE INKEY$ <> CHR$(27)

40    BEEP
50    GOSUB 110                  'Use time delay subroutine **

60 WEND

70 END

100 REM ** SUBROUTINE: One second time delay **
110 start = TIMER: WHILE TIMER < start + 1: WEND: RETURN
```

PROGRAM 8-7. Beep with Time Delay Subroutine

once every second. Press the (ESC) key to leave the WHILE...WEND loop. The computer then ends the program at line 70. Without line 70, the computer would go on to the subroutine in line 110, and you would see a "RETURN without GOSUB" error message. To see this happen, delete line 70, run the program, and press (ESC).

REMEMBER: If a subroutine follows a main program, use an END statement between the main program and the subroutine.

Examples

1. **Variable time delay subroutine** The time delay subroutine used in Program 8-7, DELAY02, provides a fixed time delay of one second. Here is a variable time delay subroutine:

```
100 REM ** SUBROUTINE: Variable time delay **
110 start = TIMER: WHILE TIMER < start + delay: WEND: RETURN
```

To use this subroutine, first assign the amount of delay (in seconds) as the value of *delay*, and then call the subroutine. For example, for a one-second delay, include this:

```
delay = 1: GOSUB 110
```

Program 8-8, DELAY03 (Beep with Variable Time Delay Subroutine), demonstrates the use of the time delay subroutine. Enter and run this program. Press the (ESC) key to exit from the WHILE...END loop. The program then executes the END statement in line 70, and the program ends.

2. **The LOCASE subroutine** Suppose you are writing a trivia program. One of the questions is, "What are the colors of a rainbow?" Red is one of the colors, and people might enter it as **red** or **RED** or **Red**, or perhaps even **ReD**. This could make it difficult for the program to determine if the answer is correct.

The LOCASE subroutine changes all uppercase letters in a string to lowercase. Lowercase letters and characters that are not letters are unchanged. You can use Program 8-9, LOCASE01 (Demonstrate LOCASE Subroutine), to see how the subroutine works.

A sample run follows. For the string R2D2, notice that the subroutine leaves unchanged all characters that are not letters. Uppercase letters are changed to lowercase. Lowercase letters are not changed.

```
String, please? RED
LOCASE string:  red

String, please? Red
LOCASE string:  red

String, please? R2D2
LOCASE string:  r2d2
```

The subroutine uses the integer variable *kk%*, and two string variables, *strng$* and *character$*. Only one of the variables (*strng$*) appears in the main program. The value of *strng$* in the main program can be changed by the subroutine.

```
1 REM ** Beep with Variable Time Delay Subroutine **
2 ' Teach Yourself GW-BASIC, Chapter 8. Filename: DELAY03.BAS

10 CLS
20 PRINT "You'll hear a beep every second (Press ESC to quit)"

30 WHILE INKEY$ <> CHR$(27)

40    BEEP
50    delay = 1: GOSUB 110          'Use time delay subroutine **

60 WEND

70 END

100 REM ** SUBROUTINE: Variable time delay **
110 start = TIMER: WHILE TIMER < start + delay: WEND: RETURN
```

PROGRAM 8-8. Beep with Variable Time Delay Subroutine

```
1 REM ** Demonstrate LOCASE Subroutine **
2 ' Teach Yourself GW-BASIC, Chapter 8. Filename: LOCASE01.BAS

100 REM ** Define FNLower$ to change uppercase to lowercase **
110 DEF FNLower$(upper$) = CHR$(ASC(upper$) + 32)

200 REM ** Main program **
210 CLS
220 WHILE 1
230 INPUT "String, please"; strng$
235   IF strng$ = "" THEN END            'END if empty string
240   GOSUB 910                          'Use LOCASE subroutine
250   PRINT "LOCASE string:  "; strng$
260   PRINT
270 WEND
280 END

900 REM ** SUBROUTINE: LOCASE **
905 ' Changes letters in strng$ to lowercase
910 FOR kk% = 1 TO LEN(strng$)
920   character$ = MID$(strng$, kk%, 1)
930   IF character$ < "A" OR character$ > "Z" THEN 960
940   character$ = FNLower$(character$)
950   MID$(strng$, kk%, 1) = character$
960 NEXT kk%
970 RETURN
```

PROGRAM 8-9.   Demonstrate LOCASE Subroutine

The following variation of the main program's WHILE...WEND loop preserves the value of the string you enter:

```
220 WHILE 1
230   INPUT "String, please"; ThinRope$
240   IF ThinRope$ = "" THEN END   'END if empty string
250   strng$ = ThinRope$: GOSUB 910 'Use LOCASE subroutine
260   PRINT "LOCASE string:  "; strng$
270   PRINT
280 WEND
```

Line 240 assigns the value of *ThinRope$* as the value of *strng$* and calls the subroutine. Since the variable *ThinRope$* is not used in the subroutine, its value remains unchanged by the execution of the subroutine. Enter this version of the main program and run the resulting program to see how it works.

The LOCASE subroutine is shown here.

```
900 REM ** SUBROUTINE: LOCASE **
905 ' Changes letters in strng$ to lowercase
910 FOR kk% = 1 TO LEN(strng$)
920   character$ = MID$(strng$, kk%, 1)
930   IF character$ < "A" OR character$ > "Z" THEN 960
940   character$ = FNLower$(character$)
950   MID$(strng$, kk%, 1)= character$
960 NEXT kk%
970 RETURN
```

The subroutine consists of a FOR...NEXT loop that extracts each character of *strng$* and checks to see if it is an uppercase letter. Any uppercase letter is changed to lowercase and inserted back into the string by lines 940 and 950. Other characters are left unchanged.

The program line

```
930   IF character$ < "A" OR character$ > "Z" THEN 960
```

tells the computer to go to line 960 if the value of *character$* is less than A or greater than Z. In other words, go to line 960 if the value of *character$* is not an uppercase letter. Any character whose ASCII code is less than 65 is also less than A. Any character whose ASCII code is greater than 90 is also greater than Z.

NOTE: The condition in line 930 is an example of a *compound condition:* it consists of two simple conditions connected by the keyword OR.

If the value of *character$* is an uppercase letter (A to Z), the condition in line 930 is false, and the computer executes lines 940 and 950. Line 940 changes the letter to lowercase. Line 950 inserts the lowercase letter into the value of *strng$*.

In line 950, MID$ is used as a statement, not as a function. The statement

```
MID$(strng$, kk%, 1)= character$
```

replaces the character at position *kk%* in *strng$* with the value of *character$*. For example, suppose *strng$* is RED, *kk%* is 1, and *character$* is r. The MID$ statement replaces R with r in position 1.

Exercises

1. The LOCASE subroutine shown in Example 2 requires the use of the FNLower$ user-defined function. Write a completely self-contained LOCASE subroutine that does not require the use of FNLower$.

2. Design and write a subroutine, called UPCASE, that changes all lowercase letters in *strng$* to uppercase letters.

| 8.6 | **RELAX WITH WORDSWORTH** |

This has been a long chapter, containing many new ideas and many programs. Now take some time for a recreational activity called Wordsworth. Assign a letter score to each letter of the alphabet, *A* through Z, as follows:

A=1	E=5	I=9	M=13	Q=17	U=21	Y=25
B=2	F=6	J=10	N=14	R=18	V=22	Z=26
C=3	G=7	K=11	O=15	S=19	W=23	
D=4	H=8	L=12	P=16	T=20	X=24	

For any dictionary word you choose, compute two numbers, called *Wordsworth +* and *Wordsworth **, as follows:

- *Wordsworth +* is the numerical value of a word obtained by *adding* the letter scores of all the letters in the word. For example:

"hobbit" is worth 8 + 15 + 2 + 2 + 9 + 20 = 56 points
"dragon" is worth 4 + 18 + 1 + 7 + 15 + 14 = 59 points

- *Wordsworth* * is the numerical value of a word obtained by *multiplying* the letter scores of all the letters in the word. For example:

"hobbit" is worth 8 * 15 * 2 * 2 * 9 * 20 = 86,400 points
"dragon" is worth 4 * 18 * 1 * 7 * 15 * 14 = 105,840 points

In other words, *Wordsworth* + is the sum of the letter scores of all the letters in a word; *Wordsworth* * is the product of the letter scores of all the letters in a word. You can use Program 8-10, WRDWRTH1 (Wordsworth), to compute and print *Wordsworth* + and *Wordsworth* * for a word entered from the keyboard.

This program uses the FNLower$ function and the LOCASE subroutine introduced previously. In the annotated run in Figure 8-2, note that words can be entered in all uppercase letters, all lowercase letters, or a mixture of both. The program ignores characters that are not letters.

Exercises

Use Program WRDWRTH1 to help you answer one or more of the following questions. An answer must be a real dictionary word.

1. What three-letter word has the smallest *Wordsworth* +? *Wordsworth* *? What four-letter word?

2. What three-letter word has the largest *Wordsworth* +? *Wordsworth* *? What four-letter word?

3. What is the first word (alphabetically) to have a *Wordsworth* + of exactly 100? A *Wordsworth* * of exactly 100?

4. What is the last word (alphabetically) to have a *Wordsworth* + of exactly 100? A *Wordsworth* * of exactly 100?

5. In the entire dictionary, what word has the largest *Wordsworth* +? *Wordsworth* *?

6. What is the longest word (most letters) that has a *Wordsworth* + equal to the number of weeks in a year?

7. What word has a *Wordsworth* * closest to one million? (The value can be less than one million or greater than one million.)

```
1 REM ** Wordsworth **
2 ' Teach Yourself GW-BASIC, Chapter 8. File: WRDWRTH1.BAS

100 REM ** Define FNLower$ to change uppercase to lowercase **
110 DEF FNLower$(upper$) = CHR$(ASC(upper$) + 32)

200 REM ** Set up **
210 CLS

300 REM ** Get a word. To quit, just press ENTER **
310 INPUT "Your word"; strng$
340 IF strng$ = "" THEN END        'END if empty string
330 GOSUB 910                      'Use LOCASE subroutine

400 REM ** Set Wordsworth sum and product to zero **
410 Sum = 0
420 Product# = 1         'Product# is double precision

500 REM ** Compute Wordsworth + and Wordsworth * **
510 FOR k% = 1 TO LEN(strng$)
520    Letter$ = MID$(strng$, k%, 1)
530    IF Letter$ < "a" OR Letter$ > "z" THEN 570
540    Lscore = ASC(Letter$) - 96
550    Sum = Sum + Lscore
560    Product# = Product# * Lscore
570 NEXT k%

600 REM ** Print Wordsworth + and *, go to top of loop **
610 PRINT "Wordsworth + is"; Sum
620 PRINT "Wordsworth * is"; Product#
630 PRINT : GOTO 310

900 REM ** SUBROUTINE: LOCASE **
905 ' Changes letters in strng$ to lowercase
910 FOR kk% = 1 TO LEN(strng$)
920    character$ = MID$(strng$, kk%, 1)
930    IF character$ < "A" OR character$ > "Z" THEN 960
940    character$ = FNLower$(character$)
950    MID$(strng$, kk%, 1) = character$
960 NEXT kk%
970 RETURN
```

PROGRAM 8-10.	Wordsworth

```
Your word? dragon          (Word entered in all lowercase letters)
Wordsworth + is 59
Wordsworth * is 105840

Your word? DRAGON          (Word entered in all uppercase letters)
Wordsworth + is 59
Wordsworth * is 105840

Your word? Dragon          (Word entered in mixture of upper- and
Wordsworth + is 59              lowercase)
Wordsworth * is 105840

Your word? R2D2            (Characters other than letters are ignored)
Wordsworth + is 22
Wordsworth * is 72
```

FIGURE 8-2.   An annotated run of Program WRDWRTH1

Most of the work and play in answering these questions is people play: browsing through a dictionary, thinking about what to do, creating strategies—all most enjoyable! People do this well. Some of the work, such as looking up letter scores and calculating, is grungy stuff. Let your computer do those things.

EXERCISES

MASTERY
SKILLS
CHECK

1. Suppose you are in a room with 30 people, including yourself. What is the probability that two or more people have their birthdays on the same day of the year? One way to explore this problem is to generate 30 random integers, each in the range 1 to 365, and then check to see if two or more are equal.

   Complete lines 10 and 40 in the following program. In line 10, compose the DEF FN statement to define the FNday function to return a random integer in the range 1 to 365. In line 40, use this function to print one random number: the value of FNday.

```
10 DEF _____

20 RANDOMIZE TIMER: CLS

30 FOR k = 1 TO 30

40    PRINT _____

50 NEXT k
```

A sample run is shown below. Note that the number 13 occurs twice. For this simulation, two people have the same birthday, January 13. Is this a likely or unlikely occurrence?

32	230	184	28	264
319	208	208	157	351
348	326	97	281	306
210	172	235	361	13
219	359	13	340	335
21	356	328	14	33

2. The value of TIME$ is a string with a length of eight characters, as follows: the hour (00 to 23), a colon (:), the minutes (00 to 59), a colon (:), and the seconds (00 to 59). You can verify this by means of the following direct PRINT statement:

```
PRINT TIME$, LEN(TIME$)
07:29:34        8
```

Define three string functions, FNhr$, FNmin$, and FNsec$, as follows:

a. The value of FNhr$ is the number of hours in the value of TIME$, expressed as a string (07 in the PRINT statement result).

b. The value of FNmin$ is the number of minutes in the value of TIME$, expressed as a string (29 in the PRINT statement result).

c. The value of FNsec$ is the number of seconds in the value of TIME$, expressed as a string (34 in the PRINT statement result).

3. Write a DEF FN statement to define each of the following functions:

   a. Volume of a sphere as a function of the radius.

   $$V = \frac{4}{3} \pi r^3$$

   where V = volume

   r = radius

   π = approximately 3.14159

   b. Volume of a cylinder as a function of radius and height.

   $$V = \pi r^2 h$$

   where V = volume

   r = radius

   h = height

   π = approximately 3.14159

   c. The nth power of n (see Exercise 9 in the Mastery Skills Check, Chapter 5). Make this a double precision function, FNnpwrn#, of the double precision argument, n#.

   d. The distance between two points in the xy-plane. One point is located at coordinates (x1, y1). The other point is located at coordinates (x2, y2). The distance (d) between the two points is:

   $$d = \sqrt{(x1 - x2)^2 + (y1 - y2)^2}$$

   Call this function FNd. It is a function of the four arguments: *x1, y1, x2, y2.*

4. Design a string function, called FNsuit$, that returns a card symbol (♥ ♦ ♣ ♠) as its value. FNsuit$ is a function of one argument. The value of the argument must be an integer from 1 to 4. The ASCII codes for the card symbols are 3 for hearts (♥), 4 for diamonds (♦), 5 for clubs (♣), and 6 for spades (♠). A sample run of a program that uses FNsuit$ is shown next.

```
Suit number (1 to 4)? 1
Your suit is: ♥
```

```
Suit number (1 to 4)? 2
Your suit is: ◆

Suit number (1 to 4)? 5
Your suit is:                (Nothing is printed)
```

5. Design a string function, called FNcard$, whose value is a "card" selected from the string shown here:

```
" A 2 3 4 5 6 7 8 910 J Q K"
```

This string has 13 items, each occupying two character positions. The first item is a space and *A*, the second item is a space and 2, and so on. The tenth item is 10, and the thirteenth item is a space and *K*.

FNcard$ is a function of one argument, which must have an integer value in the range 1 to 13. A sample run of a program to test FNcard$ might go like this:

```
Card number (1 to 13)? 1
Your card is:   A

Card number (1 to 13)? 13
Your card is:   K

Card number (1 to 13)? 14
Your card is:               (Nothing is printed)
```

6. You have seen, or designed, functions that roll a fixed number of six-sided dice. Now write a subroutine to simulate rolling any number of dice. Use *NmbrD6* to designate the number of dice. Your subroutine should compute the value of *DiceTotal*, the sum of the rolls of all of the dice. Use the following program to test your subroutine. In line 30, supply the line number for the GOSUB statement.

```
10 RANDOMIZE TIMER: CLS
20 INPUT "How many dice to roll"; NmbrD6
30 GOSUB _____
40 PRINT "The total roll is:   "; DiceTotal
50 PRINT : GOTO 20
```

A sample run of the program, using your subroutine, might go like this:

```
How many dice to roll? 1
The total roll is:     5

How many dice to roll? 3
The total roll is:     15

How many dice to roll? 10
The total roll is:     39
```

7. In the Prince Valiant role-playing game, the outcomes of many events are determined by flipping several coins. The number of coins varies with the character's skills; a larger number of coins indicates a greater skill.

    Write a subroutine to simulate flipping a bunch of coins. Use *NmbrCoins* as the variable for the number of coins. Your subroutine should compute the values of the following variables:

NmbrHeads	Number of heads
NmbrTails	Number of tails
PctHeads	Percent of total throws that were heads
PctTails	Percent of total throws that were tails

    Use the program shown here to test your subroutine. In line 30, supply the line number for the GOSUB statement.

```
10 RANDOMIZE TIMER: CLS
20 INPUT "How many coins to flip"; NmbrCoins
30 GOSUB _____
40 PRINT
50 PRINT "Number of heads: "; NmbrHeads
60 PRINT "Number of tails: "; NmbrTails
70 PRINT "Percent heads:   "; PctHeads
80 PRINT "Percent tails:   "; PctTails
90 END
```

    A possible sample run is shown next.

```
How many coins to flip? 7

Number of heads:   3
Number of tails:   4
Percent heads:     42.85714
Percent tails:     57.14286
```

To see the results printed more neatly, modify the main program so that the percentages are rounded to the nearest percent.

Data Structures: Data Lists and Arrays

▶9◀

CHAPTER OBJECTIVES

- ▶ Use READ and DATA to acquire values
  of variables   9.1
- ▶ Restore data for repetitive use   9.2
- ▶ Learn about arrays and array variables   9.3
- ▶ Use arrays in programs   9.4
- ▶ Use arrays to count things   9.5
- ▶ Add another dimension   9.6

In this chapter, you will learn another way to store numbers and strings—in DATA statements as part of your program—and how to use READ statements to read these numbers and strings as values of variables.

This chapter also introduces a new kind of variable—the *array variable*—and arrays of array variables. Arrays give you the means to store and process large amounts of data.

SKILLS
CHECK

EXERCISES

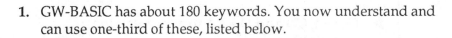

You now know a good deal about GW-BASIC, and have already acquired the following skills:

1. GW-BASIC has about 180 keywords. You now understand and can use one-third of these, listed below.

ABS	EXP	LIST	RANDOMIZE	TAN
ASC	FIX	LLIST	REM	THEN
ATN	FOR	LOCATE	RETURN	TIME$
BEEP	GOSUB	LOG	RND	TIMER
CHR$	GOTO	LPRINT	RUN	TO
CIRCLE	IF	MID$	SCREEN	USING
CLS	INKEY$	NEW	SIN	WEND
COLOR	INPUT	NEXT	SOUND	WHILE
COS	INPUT$	OFF	SPACE$	WIDTH
DATE$	INT	ON	SQR	
DEF FN	KEY	OR	STEP	
ELSE	LEN	PRINT	SYSTEM	
END	LINE	PSET	TAB	

2. You can read and understand programs that include the above keywords, along with numbers, strings, variables, and functions.

3. You can modify programs to suit your needs and programming style. Modifying a program is a good way for you to make sure you understand how a program works. Try writing your own versions of programs you see in this book.

4. You can design user-defined functions and subroutines.

5. You can design and write original programs—programs that tell the computer what to do and how to do it, the way you want it done. The best way to learn how to program is to write programs and make them work.

USE READ AND DATA TO ACQUIRE VALUES OF VARIABLES

9.1

The program shown below introduces two new statements: a DATA statement and a READ statement. A DATA statement stores number or string values to be assigned to a variable. A DATA statement can contain two or more values, separated by commas. You can use a READ statement to read the data stored in DATA statements as values of a variable, as shown here:

```
10 CLS
20 WHILE 1
30    READ number
40    DATA 1, 22, 333
50    PRINT number
60 WEND
```

The program line

```
30    READ number
```

tells the computer to read one number from a DATA statement as the value of *number*. Each time through the WHILE...WEND loop, line 30 reads the next number in the DATA statement and assigns it as the value of *number*. Run the program, and observe the results shown here:

```
 1
 22
 333
Out of DATA in 30
```

The program read and printed the three values in the DATA statement, and then tried to read another value. Since there are only three values in the DATA statement, an "Out of DATA" message was printed.

You can avoid an "Out of DATA" situation by reading only as many (or fewer) values as are contained in the DATA statement. For example, try this program:

```
10 CLS
20 FOR k = 1 TO 3
30    READ number
40    DATA 1, 22, 333
50    PRINT number
60 NEXT k
```

The FOR...NEXT loop causes *exactly* three values to be read from the DATA statement and printed. No "Out of DATA" message occurs, as you can see from this sample run:

```
1
22
333
```

The DATA statement in line 40 contains three numbers, separated by commas, as shown here:

```
40    DATA 1, 22, 333
```

Commas between numbers

In the programs shown previously, the DATA statement follows the READ statement. A DATA statement may appear anywhere in a program, as in the following two programs shown side by side:

```
10 CLS                    10 CLS
20 DATA 1, 22, 333        20 FOR k = 1 TO 3
30 FOR k = 1 TO 3         30    READ number
40    READ number         40    PRINT number
50    PRINT number        50 NEXT k
60 NEXT k                 60 DATA 1, 22, 333
```

You can also store strings in DATA statements, and then use a READ statement to read a string as the value of a string variable.

```
10 CLS
20 WHILE 1
30   READ strng$
40   PRINT strng$
50 WEND
60 DATA one, two, three
```

Run the foregoing program and see the following on the screen:

```
one
two
three
Out of DATA in 30
```

Items in a DATA statement are separated by commas. Therefore, if a string contains a comma, it must be enclosed in quotation marks, as shown in line 60.

```
10 CLS
20 WHILE 1
30   READ strng$
40   PRINT strng$
50 WEND
60 DATA "Stardrake, Laran", "April 1, 1991"
```

Line 60 contains two strings, each enclosed in quotation marks. A comma separates the two strings. Run the program to see these results:

```
Stardrake, Laran
April 1, 1991
Out of DATA in 30
```

You can put two or three or more DATA statements—as many as you want—in a program. For example, this next program has two DATA statements, each containing one string.

```
10 CLS
20 WHILE 1
30   READ strng$
40   PRINT strng$
50 WEND
60 DATA "Stardrake, Laran"
70 DATA "April 1, 1991"
```

The computer begins at the first item in the first DATA statement (smallest line number). After reading all the data in the first DATA statement, it continues with the first item in the second DATA statement, and so on.

Examples

1. The READ statement in the next program reads two values from DATA statements. The first value must be a string, the value of the string variable *note$*. The second value must be a number, the value of the numeric variable *frequency*. Run the program to see what you hear and hear what you see.

```
10 CLS
20 WHILE 1
30   READ note$, frequency
40   SOUND frequency, 9
50   PRINT note$
60 WEND
70 DATA DO, 262, RE, 294, MI, 330, FA, 349
80 DATA SOL, 392, LA, 440, TI, 494, DO, 523
```

The values in the DATA statement must match the variables in the READ statement. Therefore, data must be supplied in pairs, a string followed by a number, as shown here:

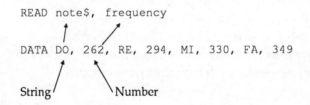

2. Have you ever used flashcards to study a language or some other subject? You can use Program 9-1, FLSHCD01 (Flashcard with Japanese-English Data), to learn some Japanese words and phrases. Here is a run of the program.

```
Press a key for Japanese word or phrase

Nihon'go

Press a key for English word or phrase

Japanese language

Press a key to continue
```

You have now seen both "sides" of the first "flashcard"—the information of the first DATA statement (line 10010). Now press a key to see "side A" of the next card, using information from the second DATA statement (line 10020). Keep pressing keys, and eventually you will see the information from the last DATA statement (line 10070).

```
Press a key for Japanese word or phrase

Sayonara

Press a key for English word or phrase

Goodbye

Press a key to continue
```

Now press a key, and the program ends with the message "Out of DATA in 120." The program has already read all the data in all the DATA statements. If you want more practice, run the program again.

Exercises

1. What will be printed when you run this program?

```
10 CLS
20 WHILE 1
```

```
30   READ strng$
40   PRINT strng$
50 WEND
60 DATA Stardrake, Laran
70 DATA April 1, 1991
```

2. Modify Program FLSHCD01 (from Example 2) so that the English word or phrase is presented first, and then the Japanese equivalent.

```
1 REM ** Flashcard with Japanese-English Data **
2 ' Teach Yourself GW-BASIC, Chapter 9. Filename: FLSHCD01.BAS

100 REM ** Read and print Japanese, then English **
110 WHILE 1
120   READ Japanese$, English$ 'Get two strings from DATA statement

130   CLS
140   LOCATE 1, 1: PRINT "Press a key for Japanese word or phrase"
150   akey$ = INPUT$(1)
160   LOCATE 3, 1: PRINT Japanese$

170   LOCATE 5, 1: PRINT "Press a key for English word or phrase"
180   akey$ = INPUT$(1)
190   LOCATE 7, 1: PRINT English$

200   LOCATE 9, 1: PRINT "Press a key to continue"
210   akey$ = INPUT$(1)
220 WEND

10000 REM ** Data: Japanese, English **
10010 DATA Nihon'go, Japanese language
10020 DATA Ohayo gozaimasu, Good morning
10030 DATA Kon'nichi wa, Hello or Good day
10040 DATA Kon'ban wa, Good evening
10050 DATA Oyasumi nasai, Good night
10060 DATA "Jaa, mata ashita", "Well, I'll see you again tomorrow"
10070 DATA Sayonara, Goodbye
```

PROGRAM 9-1.   Flashcard with Japanese-English Data

RESTORE DATA FOR REPETITIVE USE

In running a program that contains READ and DATA statements, the computer sets a *data pointer* that points to the first item of data in the first DATA statement. When an item is read by a READ statement, this pointer moves to the next item. This continues as more items are read, until eventually the data pointer moves beyond the last item in the last DATA statement. After this happens, any attempt to read data produces an "Out of DATA" message.

You can use the RESTORE statement to set the data pointer back to the first data item in the first DATA statement. A RESTORE statement appears in line 30 of the next program.

```
10 RANDOMIZE TIMER: CLS
20 WHILE INKEY$ <> CHR$(27)
30    RESTORE
40    FOR k = 1 TO INT(3 * RND)+ 1
50       READ strng$
60    NEXT k
70    PRINT strng$,
80 WEND
90 DATA one, two, three
```

This program prints strings selected from the DATA statement (line 90) in random order, as shown in the following sample run. The (ESC) key was pressed to end the program.

```
two        one        three      one        two
three      two        three      one        three
three      three      two        one
```

Lines 30 through 70 are inside a WHILE...WEND loop that continues until you press (ESC). Lines 30 through 60 read one, two, or three strings from the DATA statement. Line 30 sets the data pointer to the first item in the DATA statement. In line 40, the value of

```
INT(3 * RND) + 1
```

is 1, 2, or 3. Therefore, line 50 will be executed one, two, or three times. Each value that is read replaces the previous value of *strng$*. Line 70 then prints the final value of *strng$*.

Examples

1. Program 9-2, FLSHCD02 (Random Flashcard with READ, DATA, RESTORE), presents randomly selected Japanese and English words and phrases. You can press (ESC) to quit, or some other key to see another pair of phrases. The phrase pairs are selected randomly from the DATA statements in lines 10010 through 10070. There is one chance in seven that the first phrase pair will be the one shown here.

```
Press a key for Japanese word or phrase

Kon'ban wa

Press a key for English word or phrase

Good evening

Press a key to continue, or ESC to quit
```

2. Programs FLSHCD01 and FLSHCD02 are designed to work with exactly seven "flashcards." This is inconvenient. It would be better to have a variable number of flashcards available. Program 9-3, FLSHCD03 (A More General Flashcard Program), reads the number of flashcards (pairs of strings) from the first DATA statement (line 10005) as the value of *NmbrCards*. Line 10005 contains the number of flashcards stored in lines 10010 through 10070. This value (7) is read as the value of *NmbrCards* in block 200.

```
200 REM ** Get random flashcard **
210 RESTORE
220 READ NmbrCards
230 FOR k = 1 TO INT(NmbrCards * RND) + 1
240   READ Japanese$, English$
250 NEXT k
```

If you go to a sushi bar, you might like to know the Japanese names of some of the things you eat. Use the following data in Program FLSHCD03. The DATA statements in lines 10010

```
1 REM ** Random Flashcard with READ, DATA, RESTORE **
2 ' Teach Yourself GW-BASIC, Chapter 9. Filename: FLSHCD02.BAS

100 REM ** Set up **
110 RANDOMIZE TIMER
120 CLS

200 REM ** Get random flashcard **
210 RESTORE
220 FOR k = 1 TO INT(7 * RND) + 1
230   READ Japanese$, English$
240 NEXT k

300 REM ** Print side A, then side B **
310 CLS
320 LOCATE 1, 1: PRINT "Press a key for Japanese word or phrase"
330 akey$ = INPUT$(1)
340 LOCATE 3, 1: PRINT Japanese$

350 LOCATE 5, 1: PRINT "Press a key for English word or phrase"
360 akey$ = INPUT$(1)
370 LOCATE 7, 1: PRINT English$

400 REM ** Continue practice or quit **
410 LOCATE 9, 1: PRINT "Press a key to continue, or ESC to quit"
420 akey$ = INPUT$(1)
430 IF akey$ <> CHR$(27) THEN 210 ELSE END

10000 REM ** Data: Japanese, English **
10010 DATA Nihon'go, Japanese language
10020 DATA Ohayo gozaimasu, Good morning
10030 DATA Kon'nichi wa, Hello or Good day
10040 DATA Kon'ban wa, Good evening
10050 DATA Oyasumi nasai, Good night
10060 DATA "Jaa, mata ashita", "Well, I'll see you again tomorrow"
10070 DATA Sayonara, Goodbye
```

PROGRAM 9-2.   Random Flashcard with READ, DATA, RESTORE

```
1 REM ** A More General Random Flashcard Program **
2 ' Teach Yourself GW-BASIC, Chapter 9. Filename: FLSHCD03.BAS

100 REM ** Set up **
110 RANDOMIZE TIMER
120 CLS

200 REM ** Get random flashcard **
210 RESTORE
220 READ NmbrCards
230 FOR k = 1 TO INT(NmbrCards * RND) + 1
240    READ Japanese$, English$
250 NEXT k

300 REM ** Print side A, then side B **
310 CLS
320 LOCATE 1, 1: PRINT "Press a key for Japanese word or phrase"
330 akey$ = INPUT$(1)
340 LOCATE 3, 1: PRINT Japanese$

350 LOCATE 5, 1: PRINT "Press a key for English word or phrase"
360 akey$ = INPUT$(1)
370 LOCATE 7, 1: PRINT English$

400 REM ** Continue practice or quit **
410 LOCATE 9, 1: PRINT "Press a key to continue, or ESC to quit"
420 akey$ = INPUT$(1)
430 IF akey$ <> CHR$(27) THEN 210 ELSE END

10000 REM ** Data: Japanese, English **
10005 DATA 7
10010 DATA Nihon'go, Japanese language
10020 DATA Ohayo gozaimasu, Good morning
10030 DATA Kon'nichi wa, Hello or Good day
10040 DATA Kon'ban wa, Good evening
10050 DATA Oyasumi nasai, Good night
10060 DATA "Jaa, mata ashita", "Well, I'll see you again tomorrow"
10070 DATA Sayonara, Goodbye
```

PROGRAM 9-3. A More General Random Flashcard Program

through 10040 each contain two data pairs, for a total of eight pairs, as specified in line 10005.

```
10000 REM ** Data: Japanese, English **
10005 DATA 8
10010 DATA buri, yellowtail, kaki, oyster
10020 DATA tako, octopus, anago, sea eel
10030 DATA maguro, tuna, kurumaebi, prawn
10040 DATA saba, mackerel, tomago, egg
```

Exercises

1. The flashcard programs shown so far are designed for the study of Japanese. Rewrite Program FLSHCD03 so that it becomes a general flashcard program, as described here:

   a. Instead of *Japanese$* and *English$*, use *SideA$* and *SideB$* as variable names.

   b. Change the instruction printed by line 320 to "Press a key for side A."

   c. Change the instruction printed by line 350 to "Press a key for side B."

   d. Create your own data block.

2. Write a program named FLSHCD05, Random Flashcard Program with Time Delay. Have the program show side A, wait five seconds (or another number of seconds) and then show side B. Use the time delay subroutine shown in Chapter 8 in Program 8-8, DELAY03.

LEARN ABOUT ARRAYS AND ARRAY VARIABLES
9.3

You have used simple numeric and string variables, for example:

Numeric Variables	String Variables
number	*akey$*
k	*vowel$*
Pop1990	*word$*
Value#	*Naym$*

Now you will learn about *arrays* and *array variables*. An array is a set, or collection, of array variables. Each individual array variable in an array is called an *element* of the array. An array has a name. An array variable consists of the name of the array followed by a *subscript*. The subscript is enclosed in parentheses.

All array variables in an array have the same variable name, which is also the name of the entire array. An array variable can be numeric or string. For example:

Numeric Array Variables	String Array Variables
temperature(3)	*StateName$(50)*
AcctBalance#(5)	*word$(23)*

Note that a *string array* variable name ends in a dollar sign ($). A *numeric array* variable name may end in a numeric type designator (%, !, or #). These characters designate the array as either an integer array (%), single precision array (!), or double precision array (#). If a numeric array variable name does not end in a type designator, it is automatically a single precision array.

The *subscript* of an array variable is the number enclosed in parentheses following the variable name, as shown here:

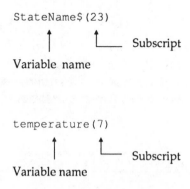

A subscript can be a number, a numeric variable, or a numeric expression consisting of any legal combination of numbers, numeric variables, and numeric functions. The value of a subscript must be an integer. If you use a subscript that is not an integer, GW-BASIC will round it to the nearest integer.

REMEMBER: An array variable consists of these parts, in this order:

	Numeric	String
1. a variable name:	*number*	*word$*
2. left (open) parenthesis:	*number(*	*word$(*
3. a numeric subscript:	*number(3*	*word$(3*
4. right (close) parenthesis:	*number(3)*	*word$(3)*

An array is a list of array variables. In the following numeric array with four array variables, note that the subscripts begin with 0, followed by 1, 2, and 3.

```
number(0)        number(1)        number(2)        number(3)
```

A string array with three array variables is shown next. The subscripts are 0, 1, and 2.

```
word$(0)        word$(1)        word$(2)
```

Unless you tell it otherwise, GW-BASIC assumes that an array has 11 elements, with subscripts 0 through 10. You use the DIM statement to specify a maximum subscript other than 10. The keyword DIM is a shortened form of the word "dimension." Some examples of DIM statements are

```
DIM temperature(7)
DIM DaysInMonth%(12)
DIM AcctBalance#(1000)
DIM StateName$(50)
```

- The statement

  ```
  DIM temperature(7)
  ```

  defines a single precision numeric array of eight elements, *temperature(0)* through *temperature(7)*. You could also use an exclamation point (!) to define this array as a single precision array:

  ```
  DIM temperature!(7)
  ```

- The statement

```
DIM DaysInMonth%(12)
```

defines an integer array of 13 elements, *DaysInMonth%(0)* through *DaysInMonth%(12)*.

- The statement

```
DIM AcctBalance#(1000)
```

defines a double precision numeric array of 1001 elements; that is, *AcctBalance#(0)* through *AcctBalance#(1000)*.

- The statement

```
DIM StateName$(50)
```

defines a string array of 51 elements, *StateName$(0)* through *StateName$(50)*.

In this book, an array name followed by an empty set of parentheses refers to an entire array. This convention is used so you can easily distinguish an array from a simple variable or a single array variable, as compared here:

Simple Variables	Single Array Variables	Entire Array
number	*number(7)*	*number()*
word$	*word$(7)*	*word$()*

For example, *DaysInMonth%()* is an integer array defined by the following DIM statement:

```
DIM DaysInMonth%(12)
```

DaysInMonth%(), then, refers to the entire array of 13 elements, from *DaysInMonth%(0)* to *DaysInMonth%(12)*. The DIM statement reserves memory space for the specified number of array elements, and clears this space to zeros for numeric arrays, or to null strings for string arrays.

- The statement

```
DIM temperature(7)
```

allocates memory space for 8 single precision array variables, *temperature(0)* through *temperature(7)*. A single precision number requires 4 bytes of memory; therefore, 32 bytes are reserved.

- The statement

```
DIM DaysInMonth%(12)
```

allocates memory space for 13 integer array variables, from *DaysInMonth%(0)* through *DaysInMonth%(12)*. An integer requires 2 bytes of memory; therefore, 26 bytes are reserved.

- The statement

```
DIM LotsaBucks#(1000)
```

allocates memory space for 1001 double precision array variables, *LotsaBucks#(0)* through *LotsaBucks#(1000)*. A double precision number requires 8 bytes of memory; therefore, 8008 bytes are reserved.

- The statement

```
DIM word$(100)
```

tells the computer that *word$()* is a string array with 101 elements, *word$(0)* through *word$(100)*. Strings are variable in length, from no bytes (the null string) to a maximum of 255 bytes. The DIM statement allocates a 3-byte *string pointer* for each array variable. Additional memory is allocated later when string array variables are assigned values.

Exercises

1. What are the elements of the array *VoteTally()* defined by the following DIM statement?

```
DIM VoteTally(3)
```

2. A single precision array has the elements *frequency(0)*, *frequency(1)*, and so on, up to *frequency(13)*. Write a DIM statement to allocate memory space for this array. How much memory space is required?

3. The string array *word$()* is dimensioned as follows:

```
DIM word$(100)
```

Suppose that a three-letter word has been assigned to every element of *word$()*. How many bytes of memory are occupied by this array?

9.4 USE ARRAYS IN PROGRAMS

Arrays add a new dimension to your ability to make the computer do what you want it to do, the way you want it done. You can use arrays to write programs that would be impractical, or even impossible, to write without arrays.

The following program reads values for array variables *frequency(0)* through *frequency(7)*, and then prints all the values in the entire array.

```
10 CLS
20 FOR k = 0 TO 7
30    READ frequency(k)
40 NEXT k
50 DATA 262, 294, 330, 349, 392, 440, 494, 523
60 FOR k = 0 TO 7
70    PRINT frequency(k);
80 NEXT k
```

Since line 70 ends in a semicolon (;), the values of *frequency(0)* through *frequency(7)* are printed on a single line, like this:

```
 262   294   330   349   392   440   494   523
```

You can use direct PRINT statements to verify that values have been assigned to array variables. For example, to see the values of *frequency(0)* and *frequency(7)*,

Type **PRINT frequency(0), frequency(7)**
and press (ENTER)

Your PRINT statement and its results will appear on the screen, as shown here:

```
PRINT frequency(0), frequency(7)
 262           523
```

The foregoing program does not contain a DIM statement. Therefore, the array has the default dimension of 10, with the elements *frequency(0)* through *frequency(10)*. The program assigned values to *frequency(0)* through *frequency(7)*. The remaining elements (8, 9, and 10) all have the value zero, which can be verified by the following direct PRINT statement:

```
PRINT frequency(8), frequency(9), frequency(10)
 0              0              0
```

If you try to use a subscript greater than 10 with a *frequency()* element, you will see a "Subscript out of range" error message.

```
PRINT frequency(11)
Subscript out of range
```

It is good programming practice to always use a DIM statement to define an array used in a program—even if the largest subscript is less than or equal to 10. The DIM statement should be near the beginning of the program, before the array is used.

Examples

1. The random flashcard programs shown previously in this chapter access data *sequentially* to obtain the randomly selected data. Suppose that a program's DATA statements contained 1000 sets of data. To get the 997th set, the computer would first read, but not use, the first 996 pairs of values. This could take a few seconds.

   Program 9-4, FLSHCD06 (Random Flashcard with Arrays and Time Delay), solves this problem. It reads the flashcard data into arrays, *SideA$()* and *SideB$()*, and then selects randomly from the arrays. The flashcard data is read into arrays by block 200, shown here:

```
200 REM ** Read data into SideA$()and SideB$() arrays **
210 READ NmbrCards
```

```
220 DIM SideA$(NmbrCards), SideB$(NmbrCards)
230 FOR card = 1 TO NmbrCards
240   READ SideA$(card), SideB$(card)
250 NEXT card
```

```
1 REM ** Random Flashcard with Arrays and Time Delay **
2 ' Teach Yourself GW-BASIC, Chapter 9. Filename: FLSHCD06.BAS

100 REM ** Set up **
110 RANDOMIZE TIMER

200 REM ** Read data into SideA$() and SideB$() string arrays **
210 READ NmbrCards
220 DIM SideA$(NmbrCards), SideB$(NmbrCards)
230 FOR card = 1 TO NmbrCards
240   READ SideA$(card), SideB$(card)
250 NEXT card

300 REM ** Random card: Show side A, delay, then show side B **
310 CLS
320 CardNmbr = INT(NmbrCards * RND) + 1 'Random subscript
330 LOCATE 1, 1: PRINT SideA$(CardNmbr) 'Show side A
340 delay = 5: GOSUB 510                 'Time delay subroutine
350 LOCATE 3, 1: PRINT SideB$(CardNmbr) 'Show side B

400 REM ** Continue practice or quit **
410 LOCATE 5, 1: PRINT "Press a key to continue, or ESC to quit"
420 akey$ = INPUT$(1)
430 IF akey$ <> CHR$(27) THEN 310 ELSE END

500 REM ** SUBROUTINE: Variable time delay **
510 start = TIMER: WHILE TIMER < start + delay: WEND: RETURN

10000 REM ** Data: SideA$, SideB$ **
10005 DATA 7
10010 DATA Nihon'go, Japanese language
10020 DATA Ohayo gozaimasu, Good morning
10030 DATA Kon'nichi wa, Hello or Good day
10040 DATA Kon'ban wa, Good evening
10050 DATA Oyasumi nasai, Good night
10060 DATA "Jaa, mata ashita", "Well, I'll see you again tomorrow"
10070 DATA Sayonara, Goodbye
```

PROGRAM 9-4.   Random Flashcard with Arrays and Time Delay

Line 210 reads the number of flashcards as the value of *Nmbr-Cards*. Line 220 uses the value of *NmbrCards* to dimension both the *SideA$()* and *SideB$()* arrays. You can use a single DIM statement to allocate space for two or more arrays. Use a comma (,) to separate the arrays.

The FOR...NEXT loop in lines 230 through 250 reads the values of the array variables *SideA$(1), SideB$(1), SideA$(2), SideB$(2),* and so on. This program does not use array variables *SideA$(0)* and *SideB$(0)*.

Block 300, shown below, picks a random flashcard, displays side A, delays five seconds, and displays side B.

```
300 REM ** Random card: Show side A, delay, then show side B **
310 CLS
320 CardNmbr = INT(NmbrCards * RND)+ 1   'Random subscript
330 LOCATE 1, 1: PRINT SideA$(CardNmbr) 'Show side A
340 delay = 5: GOSUB 510                  'Time delay subroutine
350 LOCATE 3, 1: PRINT SideB$(CardNmbr) 'Show side B
```

This program provides "equal-time" random access to any flashcard. This access time is independent of the number of flashcards.

2. Program 9-5, STAT01 (High, Low, and Average for One Week), is a simple statistics program. Arrays are very useful for this type of application. A sample run of the program is shown in Figure 9-1.

Program block 100 includes a DIM statement to dimension the *temperature()* array.

```
110 DIM temperature(7)     'Dimension temperature() array
```

The program processes temperature data for one week, Sunday through Saturday. Block 200 reads the temperatures into array variables *temperature(0)* through *temperature(7)*.

```
200 REM ** Read data into array **
210 FOR day = 1 TO 7
220    READ temperature(day)
230 NEXT day
240 DATA 68, 67, 70, 72, 75, 80, 77
```

```
1 REM ** High, Low, and Average Temperature for One Week **
2 ' Teach Yourself GW-BASIC, Chapter 9. Filename: STAT01.BAS

100 REM ** Set up **
110 DIM temperature(7)        'Dimension temperature() array
120 CLS

200 REM ** Read data into array **
210 FOR day = 1 TO 7
220   READ temperature(day)
230 NEXT day
240 DATA 68, 67, 70, 72, 75, 80, 77

300 REM ** Find high temperature **
310 High = temperature(1)
320 FOR day = 2 TO 7
330   IF temperature(day) > High THEN High = temperature(day)
340 NEXT day

400 REM ** Find low temperature **
410 Low = temperature(1)
420 FOR day = 2 TO 7
430   IF temperature(day) < Low THEN Low = temperature(day)
440 NEXT day

500 REM ** Compute average temperature **
510 Total = 0
520 FOR day = 1 TO 7
530   Total = Total + temperature(day)
540 NEXT day
550 Average = Total / 7

600 REM ** Print temperatures, Sunday thru Saturday **
610 FOR day = 1 TO 7
620   READ DayOfWeek$
630   PRINT DayOfWeek$, temperature(day)
640 NEXT day
650 DATA Sunday, Monday, Tuesday, Wednesday
660 DATA Thursday, Friday, Saturday

700 REM ** Print high, low, and average temperatures **
710 PRINT
720 PRINT "High:", High
730 PRINT "Low:", Low
740 PRINT "Average:", Average
```

PROGRAM 9-5.   High, Low, and Average Temperature for One Week

```
Sunday        68
Monday        67
Tuesday       70
Wednesday     72
Thursday      75
Friday        80
Saturday      77

High:         80
Low:          67
Average:      72.71429
```

FIGURE 9-1.	Sample run of Program STAT01

Block 300 searches the array to find the highest temperature.

```
300 REM ** Find high temperature **
310 High = temperature(1)
320 FOR day = 2 TO 7
330    IF temperature(day) > High THEN High = temperature(day)
340 NEXT day
```

The value of *High* is set equal to the first number in the array—the value of *temperature(1)*. The FOR...NEXT loop then searches the rest of the array (subscripts 2 through 7). If any value in the array is higher than the value of *High*, it is assigned as the new value of *High*.

Block 400 uses a similar method to find the lowest temperature and assign it as the value of *Low*, as follows:

```
400 REM ** Find low temperature **
410 Low = temperature(1)
420 FOR day = 2 TO 7
430    IF temperature(day)< Low THEN Low = temperature(day)
440 NEXT day
```

Block 500 adds the seven temperatures, then divides by 7 to obtain the average temperature. It first sets the value of *Total* to zero, and then uses a FOR...NEXT loop to add the temperatures. Each value in *temperature()* is added to *Total* as the value of *day* goes from 1 to 7. The final value of *Total* is divided by 7 to obtain the value of *Average*.

```
500 REM ** Compute average temperature **
510 Total = 0
520 FOR day = 1 TO 7
530   Total = Total + temperature(day)
540 NEXT day
550 Average = Total / 7
```

This completes the processing. Now it is time to print the results. Block 600 prints the days of the week, Sunday through Saturday, and the temperature for each day, as follows:

```
600 REM ** Print temperatures, Sunday thru Saturday **
610 FOR day = 1 TO 7
620   READ DayOfWeek$
630   PRINT DayOfWeek$, temperature(day)
640 NEXT day
650 DATA Sunday, Monday, Tuesday, Wednesday
660 DATA Thursday, Friday, Saturday
```

The names of the days of the week are read from DATA statements. Therefore, the data pointer must be pointing at the first string (Sunday) in the first DATA statement (line 650) when this block begins. Look again at block 200. It read all the data (seven values) in the DATA statement in line 240; thus, the data pointer is properly positioned. To be absolutely certain, however, you could use this variation of the RESTORE statement:

```
605 RESTORE 650
```

This RESTORE statement tells the computer to move the data pointer to the first item in line 650, which, of course, must be a DATA statement.

Only one easy block remains. Block 700, shown here, prints the high, low, and average temperatures that were computed in blocks 300, 400, and 500, respectively.

```
700 REM ** Print high, low, and average temperatures **
710 PRINT
720 PRINT "High:", High
730 PRINT "Low:", Low
740 PRINT "Average:", Average
```

Exercises

1. The program below dimensions the array *nzp$()*, and reads values for the array variables.

```
10 DIM nzp$(3)
20 CLS
30 FOR k = 1 TO 3
40    READ nzp$(k)
50 NEXT k
60 DATA negative, zero, positive
```

Suppose this program has been entered and run. Make a table showing each array variable and the value assigned to it.

2. Modify Program STAT01 so that you can enter the temperatures from the keyboard. For example:

```
Sunday    ? 68
Monday    ? 67
Tuesday   ? 70
Wednesday? 72
Thursday ? 75
Friday    ? 80
Saturday ? 77
```

After you enter the data shown above, the computer prints these results:

```
High:     80
Low:      67
Average:  72.71429
```

9.5 | USE ARRAYS TO COUNT THINGS

Here's the questionnaire for a recent survey by The People's Poll:

Does your computer understand you?
Circle the number of your answer.

1. Yes

2. No

You can use Program 9-6, POLL01 (The People's Poll), to tally the answers. A test run is shown in Figure 9-2. No valid answers were entered in this test run; it merely tests for invalid answers and for the entry of zero to end the data entry part of the program.

Figure 9-3 shows another test run. Seven valid responses were entered here, and then zero to end the data entry. This program uses the array variable *Tally(1)* to count "Yes" answers and array variable *Tally(2)* to count "No" answers. Block 200, shown below, sets these variables to zero.

```
200 REM ** Set tallies to zero **
210 Tally(1) = 0                    'Tally for 'Yes' answers
220 Tally(2) = 0                    'Tally for 'No' answers
```

This block is not really necessary. The DIM statement in line 110 dimensions the array and also sets all of its variables to zero. However, this block is included to remind you that, before any answers are entered, the tallies are zero.

Block 400 is the heart of the program and does most of the work. Line 430 gets an answer to the question posed by the poll. If the answer is zero, line 440 sends control to block 500. If the response is not zero, lines 450 and 460 do a validity check.

```
450 IF answer <> FIX(answer) THEN PRINT Oop$: GOTO 420
460 IF answer < 1 OR answer > 2 THEN PRINT Oop$: GOTO 420
```

```
1 REM ** The People's Poll **
2 ' Teach Yourself GW-BASIC, Chapter 9. Filename: POLL01.BAS

100 REM ** Set up **
110 DIM Tally(2)
120 Oop$ = "Oops!    Please enter 1, 2, or 0."
130 CLS

200 REM ** Set tallies to zero **
210 Tally(1) = 0                        'Tally for 'Yes' answers
220 Tally(2) = 0                        'Tally for 'No' answers

300 REM ** Tell what to do **
310 LOCATE 1, 1: PRINT "Does your computer understand you?"
320 LOCATE 3, 1: PRINT "1 = Yes 2 = No"
330 LOCATE 5, 1: PRINT "To quit, enter zero (0) as your answer."

400 REM ** Get answers and count them **
410 WHILE 1
420    PRINT
430    INPUT "Answer (1, 2, or 0 to quit)"; answer

440    IF answer = 0 THEN 510              'If zero, go print tallies

445    ' If not a valid answer, reject it & go for another
450    IF answer <> FIX(answer) THEN PRINT Oop$: GOTO 420
460    IF answer < 1 OR answer > 2 THEN PRINT Oop$: GOTO 420
470    Tally(answer) = Tally(answer) + 1         'Count the answer
480 WEND

500 REM ** Print the final tallies **
510 PRINT
520 PRINT "Total 'Yes' answers:"; Tally(1)
530 PRINT "Total 'No' answers: "; Tally(2)
```

PROGRAM 9-6. ▊   The People's Poll

Answers must be integers. If not, line 450 prints the value of the string variable *Oop$* and sends control back to line 420 for another try. The only valid integers are 1 and 2. Otherwise, line 460 prints the value of *Oop$* and sends the computer back to line 420 for another try.

```
Does your computer understand you?

1 = Yes  2 = No

To quit, enter zero (0) as your answer.

Answer (1, 2, or 0 to quit)? -1
Oops!   Please enter 1, 2, or 0.

Answer (1, 2, or 0 to quit)? 3
Oops!   Please enter 1, 2, or 0.

Answer (1, 2, or 0 to quit)? 1.3
Oops!   Please enter 1, 2, or 0.

Answer (1, 2, or 0 to quit)? 0

Total 'Yes' answers: 0
Total 'No' answers:  0
```

FIGURE 9-2.   First test run of Program POLL01

Think of lines 440, 450, and 460 as a "filter"; only valid answers (1 or 2) can filter down to line 470.

```
470   Tally(answer)= Tally(answer) + 1    'Count the answer
```

If the value of *answer* is 1, line 470 increases the value of *Tally(1)* by one, thus increasing the tally for "Yes" answers. If the value of *answer* is 2, line 470 increases the value of *Tally(2)* by one, thus increasing the tally for "No" answers.

Examples

1. Program 9-7, POLL02 (The People's Poll #2), shows another way to count answers to the questionnaire. Both valid and invalid answers are stored in the following DATA statement:

```
1000 REM ** Data: valid answer is 1 or 2, or 0 to quit **
1010 DATA 1, 2, -1, 2, 1, 2, 1.3, 1, 1, 0
```

```
Does your computer understand you?

1 = Yes   2 = No

To quit, enter zero (0) as your answer.

Answer (1, 2, or 0 to quit)? 1

Answer (1, 2, or 0 to quit)? 2

Answer (1, 2, or 0 to quit)? 2

Answer (1, 2, or 0 to quit)? 1

Answer (1, 2, or 0 to quit)? 2

Answer (1, 2, or 0 to quit)? 1

Answer (1, 2, or 0 to quit)? 1

Answer (1, 2, or 0 to quit)? 0

Total 'Yes' answers: 4
Total 'No' answers:  3
```

FIGURE 9-3.	Second test run of Program POLL01

Run Program 9-7. The valid answers (1 and 2) are tallied, and the following results printed:

```
Total 'Yes' answers: 4
Total 'No' answers:  3
```

2. If you roll a six-sided die 6000 times, you might expect to see each possible value (1 through 6) come up about 1000 times. The next program simulates this experiment.

```
10 RANDOMIZE TIMER: CLS
20 DIM Tally(6)
30 FOR roll = 1 TO 6000
40   die = INT(6 * RND) + 1
```

```
50    Tally(die) = Tally(die)+ 1
60 NEXT roll
70 FOR k = 1 TO 6
80    PRINT k, Tally(k)
90 NEXT k
```

```
1 REM ** The People's Poll #2 **
2 ' Teach Yourself GW-BASIC, Chapter 9. Filename: POLL02.BAS

100 REM ** Set up **
110 DIM Tally(2)
120 Oops$ = "Oops! Please enter 1,2, or 0."
130 CLS

200 REM ** Set tallies to zero **
210 Tally(1) = 0                        'Tally for 'Yes' answers
220 Tally(2) = 0                        'Tally for 'No' answers

400 REM ** Get answers and count them **
410 WHILE 1
420    READ answer
450    IF answer = 0 THEN 510           'If zero, go print tallies

455    ' If not a valid answer, reject it & go for another
460    IF answer <> FIX(answer) THEN 420
470    IF answer < 1 OR answer > 2 THEN 420

480    Tally(answer) = Tally(answer) + 1  'Count the answer
490 WEND

500 REM ** Print the final tallies **
510 PRINT
520 PRINT "Total 'Yes' answers:"; Tally(1)
530 PRINT "Total 'No' answers: "; Tally(2)

1000 REM ** Data: valid answer is 1 or 2, or 0 to quit **
1010 DATA 1, 2, -1, 2, 1, 2, 1.3, 1, 1, 0
```

PROGRAM 9-7. The People's Poll #2

Here is a sample run:

```
1          995
2          977
3          982
4          1040
5          993
6          1013
```

Exercises

1. Another People's Poll questionnaire looks like this:

```
┌─────────────────────────────────────────┐
│                                           │
│   Does your computer understand you?      │
│   Circle the number of your answer.       │
│                                           │
│   1. Yes                                  │
│                                           │
│   2. No                                   │
│                                           │
│   3. Sometimes                            │
│                                           │
└─────────────────────────────────────────┘
```

Modify Program POLL02 to tally the answers to this questionnaire. Also, count and report invalid responses. Results might
look like this:

```
Total 'Yes' answers:       7
Total 'No' answers:        10
Total 'Sometimes' answers: 23
Total invalid answers:     3
```

2. Write a program to simulate rolling 2D6 (two six-sided dice) *n*
    times, and count the number of occurrences of each possible
    value, 2 through 12. A sample run is shown in Figure 9-4.

```
How many rolls of 2D6? 1000

Outcome          Number of times
   2                29
   3                59
   4                68
   5                117
   6                142
   7                163
   8                160
   9                107
  10                82
  11                53
  12                20
```

FIGURE 9-4.   Roll 2D6 and count the outcomes

9.6 ADD ANOTHER DIMENSION

Original Dartmouth BASIC had one-dimensional and two-dimensional arrays. In the documentation, one-dimensional arrays were called lists or vectors, and two-dimensional arrays were called tables or matrices. GW-BASIC arrays can have one, two, or even more dimensions. A two-dimensional array variable has two subscripts, separated by a comma. Some two-dimensional array variables are shown here:

```
Tally(1, 2)        Chess$(8, 3)        Go(13, 17)
```

Think of a two-dimensional array as an arrangement of rows and columns of array variables, with the first subscript denoting the row, and the second subscript the column. For example:

```
TicTacToe(0, 0)        TicTacToe(0, 1)      TicTacToe(0, 2)

TicTacToe(1, 0)        TicTacToe(1, 1)      TicTacToe(1, 2)

TicTacToe(2, 0)        TicTacToe(2, 1)      TicTacToe(2, 2)
```

This array has nine elements. It is dimensioned like this:

```
DIM TicTacToe(2, 2)
```

The *TicTacToe()* array is a *square array*. It has the same number of rows and columns: three of each. The array shown below has twelve elements arranged in three rows and four columns.

```
array(0, 0)     array(0, 1)     array(0, 2)     array(0, 3)

array(1, 0)     array(1, 1)     array(1, 2)     array(1, 3)

array(2, 0)     array(2, 1)     array(2, 2)     array(2, 3)
```

Dimension the array called *array()*, as follows:

```
DIM array(2, 3)
```

Example

1. The results of previous "Does your computer understand you?" surveys were very interesting. Some people said yes, and some said no. Does age make a difference? Here is the latest questionnaire:

> Does your computer understand you?
>
> 1. Yes   2. No   3. Sometimes
>
> How old are you?
>
> 1. 18 or younger   2. Older than 18

The first question has three possible answers (1, 2, or 3), and the second question has two possible answers (1 or 2). Each completed questionnaire provides a pair of numbers that can be used as subscripts to select the appropriate two-dimensional array variables.

	18 or under	Over 18
Yes	Tally(1, 1)	Tally(1, 2)
No	Tally(2, 1)	Tally(2, 2)
Sometimes	Tally(3, 1)	Tally(3, 2)

Answers from 32 questionnaires are shown in the DATA statements that follow. There are 32 pairs of answers, followed by an "end of data" pair (0, 0). A comma, but no space, separates the two numbers of each pair. A comma *and* a space follow each pair so that you can more easily distinguish them. The computer ignores this space.

```
1000 REM ** Data: answer to question 1, answer to question 2 **
1010 DATA 1,2, 2,1, 3,2, 1,1, 2,2, 2,2, 1,1, 2,1, 1,2, 2,2
1020 DATA 2,2, 3,1, 2,2, 1,1, 1,1, 2,2, 1,2, 3,2, 2,2, 2,1
1030 DATA 1,1, 1,1, 1,1, 1,2, 1,1, 1,2, 2,1, 1,2, 2,2, 1,1
1040 DATA 3,1, 1,1, 0,0
```

Program 9-8, POLL03 (The People's Poll #3), processes this data and prints the following summary report:

Answer	18 or under	Over 18
Yes	10	6
No	4	8
Sometimes	2	2

Exercises

1. Modify Program POLL03 (in Example 1) so that the summary report includes row totals and column totals, as shown here:

Answer	18 or under	Over 18	Row totals
Yes	10	6	16
No	4	8	12
Sometimes	2	2	4
Column totals	16	16	32

   Call this Program POLL04, The People's Poll #4.

2. Write Program POLL05, The People's Poll #5, to process data from a questionnaire that has these questions:

   ```
   Does your computer understand you?

   1. Yes   2. No   3. Sometimes   4. None of these

   What is your age group?

   1. 18 or younger   2. 19 to 29   3. 30 or over
   ```

EXERCISES

1. Each of these DATA statements has a problem. Identify what is wrong with each one.

   ```
   DATA, one, two, three
   DATA 1, 22, 333,
   DATA 262; 294; 330; 349; 392; 440; 494; 523
   ```

2. The number 1E38 is a most unlikely number. Therefore, it is a good number to use as a "flag" that signals the end of data. For example:

   ```
   DATA 68, 67, 70, 72, 75, 80, 77, 1E38
   ```

```
1 REM ** The People's Poll #3 **
2 ' Teach Yourself GW-BASIC, Chapter 9. Filename: POLL03.BAS

100 REM ** Set up **
110 DIM Tally(3, 2)                            'Two-dimensional array
120 CLS

200 REM ** Set tallies to zero **
210 FOR row = 0 TO 3
220   FOR col = 0 TO 2
230       Tally(row, col) = 0
240   NEXT col
250 NEXT row

400 REM ** Get answers and count them **
410 WHILE 1
420   READ ans1, ans2
450   IF ans1 = 0 THEN 510                      'Exit if zero
480   Tally(ans1, ans2) = Tally(ans1, ans2) + 1 'Count the answer
490 WEND

500 REM ** Print the final tallies **
510 PRINT
520 PRINT "Answer", "18 or under", "Over 18"
530 PRINT
540 PRINT "Yes", Tally(1, 1), Tally(1, 2)
550 PRINT "No", Tally(2, 1), Tally(2, 2)
560 PRINT "Sometimes", Tally(3, 1), Tally(3, 2)

1000 REM ** Data: answer to question 1, answer to question 2 **
1010 DATA 1,2, 2,1, 3,2, 1,1, 2,2, 2,2, 1,1, 2,1, 1,2, 2,2
1020 DATA 2,2, 3,1, 2,2, 1,1, 1,1, 2,2, 1,2, 3,2, 2,2, 2,1
1030 DATA 1,1, 1,1, 1,1, 1,2, 1,1, 1,2, 2,1, 1,2, 2,2, 1,1
1040 DATA 3,1, 1,1, 0,0
```

PROGRAM 9-8. | The People's Poll #3

a. Write a program to *read and print* all numbers that appear prior to 1E38 in a DATA statement or statements.

b. Write a program to *read and compute* the sum of all numbers that appear prior to 1E38 in a DATA statement or statements. (For the data in this example, the sum is 509.)

c. Write a program to *read and count* the number of numbers prior to 1E38 in a DATA statement or statements. (For this data, the result is 7.)

d. Combine the programs you just wrote into a single program that computes the sum, number of numbers, and average of all numbers prior to 1E38 in a DATA statement or statements.

3. Weights in pounds and ounces can be stored in DATA statements as follows:

```
DATA 7,12,  0,6,  5,0,  3,13,  10,8,  -1,-1
```

The first item is 7 pounds, 12 ounces; the second is 0 pounds, 6 ounces; and so on. The last item (–1,–1) is not part of the data. It is the "end-of-data" flag, signalling "no more data."

Write a program to read the data in a DATA statement like the foregoing one, and compute the total weight in pounds and ounces. In the final total, the number of ounces should be less than 16. Print the data and the total, as follows:

Pounds	Ounces
7	12
0	6
5	0
3	13
10	8
----	----
27	7

4. Write a program to play Guess My Word. The computer thinks of a three-letter word, and the player tries to guess the word. The game might begin like this:

```
I'll think of a 3-letter word. You try to guess my word.
If you miss, I'll give you a hint like the ones below:

   'Higher' means higher in the alphabet, towards z

   'Lower' means lower in the alphabet, towards a

Ok, I've got a secret word. Good luck!

What is your guess? _
```

Your program should select a random word from the list shown in the following DATA statements, or from a word list you choose. The last item in the list below is the end-of-data flag, "zzz."

```
DATA aha, auk, baa, boy, cat, cry, dog, duo, elf, erg
DATA fez, fun, gee, gnu, hex, hum, icy, ivy, jib, joy
DATA key, kid, lei, leu, mew, mom, nay, nub, obi, owl
DATA pal, pry, rho, rue, sea, sty, toy, try, ugh, use
DATA vex, via, wan, win, yak, yew, zen, zoo, zzz
```

After any incorrect guess, give a hint such as "Try a higher word," or "Try a lower word."

5. The table below shows five quiz scores and their deviations from the mean, or average, score. In this case, the average is 79.2. To obtain the deviation, subtract the average from the score.

Score	Deviation
77	−2.2
83	3.8
68	−11.2
73	−6.2
95	15.8

Write a program to do these things:

a. Read scores from DATA statements into the array named *score()*.

b. Compute the average of the scores.

c. Print the scores and deviations as shown in the preceding table.

6. In a small class of five students, each student has taken three quizzes. Here are their scores.

	Quiz 1	Quiz 2	Quiz 3
Student 1	65	57	71
Student 2	81	90	91
Student 3	45	38	44
Student 4	70	68	83
Student 5	98	92	100

Write a program that will

a. Read the above information into a two-dimensional array.

b. Compute each student's average score for the three quizzes.

c. For each quiz, compute the average score among all five students.

d. Print a report that shows the information from the table plus all the averages you computed.

7. Suppose a group of students take a multiple-choice quiz that has ten questions, with four possible answers per question. Here are the answers given by seven students. Each student's answers are in a separate DATA statement.

```
DATA 2, 3, 1, 1, 1, 2, 4, 3, 4, 1
DATA 2, 3, 2, 4, 1, 2, 4, 2, 1, 3
DATA 2, 3, 3, 1, 1, 4, 3, 3, 4, 1
DATA 3, 2, 4, 1, 1, 2, 3, 3, 4, 2
DATA 2, 3, 4, 1, 1, 3, 4, 3, 4, 1
DATA 2, 1, 2, 3, 1, 2, 4, 3, 4, 1
DATA 3, 4, 1, 1, 1, 4, 3, 1, 4, 2
```

Write a program to

a. Read the above data into a two-dimensional array.

b. Print a report showing the number of students who gave each answer to each question. For example, the first few lines of the report might look like this:

```
            Answer 1   Answer 2   Answer 3   Answer 4

Question 1     0          5          2          0
Question 2     1          1          4          1
Question 3     2          2          1          2
```

Your BASIC Backpack: Additional Keywords

In Chapters 1 through 9 of this book, you learned how to use elements of the GW-BASIC language by performing tasks and solving problems. You now know how to use the following GW-BASIC keywords:

ABS	ELSE	LEN	PRINT	SQR
ASC	END	LINE	PSET	STEP
ATN	EXP	LIST	RANDOMIZE	SYSTEM
BEEP	FIX	LLIST	READ	TAB
CHR$	FOR	LOCATE	REM	TAN
CIRCLE	GOSUB	LOG	RESTORE	THEN
CLS	GOTO	LPRINT	RETURN	TIME$
COLOR	IF	MID$	RND	TIMER
COS	INKEY$	NEW	RUN	TO
DATA	INPUT	NEXT	SCREEN	USING
DATE$	INPUT$	OFF	SIN	WEND
DEF FN	INT	ON	SOUND	WHILE
DIM	KEY	OR	SPACE$	WIDTH

This appendix briefly introduces some additional GW-BASIC keywords, with examples of their use. You will explore the following keywords:

AUTO	INSTR	RENUM	STR$	VAL
CONT	KILL	RIGHT$	STRING$	
DELETE	LEFT$	SGN	TROFF	
EDIT	NAME	STOP	TRON	

You can learn more about the above keywords, and about keywords not covered in this book, by consulting a GW-BASIC reference guide. The following guides each contain a complete description of the GW-BASIC language:

Inman, Don and Bob Albrecht. *The GW-BASIC Reference*. Berkeley: Osborne/McGraw-Hill, 1990.

Microsoft. *GW-BASIC User's Guide and Reference*. Redmond: Microsoft Press, 1989.

Schneider, David I. *Handbook of BASIC*. 3d ed. New York: Brady Press, 1988.

THE AUTO, EDIT, DELETE, AND RENUM STATEMENTS

These statements can help you create and edit programs. Use AUTO to tell the computer to automatically type line numbers, EDIT to list a line or block of lines for editing, DELETE to delete a line or block of lines, and RENUM to renumber a line or block of lines.

AUTO

Use AUTO as a direct statement to tell the computer to automatically type the line numbers that begin program lines. The computer types each line number, and then you can type the rest of the program line and press (ENTER). After you enter the last line of the program, press (CTRL)-(BREAK) to end the automatic line numbering.

In the example that follows, the computer automatically typed the line numbers 10, 20, and 30.

```
AUTO
10 PRINT "To stop, press CTRL BREAK"
20 GOTO 10
30 _
```

This program has only two lines: 10 and 20. Press (CTRL)-(BREAK) to end the AUTO statement. The screen will then look like this:

```
AUTO
10 PRINT "To stop, press CTRL BREAK"
20 GOTO 10
30
Ok
—
```

The AUTO statement shown here begins numbering at line 10 and increments by 10 to obtain each new line number. You can specify the starting line number, the increment, or both. Some examples are

AUTO Statement	Line Number Sequence
AUTO	10, 20, 30, 40, 50. . .
AUTO 100	100, 110, 120, 130, 140. . .
AUTO 100, 5	100, 105, 110, 115, 120. . .

REMEMBER: To end an AUTO statement, press (CTRL)-(BREAK).

EDIT

The EDIT statement displays a program line and puts the cursor under the first digit of the line number, ready for editing. For example, suppose the following program is already stored in memory, with "PRINT" misspelled as "PTINT":

```
10 PTINT "To stop, press CTRL BREAK"
20 GOTO 10
```

You can use an EDIT statement to display line 10 and put the cursor on the first digit (1) of the line number, as shown here:

```
EDIT 10
10 PTINT "To stop, press CTRL BREAK"
```

You can now correct the mistake. Move the cursor to the incorrect *T*, type **R**, and press (ENTER).

DELETE

You already know one way to delete a program line: type the line number by itself and press (ENTER). You can also use the DELETE statement to delete either a single program line or a block of program lines. Here are some examples.

DELETE Statement	Lines Deleted
DELETE	All program lines (the entire program)
DELETE 15	Line 15 only
DELETE 200-240	All lines from line 200 through line 240
DELETE 500-	All lines from line 500 to the end of the program
DELETE -499	All lines from the lowest-numbered line through line 499

RENUM

You can use the RENUM statement to automatically renumber a program line, a block of program lines, or the entire program. For example, suppose you have entered a short program and then added some lines, so that it is stored as follows:

```
10 RANDOMIZE TIMER:  CLS
15 COLOR INT(15 * RND) + 1
17 SOUND 3000 * RND + 1000, .25
20 PRINT "Rory  ";
30 GOTO 15
```

Use RENUM to renumber the program lines, and then list the renumbered program.

```
RENUM 10, 10, 10
Ok
LIST
10 RANDOMIZE TIMER: CLS
20 COLOR INT(15 * RND) + 1
30 SOUND 3000 * RND + 1000, .25
40 PRINT "Rory  ";
50 GOTO 20
Ok
—
```

Note that the line number following the keyword GOTO has been changed; it now refers to the new line number of the COLOR statement.

The RENUM statement shown above is in this form:

RENUM *new number, old number, increment*

This statement renumbers program lines beginning at *old number*. The newly numbered lines begin with *new number* and are spaced by the number used for *increment*. Here are additional examples of the RENUM statement:

RENUM Statement	Action
RENUM	Renumbers entire program. The new line numbers are 10, 20, 30, and so on.
RENUM 100, 10, 20	Renumbers from old line number 10. The new sequence is 100, 120, 140, and so on.
RENUM 100, 10	Renumbers from old line number 10. The default increment is 10, so the new line number sequence is 100, 110, 120, and so on.

THE CONT AND STOP STATEMENTS

The CONT statement resumes execution of a program that has been stopped by pressing (CTRL)-(BREAK), or by a STOP or END statement in the program. You can press the (F5) function key to execute a CONT instruction. The keyword CONT is an abbreviation of CONTINUE.

A STOP statement in a program line causes the program to stop. You can press (F5) to continue the program. Here, the STOP statement is in line 30:

```
10 CLS
20 BEEP
30 STOP
40 GOTO 20
```

Enter and run the foregoing program. When it stops, press (F5) to continue it. It will stop again; press (F5) to continue. After the third stop, the screen looks like this:

```
Break in 30
Ok
CONT
Break in 30
Ok
CONT
Break in 30
Ok
_
```

You can use the STOP statement to help you find an error in any misbehaving program. Put STOP statements in carefully chosen places in your program, and then run it. When the program stops, use direct PRINT statements to print the values of key variables and compare them with expected values. Use a CONT statement (press (F5)) to continue the program. After you find and correct the error, delete the STOP statements.

TRACING A PROGRAM: TRON AND TROFF STATEMENTS

A program executes its lines in line number order, except when the order is redirected by statements such as GOTO and GOSUB, or when the program contains statements in a WHILE...WEND or FOR...NEXT loop.

GW-BASIC has the ability to *trace* a program for you by printing the line number of each line as it is executed. You use the (F7) function key to turn the trace on, and the (F8) function key to turn the trace off. When you turn the trace on and run the program, the computer prints the line number of each line it executes.

The program shown next prints information on the screen about the trace on (TRON) and trace off (TROFF) statements. The main program is in lines 10 through 90. Line 70 calls a time-delay subroutine in line 100. The subroutine then returns to line 80.

```
10 CLS
20 PRINT "Press F7 to turn the trace on (TRON)."
30 PRINT "Press F8 to turn the trace off (TROFF)."
40 PRINT "When the trace is on, the computer prints"
50 PRINT "the line number of each line it executes."
60 PRINT
70 GOSUB 100    'Use time delay subroutine
80 GOTO 20
90 END
100 start = TIMER: WHILE TIMER < start + 1: WEND: RETURN
```

Figure A-1 shows a run of the program with the trace off. Only when the program is not running can you turn the trace on or off. Press (F7) to turn the trace on, or (F8) to turn the trace off.

Now turn the trace on and run the program. Figure A-2 shows a trace of the program. The trace was interrupted by pressing (CTRL)-(BREAK).

NOTE: Although you cannot use (F8) to stop a trace while the program is running, you can interrupt a trace with (CTRL)-(BREAK). Then press (F8) to turn off the trace (unless you want to trace again). Alternatively, you can use STOP statements in the program to make

```
Press F7 to turn the trace on (TRON).
Press F8 to turn the trace off (TROFF).
When the trace is on, the computer prints
the line number of each line it executes.

Press F7 to turn the trace on (TRON).
Press F8 to turn the trace off (TROFF).
When the trace is on, the computer prints
the line number of each line it executes.

Break in 100
Ok
—
```

FIGURE A-1.　Sample run with trace off

it stop where you want it to stop. While the program is stopped, you can turn the trace off or on, and then press (F5) to continue running the program.

```
[20]Press F7 to turn the trace on (TRON).
[30]Press F8 to turn the trace off (TROFF).
[40]When the trace is on, the computer prints
[50]the line number of each line it executes.
[60]
[70][100][80][20]Press F7 to turn the trace on (TRON).
[30]Press F8 to turn the trace off (TROFF).
[40]When the trace is on, the computer prints
[50]the line number of each line it executes.
[60]
[70][100]
Break in 100
Ok
—
```

FIGURE A-2.　Sample run with trace on

THE KILL AND NAME STATEMENTS

You can use the KILL statement to erase a file from a disk, and the NAME statement to change the name of a file on a disk. Here are some examples.

- The statement

```
KILL "OBSOLETE.BAS"
```

erases the file named OBSOLETE.BAS from the disk in the default disk drive. If the file does not exist on that disk, you will see a "File not found" message. In a KILL statement, you must use the entire filename, including the filename extension, enclosed in quotation marks.

- The statement

```
KILL "B:OBSOLETE.BAS"
```

erases the file named OBSOLETE.BAS from the disk in drive B. If the file does not exist on that disk, you will see a "File not found" message.

- The statement

```
NAME "OLDFILE.BAS" AS "NEWFILE.BAS"
```

changes the name of the file called OLDFILE.BAS to NEW-FILE.BAS on the default disk drive. If the file named OLDFILE.BAS does not exist on that disk, you will see a "File not found" message. If that disk already contains a file named NEW-FILE.BAS, you will see a "File already exists" message. In a NAME statement, you must use the entire filename, including the filename extension, enclosed in quotation marks.

- The statement

```
NAME "B:OLDFILE.BAS" AS "NEWFILE.BAS"
```

changes the name of the file called OLDFILE.BAS to NEW-FILE.BAS on the disk in drive B. If OLDFILE.BAS does not exist on that disk, you will see a "File not found" message. If that disk

| TABLE A-1. | | Values of INSTR for Several Pairs of Arguments |

INSTR Function	Value	Result
INSTR("abc","a")	1	Match at position 1 of first argument
INSTR("abc","b")	2	Match at position 2 of first argument
INSTR("abc","c")	3	Match at position 3 of first argument
INSTR("abc","*")	0	No match; no asterisk in first argument
INSTR("abc","A")	0	No match; no A in first argument
INSTR("abc","ab")	1	Match at position 1 of first argument
INSTR("abc","bc")	2	Match at position 2 of first argument
INSTR("abc","abc")	1	Match at position 1 of first argument
INSTR("ab","abc")	0	No match; *abc* is not in first argument

already contains a file called NEWFILE.BAS, you will see a "File already exists" message.

A FLOCK OF FUNCTIONS

You already know how to use many of GW-BASIC's functions. This section briefly introduces seven more functions, listed here:

INSTR LEFT\$ RIGHT\$ SGN STR\$ STRING\$ VAL

The INSTR Numeric Function

INSTR is a numeric function of two string arguments. INSTR returns a numeric value that depends on whether the second argument is a substring of the first argument. If not, the value of INSTR is zero (0); if there is a match, the value of INSTR is the position in the first argument where the second argument matches. Table A-1 shows values of INSTR for several pairs of arguments.

INSTR appears in line 50 of the following program:

```
10 CLS
20 rainbow$ = "redorangeyellowgreenblueviolet"
30 PRINT
40 INPUT "Enter a rainbow color: ", kolor$
50 IF INSTR(rainbow$, kolor$) = 0 THEN GOSUB 80 ELSE GOSUB 90
60 GOTO 30
70 END
80 PRINT "Sorry, "; kolor$; " is not in my rainbow.": RETURN
90 PRINT "Yes, "; kolor$; " is in my rainbow.": RETURN
```

This is a very simple quiz program about colors of the rainbow. Answers must be entered in lowercase letters, as shown in the following sample run:

```
Enter a rainbow color: green
Yes, green is in my rainbow.

Enter a rainbow color: GREEN
Sorry, GREEN is not in my rainbow.

Enter a rainbow color: hot pink
Sorry, hot pink is not in my rainbow.

Enter a rainbow color: _
```

Try other rainbow colors, but be sure to enter them in lowercase and spell them correctly.

The LEFT$ and RIGHT$ String Functions

Think of the LEFT$ and RIGHT$ functions as specialized versions of the MID$ function. Use LEFT$ to extract a substring from the left end of a string, and RIGHT$ to obtain a substring from the right end of a string.

LEFT$ and RIGHT$ are both string functions of two arguments (a string argument followed by a numeric argument). Table A-2 shows examples of both functions.

• The value of

  LEFT$(*strng$, number*)

  is a string consisting of the leftmost *number* of characters of *strng$*.

- The value of

  RIGHT$(*strng$, number*)

  is a string consisting of the rightmost *number* of characters of *strng$*.

  The next program uses LEFT$, RIGHT$, and MID$ to acquire a three-letter word, and then print it with the letters reversed.

```
10 CLS
20 INPUT "Enter a 3-letter word: ", wrd$
30 rvrs$ = RIGHT$(wrd$, 1) + MID$(wrd$, 2, 1) + LEFT$(wrd$, 1)
40 PRINT "The reverse word is: <> "; rvrs$
50 PRINT : GOTO 20
```

The sample run shown here displays two semordnilaps, which are words whose reversed spellings are also words.

```
Enter a 3-letter word: pot
The reverse word is:   top

Enter a 3-letter word: won
The reverse word is:   now
```

| TABLE A-2. | Values of LEFT$ and RIGHT$ Functions |

Function	Value of function
LEFT$("abc", 1)	a
LEFT$("abc", 2)	ab
LEFT$("abc", 3)	abc
LEFT$("abc", 4)	abc
RIGHT$("abc", 1)	c
RIGHT$("abc", 2)	bc
RIGHT$("abc", 3)	abc
RIGHT$("abc", 4)	abc

The SGN Numeric Function

SGN is a numeric function of one numeric argument. Its value is −1, 0, or 1, as defined here:

If *number* is negative, then SGN(*number*) is −1.

If *number* is zero, then SGN(*number*) is 0.

If *number* is positive, then SGN(*number*) is 1.

In Chapter 6 you saw Program 6-3, NZP01 (Negative, Zero or Positive with IF Statements). That program identified a number entered from the keyboard as being negative, zero, or positive. The following performs the same task, using the SGN function and a small array called *nzp$()*.

```
10 CLS
20 nzp$(1) = "negative"
30 nzp$(2) = "zero"
40 nzp$(3) = "positive"
50 INPUT "Enter a number: ", number
60 PRINT nzp$(SGN(number) + 2)
70 PRINT : GOTO 50
```

Lines 20, 30, and 40 assign the words "negative," "zero," and "positive" as the values of array variables *nzp$(1)*, *nzp$(2)*, and *nzp$(3)*. After you enter a number for the value of *number*, line 60 selects and prints the value of the appropriate array variable. For example:

If the value of *number* is negative, then SGN(*number*) is −1, and SGN(*number*) + 2 is 1. The value of *nzp$(1)* is printed.

If the value of *number* is zero, then SGN(*number*) is 0, and SGN(*number*) + 2 is 2. The value of *nzp$(2)* is printed.

If the value of *number* is positive, then SGN(*number*) is 1, and SGN(*number*) + 2 is 3. The value of *nzp$(3)* is printed.

You can use the SGN function with the FIX or INT function to round a number. This next program rounds a number to two decimal places.

```
10 CLS
20 INPUT "Number, please"; nmbr
30 rounded = SGN(nmbr) * FIX(100 * ABS(nmbr) + .5) / 100
40 PRINT "Rounded value: "; rounded
50 PRINT : GOTO 20
```

To round a number to one decimal place, replace 100 with 10 in line 30. To round to three decimal places, replace 100 with 1000. For four decimal places, use 10000, and so on.

The STRING$ String Function

STRING$ is a string function of two numeric arguments, or a numeric argument followed by a string argument. Its value is a string of up to 255 characters, all the same character. Here are some examples.

```
PRINT STRING$(13, "*")
*************

PRINT STRING$(30, "A")
AAAAAAAAAAAAAAAAAAAAAAAAAAAAAA

PRINT STRING$(30, 65)
AAAAAAAAAAAAAAAAAAAAAAAAAAAAAA
```

The first argument is numeric and specifies the length of the value of STRING$ (the number of characters). The second argument can be string or numeric. It can be a single character or the ASCII code of a character. The value of STRING$ is this character repeated the number of times specified by the first argument.

For a colorful demonstration of the STRING$ function, run the program shown below. It displays color bars across the screen in the 15 colors numbered 1 through 15. Each color bar is 80 characters long, using the character whose ASCII code is 219.

```
10 CLS
20 FOR kolor = 1 TO 15
30   COLOR kolor
40   PRINT STRING$(80, 219);
50 NEXT kolor
```

The STR$ and VAL Functions

STR$ is a string function of a numeric argument; VAL is a numeric function of a string argument. These functions are the opposites of each other. You use STR$ to obtain a string that corresponds to a number, and VAL to obtain a number that corresponds to a string.

Here are two examples using the VAL numeric function.

```
PRINT VAL("123456789"), VAL:("1E15"), VAL("1E16")
 123456789      1000000000000000           1D+16

PRINT VAL("123abc"), VAL("abc123")
 123          0
```

From these examples, note the following things:

- The value of VAL is a double precision number. If the value has more than 16 digits, it is printed in floating point notation.

- If the string contains non-numeric characters (such as "123abc"), VAL returns any number that appears on the left end of the string. If the first character of the string is non-numeric, then VAL returns zero (0).

Next, here are some examples of the STR$ string function.

```
NmbrStrng$ = STR$(123): PRINT NmbrStrng$, LEN(NmbrStrng$)
 123          4

NmbrStrng$ = STR$(-123.45): PRINT NmbrStrng$, LEN(NmbrStrng$)
-123.45        7

NmbrStrng$ = STR$(1E6): PRINT NmbrStrng$, LEN(NmbrSrng$)
 1000000        8
```

From these examples, note the following things:

- The value of STR$ includes a leading space for non-negative numbers, or a minus sign (–) for negative numbers. For an integer argument, the length of the value of STR$ is one more than the number of digits in the argument.

- If the argument has a decimal point, it appears as a character in the value of STR$. The length of STR$(−123.45) is seven characters—two more than the number of digits in the argument.

- The single precision floating point number, 1E6, was printed in ordinary notation. However, try 1E7 or 1E8 and see what happens. Also try numbers with more than seven digits, and double precision floating point numbers such as 1D16.

Both VAL and STR$ appear in the next program. This program computes and prints the sum of the digits of a number entered from the keyboard.

```
10 CLS
20 INPUT "Number, please"; number
30 NmbrStrng$ = STR$(number)
40 SumDigits = 0
50 FOR k = 2 TO LEN(NmbrSrng$)
60    SumDigits = SumDigits + VAL(MID$(NmbrStrng$, k, 1))
70 NEXT k
80 PRINT "Sum of digits: "; SumDigits
90 PRINT : GOTO 20
```

A sample run is shown below. Note that the sum of the digits is positive, even when the number entered is negative. Will the program work for numbers that are not integers? Try it and find out.

```
Number, please? 123
Sum of digits:  6

Number, please? 1234567
Sum of digits:  37

Number, please? -123
Sum of digits:  6
```

THE END . . . OF THE BEGINNING

You now know a great deal about GW-BASIC. You can use GW-BASIC to tell the computer what to do and how to do it, the way **you** want it done.

You can continue learning about GW-BASIC by consulting reference guides such as the ones mentioned at the beginning of this appendix. Also helpful are these publications:

Albrecht, Bob and Don Inman. *GW-BASIC Made Easy*. Berkeley: Osborne/McGraw-Hill, 1989.

The BASIC Teacher. 2813 19th Street, San Francisco, California 94110. A tutorial magazine for beginners covering GW-BASIC and QuickBASIC.

The best way to learn more about GW-BASIC is to write programs and make them work. The author encourages you to write your programs in good style, so that others can read and understand them—and so that **you** can read and understand them a year later.

GW-BASIC Keywords
▶B◀

ABS	CONT	ENVIRON$	IF	LOAD
AND	COS	EOF	IMP	LOC
ASC	CSNG	EQV	INKEY$	LOCATE
ATN	CSRLIN	ERASE	INP	LOCK
AUTO	CVD	ERDEV	INPUT	LOF
BEEP	CVI	ERDEV$	INPUT#	LOG
BLOAD	CVS	ERL	INPUT$	LPOS
BSAVE	DATA	ERR	INSTR	LPRINT
CALL	DATE$	ERROR	INT	LSET
CDBL	DEF	EXP	INTER$	MERGE
CHAIN	DEFDBL	EXTERR	IOCTL	MID$
CHDIR	DEFINT	FIELD	IOCTL$	MKDIR
CHR$	DEFSNG	FILES	KEY	MKD$
CINT	DEFSTR	FIX	KEY$	MKI$
CIRCLE	DELETE	FN	KILL	MKS$
CLEAR	DIM	FOR	LEFT$	MOD
CLOSE	DRAW	FRE	LEN	MOTOR
CLS	EDIT	GET	LET	NAME
COLOR	ELSE	GOSUB	LINE	NEW
COM	END	GOTO	LIST	NEXT
COMMON	ENVIRON	HEX$	LLIST	NOT

OCT$	POS	RND	STR$	VAL
OFF	PRESET	RSET	STRIG	VARPTR
ON	PRINT	RUN	STRING$	VARPTR$
OPEN	PRINT#	SAVE	SWAP	VIEW
OPTION	PSET	SCREEN	SYSTEM	WAIT
OR	PUT	SGN	TAB	WEND
OUT	RANDOMIZE	SHARED	TAN	WHILE
PAINT	READ	SHELL	THEN	WIDTH
PALETTE	REM	SIN	TIME$	WINDOW
PCOPY	RENUM	SOUND	TIMER	WRITE
PEEK	RESET	SPACE$	TO	WRITE#
PEN	RESTORE	SPC	TROFF	XOR
PLAY	RESUME	SQR	TRON	
PMAP	RETURN	STEP	UNLOCK	
POINT	RIGHT$	STICK	USING	
POKE	RMDIR	STOP	USR	

ASCII Codes and Characters

▶C◀

TABLE C-1.	ASCII Codes and Characters

ASCII Value	Character	ASCII Value	Character
0	Null	17	◄
1	☺	18	↕
2	☻	19	‼
3	♥	20	π
4	♦	21	§
5	♣	22	▬
6	♠	23	↨
7	Beep	24	↑
8	◘	25	↓
9	Tab	26	→
10	Linefeed	27	←
11	Cursor home	28	Cursor right
12	Form-feed	29	Cursor left
13	Carriage return	30	Cursor up
14	♫	31	Cursor down
15	☼	32	Space
16	►	33	!

TABLE C-1.	ASCII Codes and Characters (*continued*)

ASCII Value	Character	ASCII Value	Character
34	"	68	D
35	#	69	E
36	$	70	F
37	%	71	G
38	&	72	H
39	'	73	I
40	(	74	J
41	)	75	K
42	*	76	L
43	+	77	M
44	,	78	N
45	-	79	O
46	.	80	P
47	/	81	Q
48	0	82	R
49	1	83	S
50	2	84	T
51	3	85	U
52	4	86	V
53	5	87	W
54	6	88	X
55	7	89	Y
56	8	90	Z
57	9	91	[
58	:	92	\
59	;	93	]
60	<	94	^
61	=	95	_
62	>	96	'
63	?	97	a
64	@	98	b
65	A	99	c
66	B	100	d
67	C	101	e

TABLE C-1.	ASCII Codes and Characters (*continued*)

ASCII Value	Character	ASCII Value	Character
102	f	136	ê
103	g	137	ë
104	h	138	è
105	i	139	ï
106	j	140	î
107	k	141	ì
108	l	142	Ä
109	m	143	Å
110	n	144	É
111	o	145	æ
112	p	146	Æ
113	q	147	ô
114	r	148	ö
115	s	149	ò
116	t	150	û
117	u	151	ù
118	v	152	ÿ
119	w	153	Ö
120	x	154	Ü
121	y	155	¢
122	z	156	£
123	{	157	¥
124	¦	158	Pt
125	}	159	ƒ
126	~	160	á
127		161	í
128	Ç	162	ó
129	ü	163	ú
130	é	164	ñ
131	â	165	Ñ
132	ä	166	ª
133	à	167	º
134	å	168	¿
135	ç	169	⌐

TABLE C-1.	ASCII Codes and Characters (*continued*)

ASCII Value	Character	ASCII Value	Character
170		204	╠
171	½	205	═
172	¼	206	╬
173	¡	207	╧
174	«	208	╨
175	»	209	╤
176	░	210	╥
177	▒	211	╙
178	▓	212	╘
179	│	213	╒
180	┤	214	╓
181	╡	215	╫
182	╢	216	╪
183	╖	217	┘
184	╕	218	┌
185	╣	219	█
186	║	220	▄
187	╗	221	▌
188	╝	222	▐
189	╜	223	▀
190	╛	224	α
191	┐	225	β
192	└	226	Γ
193	┴	227	π
194	┬	228	Σ
195	├	229	σ
196	─	230	μ
197	┼	231	τ
198	╞	232	φ
199	╟	233	θ
200	╚	234	Ω
201	╔	235	δ
202	╩	236	∞
203	╦	237	∅

TABLE C-1.	ASCII Codes and Characters (*continued*)

ASCII Value	Character	ASCII Value	Character
238	$\in$	247	$\approx$
239	$\cap$	248	$\circ$
240	$\equiv$	249	$\bullet$
241	$\pm$	250	$\cdot$
242	$\geq$	251	$\sqrt{}$
243	$\leq$	252	^{n}
244	$\lceil$	253	^{2}
245	$\rfloor$	254	$\blacksquare$
246	$\div$	255	(blank 'FF')

Answers

▶D◀

1. BASIC is a computer programming language created in 1964 by Dartmouth professors John G. Kemeny and Thomas E. Kurtz. The word "BASIC" is an acronym for Beginner's All-Purpose Symbolic Instruction Code. GW-BASIC is the generic form of Microsoft BASIC for any IBM-compatible computer. BASICA is the version of Microsoft BASIC distributed by IBM.

2. Syntax means rules of grammar. A complete description of GW-BASIC's syntax is contained in *The GW-BASIC Reference* by Don Inman and Bob Albrecht, an Osborne/McGraw-Hill book.

3. A BASIC program is a set of instructions written using the vocabulary and syntax of BASIC.

1.2

EXERCISES

1. DOS is the computer's Disk Operating System, a program that is in charge of all activities in the computer. Think of DOS as your computer's master control system.

2. `A>_`

3. `C>_`   *(or something similar)*

1.3

EXERCISES

1. `A>_`

2. `C>_`   *(or something similar)*

1.4

EXERCISES

1. Type **BASIC** and press (ENTER).

2. The GW-BASIC prompt is the word "Ok."

3. The GW-BASIC cursor is the underscore character (_).

4. The key line has brief descriptive labels showing the functions assigned to function keys (F1) through (F10). The key line is the bottom line of the screen, line 25.

1.6

EXERCISES

1. A direct statement is an instruction to the computer, using the vocabulary (keywords) and syntax of BASIC. You type a direct statement and press (ENTER). The computer executes (does, obeys, carries out) the statement immediately.

2. The cursor (_) and the key line.

3. The GW-BASIC prompt (Ok), the cursor (_), and the key line.

4. You will see a "Syntax error" message, followed by Ok and the cursor.

EXERCISES

1. Press (ALT)-(C). (Hold down the (ALT) key and press the (C) key.)
2. COLOR 4
3. COLOR 20
4. Type **COLOR 7** and press (ENTER). (Or, press (ALT)-(C), type **7**, and press (ENTER).)

EXERCISES

1. The COLOR, 5 statement sets the background color to magenta.
2. Clear the screen. Press (CTRL)-(L), or do a CLS direct statement.
3. There are eight background colors, numbered 0 to 7.
4. You will change the foreground color instead of changing the background color. For example:

   Change background color to blue: COLOR , 1
   Change foreground color to blue: COLOR 1

EXERCISES

1. COLOR 5, 3
2. COLOR 7, 0

EXERCISES

1. When you first load GW-BASIC, the screen is a text screen that displays 25 lines with 80 characters per line.

2. Type **WIDTH 40** and press (ENTER).

3. Press (ALT)(W). (Hold down (ALT) and press (W).)

1.12 EXERCISES

1. One way: Type **KEY OFF** and press (ENTER).
   Another way: Press (F9), type **OFF**, and press (ENTER).

2. One way: Type **KEY ON** and press (ENTER).
   Another way: Press (F9), type **ON**, and press (ENTER).

1.13 EXERCISES

1. Line number; statement.

2. A direct statement does not have a line number. When you type a direct statement and press (ENTER), the computer executes it immediately.

   A program line begins with a line number. When you type a program line, the computer does not execute it immediately. Instead, it stores the program line in its memory for later execution.

1.14 EXERCISES

1. Type **NEW** and press (ENTER).

2. Press (F1), (ENTER). (Or, type **LIST** and press (ENTER).)

3. Type the program line, beginning with its line number, and press (ENTER).

4. You can replace the incorrect line 10 by typing a correct line 10 and pressing (ENTER). You can also correct the error as follows:

   List the program.
   Use the arrow keys to put the cursor on the incorrect *T*.
   Type **R** and press (ENTER).

EXERCISES

1. Press (F2). (Or, type **RUN** and press (ENTER).)

2. Press (CTRL)(BREAK). (Hold down (CTRL) and press (BREAK).)

MASTERY SKILLS CHECK

MASTERY
SKILLS
CHECK

1. _g_ BASIC
   _h_ syntax
   _a_ program
   _i_ DOS command line
   _j_ BASIC prompt
   _d_ cursor
   _c_ key line
   _f_ syntax error
   _e_ keyword
   _b_ direct statement

2. COLOR 0, 7

3. 40 characters per line: Type **WIDTH 40** and press (ENTER).
   80 characters per line: Type **WIDTH 80** and press (ENTER).
   You can press (ALT)(W) to type **WIDTH** and a space.

4. To turn the key line off, type **KEY OFF** and press (ENTER).
   To turn the key line on, type **KEY ON** and press (ENTER).
   You can press (F9) to type **KEY** and a space.

5. A program line begins with a line number. It is not executed immediately when you press (ENTER). Instead, it is stored in the computer's memory for later execution. A direct statement does not begin with a line number. It is executed immediately when you press (ENTER).

6. Type each program line, beginning with its line number, and press (ENTER).

7. Press (F1), (ENTER).

8. Here are two ways.

  a. Enter a correct line with the same line number.

  b. List the program. Use the arrow keys to put the cursor on the line that has the error. Correct the error and press (ENTER).

9. Press (F2).

10. Press (CTRL)(BREAK).

11. The PRINT statement in line 10 tells the computer to print the message "To stop, hold down CTRL and press ENTER" on the screen. The GOTO statement in line 20 tells the computer to go to line 10. Together, these statements comprise a *GOTO loop* that continues until you press (CTRL)(BREAK).

12. Type **SYSTEM** and press (ENTER).

2.1 EXERCISES

1. A colon (:).

2. You will see an "Illegal function call" error message.

```
COLOR 14, 1 CLS
Illegal function call
```

2.2 EXERCISES

1. `PRINT TIME$, DATE$`

2. One second before midnight. At midnight, the value of TIMER is set to zero.

2.3 EXERCISES

1. Quotation marks (")

2. `PRINT "George Firedrake"`

EXERCISES

1. Question mark (?).
2. Press (ALT)(P). (Hold down (ALT) and press (P).)

EXERCISES

1. Quotation marks (").
2. Here are four possible answers.

```
DATE$ = "7-15-2010"
DATE$ = "7-15-10"
DATE$ = "7/15/2010"
DATE$ = "7/15/10"
```

EXERCISES

1. `TIME$ = "7:30:23"`
2. `TIME$ = "19:30:23"`

EXERCISES

1. Use * for multiplication. Use / for division.
2. A comma (,) or a semicolon (;).
3. `PRINT 7 + 5, 7 - 5, 7 * 5, 7 / 5`
4. `PRINT 39.95 * .06; 39.95 + 39.95 * .06`

EXERCISES

1. Highest frequency: 32767
   Lowest frequency: 37

2. a. 18.2 or 18
   b. 36.4 or 36
   c. 9.1 or 9
   d. 4.55 or 4.6

3. SOUND 5000, 18

4. SOUND 37, 6

EXERCISES 2.9

1. SCREEN 0 is a text mode screen. It can display 25 lines of characters, with 80 characters per line or 40 double-width characters per line.

2. a. A pixel is a picture element, a tiny rectangle on the screen.
   b. 320
   c. 200
   d. 40 characters

EXERCISES 2.10

1. Column number: 0 to 319
   Row number: 0 to 199

2. Answers for 2a through 2e:

```
COLOR 15, 0
PSET (160, 100), 1
PSET (150, 90), 2
PSET (170, 110), 3
PSET (160, 100), 0
```

3. Press (F10).

EXERCISES 2.11

1. LINE (0, 100) - (319, 100), 1

2. `LINE (160, 0) - (160, 199), 2`

3. There are many possible solutions. For example:

```
LINE (140, 100) - (180, 130), 1, B
LINE (120, 90) - (200, 140), 2, B
LINE (100, 80) - (220, 150), 3, B
```

4. Here is one way to do it.

```
LINE (100, 80) - (140, 150), 3, BF
LINE (140, 80) - (180, 150), 1, BF
LINE (180, 80) - (220, 150), 2, BF
```

5. Answers to 5a, 5b, and 5c:

```
LINE (100, 50) - (200, 75), 0
LINE (80, 60) - (160, 120), 0, B
LINE (20, 30) - (50, 80), 0, BF
```

EXERCISES
2.12

1. In the following solution, the centers of the circles are on the vertices of an equilateral triangle:

```
CIRCLE (160, 100), 40, 1
CIRCLE (140, 135), 40, 2
CIRCLE (180, 135), 40, 3
```

2. The following solution draws and paints the outer circle first, then the middle circle, and then the inner circle:

```
CIRCLE (160, 100), 45, 1
PAINT (160, 100), 1, 1
CIRCLE (160, 100), 30, 3
PAINT (160, 100), 3, 3
CIRCLE (160, 100), 15, 2
PAINT (160, 100), 2, 2
```

MASTERY SKILLS CHECK

MASTERY
SKILLS
CHECK

1.
```
DATE$ = "1-1-92"
TIME$ = "00:00:01"
PRINT DATE$, TIME$, "Happy New Year!"
```

2. `PRINT 1, 2, 3, 4, 5`

3. `PRINT 1; 22; 333; 4444; 55555`

4. Answers to 4a and 4b:

```
PRINT "3 + 4 ="; 3 + 4
3 + 4 = 7

PRINT "The sales tax is"; 30 * .06
The sales tax is 1.8
```

5. This sound is the same as that caused by a BEEP statement.

```
SOUND 800, 4.55 (or SOUND 800, 4.6)
```

6. `SOUND 100, 0     (or any legal frequency)`

7. a. background color (0), green (1), red (2), brown (3).
   b. background color (0), cyan (1), magenta (2), bright white (3).

8. `COLOR 2, 1`

9. `PSET (100, 120), 2`

10.
```
LINE (160, 100) - (140, 135), 3
LINE (160, 100) - (180, 135), 3
LINE (140, 135) - (180, 135), 3
```

11. The following PAINT statement fills the interior of the triangle with palette color number 2.

```
PAINT (160, 120), 2, 3
```

12.
```
LINE (110, 100) - (210, 160), 3, BF
LINE (130, 120) - (150, 140), 1, BF
LINE (170, 120) - (190, 140), 2, BF
```

13.
```
CIRCLE (160, 140), 50, 3
CIRCLE (160, 120), 15, 3
CIRCLE (160, 160), 15, 3
PAINT (160, 140), 3, 3
PAINT (160, 120), 1, 3
PAINT (160, 160), 2, 3
```

14. Use the background color (palette color number 0) and erase each figure. Answers to 14a through 14e:

```
PSET (123, 45), 0
LINE (50, 50) - (80, 50), 0
LINE (160, 100) - (319, 199), 0, B
CIRCLE (160, 100), 40, 0
PAINT (160, 100), 0, 0
```

15. Press (F10).

EXERCISES

3.1

1. A program line begins with a line number. A direct statement does not begin with a line number. When you type a direct statement and press (ENTER), the computer executes it immediately. When you enter a program line, it is not executed immediately. Instead, it is stored in the computer's memory as part of a program.

2.

```
(30) PRINT TIME$
```

EXERCISES

3.2

1. This erases, removes, or deletes any old program that might be in the computer's memory. If you don't do this, lines from an old program might get mixed up with lines from your new program, thus causing mysterious and unpredictable results when you run the program.

2. The computer stores the line for later use.

3. Press (F1), (ENTER). (Or type **LIST** and press (ENTER).)

4. Press (F2). (Or type **RUN** and press (ENTER).)

5. Type **10 BEEP** and press (ENTER). (Or put the cursor on the incorrect letter *A*, type E, and press (ENTER).)

EXERCISES

3.3

1. Type each line of the program and press (ENTER).

2. Press (F2). (Or type **RUN** and press (ENTER).)

3. You will probably see a "Syntax error" or other error message.

4. Laran's name will be printed incorrectly, exactly as it appears in the PRINT statement. For example:

```
PRINT "Loren Stardrake"
Loren Stardrake
```

3.4

EXERCISES

1. Press F4 (to type **SAVE"**), type **MYNAME**, and then press ENTER. The computer will add the .BAS filename extension.
2. `FILES "*.BAS"`

3.5

EXERCISES

1. `SAVE"A:MYNAME"`
2. `FILES "A:*.BAS"`

3.6

EXERCISES

1. `LOAD"MYNAME"` *(Press F3 to type **LOAD"**.)*
2. `LOAD"B:MYNAME"`

3.7

EXERCISES

1. Type **LLIST** and press ENTER.
2. Type **L**, and press F1, ENTER.

3.8

EXERCISES

1. Enter it with a line number that falls between the numbers of the two existing program lines. For example, to enter a line between existing lines 30 and 40, use any line number from 31 to 39 (35 is a good choice).
2. First line: Use a line number smaller than any existing line number.

Last line: Use a line number larger than any existing line number.

EXERCISES

1. Answers to 1a, 1b, and 1c:

```
SAVE"BIRTHDAY"
SAVE"BIRTHDAY", A
SAVE"BIRTHDAY.ASC", A
```

2. Answers to 2a and 2b:

```
LOAD"BIRTHDAY"
LOAD"BIRTHDAY.ASC"
```

EXERCISES

1. Function; random number; 0; 1

2. 0; 16

EXERCISES

1. Yes. In the program line

```
40 PSET (319 * RND, 199 * RND), 3 * RND
```

the value of 319 * RND can be any number *between* 0 and 319; the value of 199 * RND can be any number *between* 0 and 199. The computer rounds these values for use in a PSET statement. Therefore, a rounded value of 0 or 319 is possible for the column number; a rounded value of 0 or 199 is possible for the row number.

2. Here are the changes.

```
30 COLOR 15, 0
40 PSET (159 * RND, 99 * RND), 3 * RND
50 SOUND 3000 * RND + 1000, .25
```

After making the changes, save the program as ZAPPY02. Type **SAVE"ZAPPY02", A** and press (ENTER).

MASTERY SKILLS CHECK

1. A program line consists of a line number followed by a statement.

2. a. NEW deletes, or erases, any program still in the computer's memory. Use NEW before entering a new program.

   b. LIST lists to the screen the program in the computer's memory.

   c. LLIST lists to the printer the program in the computer's memory.

   d. RUN executes (obeys, does, carries out) the program in the computer's memory.

3. a. Press (ALT)(C).
   b. Press (ALT)(G).
   c. Press (F1).
   d. Press (L), (F1).
   e. Press (F3).
   f. Press (ALT)(P).
   g. Press (F2).
   h. Press (F4).
   i. Press (ALT)(S).
   j. Press (ALT)(W).

4.

```
RUN
 │
 ▼
10 COLOR 15 * RND, 7 * RND ◄──┐
 │                            │
 ▼                            │
20 PRINT "Rory ";             │
 │                            │
 ▼                            │
30 GOTO 10 ───────────────────┘
```

5. Type **SAVE"filename", A** and press (ENTER).

6. 10 CLS

```
20 SOUND 262, 9
30 SOUND 294, 9
40 SOUND 330, 9
50 SOUND 349, 9
60 SOUND 392, 9
70 SOUND 440, 9
80 SOUND 494, 9
90 SOUND 523, 9
```

7. See Program D-1, SOUND01 (Do, Re, Mi and Eight Background Colors).

8. Type **FILES** and press (ENTER).

9. Press (F3), type the filename of the program, and then press (ENTER).

10. a. Use a line number smaller than any existing line number.
    b. Use a line number greater than any existing line number.
    c. Use a line number between 20 and 30 (25 is a good choice).

```
10 SOUND 262, 9
20 COLOR , 1: CLS
30 SOUND 294, 9
40 COLOR , 2: CLS
50 SOUND 330, 9
60 COLOR , 3: CLS
70 SOUND 349, 9
80 COLOR , 4: CLS
90 SOUND 392, 9
100 COLOR , 5: CLS
110 SOUND 440, 9
120 COLOR , 6: CLS
130 SOUND 494, 9
140 COLOR , 7: CLS
150 SOUND 523, 9
160 COLOR , 1: CLS
170 GOTO 10
```

PROGRAM D-1.   Do, Re, Mi and Eight Background Colors

11. Type **15** and press (ENTER).

12. a. 0; 1
    b. 0; 10
    c. 262; 523

13.
```
10 SCREEN 1: CLS
20 RANDOMIZE TIMER
30 COLOR 0, 1
40 PSET (159 * RND + 80, 99 * RND + 50), 3 * RND
50 SOUND 3000 * RND + 1000, 9
60 GOTO 40
```

4.1 EXERCISES

1. a. PRINT 19.95 + 6.59 + 2.50
      29.04

   b. PRINT 123.45 – 24.95 – 12.23
      86.27001

   c. PRINT 53 * 2.2
      116.6

   d. PRINT 1000 / 1.609344
      621.3712

   e. PRINT 23 * 16 + 14
      382

   f. PRINT 12 * 3600 + 36 * 60 + 47
      45407

   g. PRINT 846 * .08882 + 589 * .13524
      154.7981

2. a. PRINT (23 * 16 + 14) * 28.3495
      10829.51

   b. PRINT (19 + 17 + 24) / 3
      20

EXERCISES

1. PRINT 1250 \ 360, 1250 MOD 360
    3   170   (*3 cycles, 170 degrees*)

2. PRINT 12345 \ 60, 12345 MOD 60
  205   45
                             (*3 hours, 25 minutes, 45 seconds*)
PRINT 205 \ 60, 205 MOD 60
  3   25

3. PRINT 10000 \ 12, 10000 MOD 12
  833   4
Ok   (*277 yards, 2 feet, 4 inches*)
PRINT 833 \ 3, 833 MOD 3
  277   2

EXERCISES

1. PRINT 3.14159 * 7 * 7, 3.14159 * 7 ^ 2
  153.9379   153.9379

2. The two ways shown here produce slightly different answers due to roundoff error:

PRINT 4 / 3 * 3.14159 * 5 ^ 3
 523.5984
Ok
PRINT 4 * 3.14159 * 5 ^ 3 / 3
 523.5983

EXERCISES

1. a. 123E9 or 123E+09 or 1.23E11 or...

   b. 1.23E–13 or 123E–15 or...

2. a. 0.000000000000000000000006643

   b. 10000000000

4.5 | EXERCISES

1. –32768; 32767

2. 1234567

3. `PRINT 1 / 7, 1 / 7#`
```
 .1428572       .1428571428571429
```

4.6 | EXERCISES

1. **a.** `LoRate = .08882`

   b. `HiRate = .13524`

   c. `PRINT 846 * LoRate + 589 * HiRate`
   ```
    154.7981
   ```

2. `BaseKwh = 846`

   `XtraKwh = 589`

   `PRINT BaseKwh * LoRate + XtraKwh * HiRate`
   ```
    154.7981
   ```

4.7 | EXERCISES

1. `20 pi = 3.141593`
   `40 PRINT pi * diameter, pi * diameter / 12`

2. `30 INPUT PricePerShare#`
   `40 Value# = NumberOfShares# * PricePerShare#`

MASTERY SKILLS CHECK

1. **a.** `PRINT 13 * 60 + 28`
   ```
    808
   ```

   b. `PRINT (8 * 60 + 37) * 60 + 42`
   ```
    31062
   ```

   c. PRINT (68 + 73 + 77) / 3
       72.66666

   d. PRINT 59.95 – 59.95 * .15
       50.9575

2. a. PRINT 73 \ 10, 73 MOD 10
      7   3

   b. PRINT –100 \ 3, –100 MOD 3
      –33   –1

   c. PRINT 99 \ 100, 99 MOD 100
      0   99

   d. PRINT 125 \ –5, 125 MOD –5
      –25   0

3. PRINT 5.3E9 * (1 + .018) ^ 20
    7.572365E+09

4. 10 CLS
    20 INPUT F
    30 C = 5 * (F – 32) / 9
    40 PRINT C

5. 10 CLS
    20 INPUT n
    30 Prize1 = n
    40 Prize2 = 1.01 ^ n
    50 PRINT Prize1
    60 PRINT Prize2

6. a. 10 CLS

   b. 20 LoRate = .08882

   c. 30 HiRate = .13524

   d. 40 INPUT BaseKwh

   e. 50 INPUT XtraKwh

   f. 60 KwhCost = BaseKwh * LoRate + XtraKwh * HiRate

   g. 70 PRINT KwhCost

5.2 EXERCISES

1. ```
   1 REM ** Distance a Bike Travels in One Wheel Turn **
   2 ' Teach Yourself GW-BASIC, Chapter 5. Filename: BIKE01.BAS
   ```

2. See Program D-2, KWH05 (Cost of Electricity at Low & High Rates).

5.3 EXERCISES

1. ```
   70 PRINT "Total cost of electricity is ";
   75 PRINT USING "####.##"; KwhCost
   ```

2. ```
   50 format$ = "##.##"
   70 PRINT USING format$; distance
   ```

5.4 EXERCISES

1. ```
   60 PRINT USING "#.###"; PctWon
   ```

2. ```
   40 format$ = "$$##,###.##"
   ```

```
1 REM ** Cost of Electricity at Low & High Rates **
2 ' Teach Yourself GW-BASIC, Chapter 5.  Filename: KWH05.BAS

10 CLS
20 LoRate = .08882
30 HiRate = .13524

40 INPUT "Enter kwh charged at low rate:  ", BaseKwh
50 INPUT "Enter kwh charged at high rate: ", XtraKwh
60 KwhCost = BaseKwh * LoRate + XtraKwh * HiRate
70 PRINT "Total cost of electricity is"; KwhCost
```

PROGRAM D-2. Cost of Electricity at Low & High Rates
```

EXERCISES

1. See Program D-3, STOCKS01 (Value of Stocks with REM Statements).

2. See Program D-4, GPA01 (Grade Point Average).

EXERCISE

See Program D-5, ZAPPY06 (Zappy Artist Draws Random Boxes Filled with Color).

```
1 REM ** Value of Stocks with REM Statements **
2 ' Teach Yourself GW-BASIC, Chapter 5.  Filename: STOCKS01.BAS

100 REM ** Set up **
110 CLS

200 REM ** Get number of shares and price per share **
210 INPUT "Number of shares"; NumberOfShares#
220 INPUT "Price per share "; PricePerShare#

300 REM ** Compute value of this block of stock **
310 Value# = NumberOfShares# * PricePerShare#

400 REM ** Print the value of this block of stock **
410 PRINT
420 PRINT "The value is ";
430 PRINT USING "$$############,.##"; Value#
```

PROGRAM D-3.   Value of Stocks with REM Statements

```
1 REM ** Grade Point Average **
2 ' Teach Yourself GW-BASIC, Chapter 5.  Filename: GPA01.BAS

100 REM ** Set up **
110 CLS
120 format$ = "####.###"

200 REM ** Get hours for each grade: A, B, C, D, F **
210 PRINT "For each letter grade, enter the number of hours."
220 PRINT
230 INPUT "Hours of A"; a
240 INPUT "Hours of B"; b
250 INPUT "Hours of C"; c
260 INPUT "Hours of D"; d
270 INPUT "Hours of F"; f

300 REM ** Compute the grade point average (gpa) **
310 TotalPoints = 4 * a + 3 * b + 2 * c + d
320 TotalHours = a + b + c + d + f
330 gpa = TotalPoints / TotalHours

400 REM ** Print total grade points, total hours, and gpa **
410 PRINT
420 PRINT "Total grade points:    ";
430 PRINT USING format$; TotalPoints
440 PRINT "Total number of hours: ";
450 PRINT USING format$; TotalHours
460 PRINT "Grade point average:   ";
470 PRINT USING format$; gpa
```

PROGRAM D-4. Grade Point Average

MASTERY SKILLS CHECK

1. The program line

   20 INPUT "Frequency"; frequency

   tells the computer to

   • Print the string "Frequency"

- Print a question mark

- Wait for a number to be entered as the value of *frequency*

2.
```
30 INPUT "Duration "; duration
40 SOUND frequency, duration
```

3.
```
10 CLS
20 INPUT "Enter a frequency from 37 to 32767:   ", frequency
30 INPUT "Enter a duration between 0 and 65535: ", duration
40 SOUND frequency, duration
```

4.
```
The integer quotient of 73 divided by 5 is 14
```

5.
```
10 CLS
20 INPUT "How many sentient beings live on Mars"; Martians
30 PRINT "The population of Mars is"; Martians; "little green people."
```

```
1 REM ** Zappy Artist Draws Random Boxes Filled with Color **
2 ' Teach Yourself GW-BASIC, Chapter 5.  Filename: ZAPPY06.BAS

100 REM ** Set up **
110 SCREEN 1: CLS
120 RANDOMIZE TIMER
130 COLOR 0, 1

200 REM ** Compute random coordinates & line color **
210 a = 319 * RND
220 b = 199 * RND
230 c = 319 * RND
240 d = 199 * RND
250 Lcolor = 3 * RND

300 REM ** Draw a line from (a, b) to (c, d) in Lcolor **
310 LINE (a, b)-(c, d), Lcolor, BF
320 SOUND 3000 * RND + 1000, .25

400 REM ** Go back for new coordinates and color **
410 GOTO 210
```

PROGRAM D-5.   Zappy Artist Draws Random Boxes Filled with Color

6. Answers to 6a through 6h:

```
PRINT USING "###"; 12
 12

PRINT USING "###"; -12
-12

PRINT USING "###"; 123
123

PRINT USING "###"; -123
%-123

PRINT USING "###"; 1234
%1234

PRINT USING "###"; .7
 1

PRINT USING "###"; .3
  0

PRINT USING "###"; -.3
 -0    (Strange, but true)
```

7. Answers to 7a through 7f:

```
PRINT USING "$$#,###.##"; 1234.567
 $1,234.57

PRINT USING "$$#,###.##"; -1234.567
-$1234.57

PRINT USING "$$#,###.##"; 123.455
   $123.46

PRINT USING "$$#,###.##"; 123.4525
   $123.45

PRINT USING "$$#,###.##"; .999
     $1.00

PRINT USING "$$#,###.##"; .993
     $0.99
```

8. See Program D-6, METRIC01 (Convert Feet and Inches to Centimeters).

```
1 REM ** Convert Feet and Inches to Centimeters **
2 ' Teach Yourself GW-BASIC, Chapter 5.  Filename: METRIC01.BAS

100 REM ** Set up **
110 CLS

200 REM ** Get feet and inches **
210 INPUT "Feet  "; feet
220 INPUT "Inches"; inches

300 REM ** Compute the number of centimeters **
310 centimeters = (12 * feet + inches) * 2.54

400 REM ** Print the number of centimeters **
410 PRINT
420 PRINT "Centimeters: ";
430 PRINT USING "###.##"; centimeters
```

PROGRAM D-6. Convert Feet and Inches to Centimeters

9. See Program D-7, NPWRN01 (Compute the nth Power of n in Double Precision). Answers to questions: 9a) the largest integer for which the printed result is exactly correct is 13; 9b) the value of 13 to the 13th is 302875106592253.

```
1 REM ** Compute the nth Power of n in Double Precision **
2 ' Teach Yourself GW-BASIC, Chapter 5.  Filename: NPWRN01.BAS
3 ' To get double precision, load GW-BASIC with /D option

100 REM ** Set up **
110 CLS

200 REM ** Get the value of n# (double precision) **
210 INPUT "Positive integer, please: ", n#

300 REM ** Compute and print n# ^ n# (double precision) **
310 PRINT
320 PRINT n#; "to the"; n#; "is"; n# ^ n#
```

PROGRAM D-7. Compute the nth Power of n in Double Precision

EXERCISES

6.1

1.
```
PRINT FirstName$, MiddleName$, LastName$
Christopher    John            Hassenpfeffer

PRINT FirstName$; MiddleName$; LastName$
ChristopherJohnHassenpfeffer

PRINT FirstName$ + MiddleName$ + LastName$
ChristopherJohnHassenpfeffer
```

2. Two ways are shown for 2a, followed by two ways for 2b.
```
PRINT FirstName$ + " " + MiddleName$ + " " + LastName$
Christopher John Hassenpfeffer

PRINT FirstName$; " "; MiddleName$; " "; LastName$
Christopher John Hassenpfeffer

PRINT LastName$ + ", " + FirstName$ + " " + MiddleName$
Hassenpfeffer, Christopher John

PRINT LastName$; ", "; FirstName$; " "; MiddleName$
Hassenpfeffer, Christopher John
```

EXERCISES

6.2

1. Enclose it in quotation marks.

2.
```
10 CLS
20 INPUT "Name  "; Naym$
30 INPUT "Phrase"; Phrase$
40 WHILE 1
50    COLOR 16 * RND
60    PRINT Naym$ + " ";
70    COLOR 16 * RND
80    PRINT Phrase$
90 WEND
```

EXERCISES

1. See Program D-8, THERMS01 (Cost of Gas with IF Statement).
2. See Program D-9, ENERGY01 (Cost of Energy, Gas & Electricity).

EXERCISES

1. The odd integers 1, 3, 5, 7, and 9.

2.
```
10 CLS
20 INPUT "Count by twos to what number"; Limit
30 number = 2
40 WHILE number <= Limit
50    PRINT number,
60    number = number + 2
70 WEND
```

```
1 REM ** Cost of Gas with IF Statement **
2 ' Teach Yourself GW-BASIC, Chapter 6.  Filename: THERMS01.BAS

100 REM ** Set up **
110 CLS
120 LoRate = .44826
130 HiRate = .84849
140 format$ = "$$###,###.##"

200 REM ** Get number of therms of gas **
210 INPUT "Enter number of therms of gas: ", therms

300 REM ** Compute cost of gas **
310 IF therms <= 84 THEN GasCost = therms * LoRate: GOTO 410
320 GasCost = 84 * LoRate + (therms - 84) * HiRate

400 REM ** Print cost of gas **
410 PRINT
420 PRINT "Total cost of gas is";
430 PRINT USING format$; GasCost
```

PROGRAM D-8.   Cost of Gas with IF Statement

```
1 REM ** Cost of Energy, Gas & Electricity **
2 ' Teach Yourself GW-BASIC, Chapter 6.  Filename: ENERGY01.BAS

100 REM ** Set up **
110 CLS
120 GasLoRate = .44826
130 GasHiRate = .84849
140 KwhLoRate = .08882
150 KwhHiRate = .13524
160 format$ = "$$###,###.##"

200 REM ** Get number of therms and kilowatt-hours **
210 INPUT "Enter number of therms of gas:        ", therms
220 INPUT "Enter kilowatt-hours of electricity: ", kwh

300 REM ** Compute cost of gas **
310 IF therms <= 84 THEN GasCost = therms * GasLoRate: GOTO 410
320 GasCost = 84 * GasLoRate + (therms - 84) * GasHiRate

400 REM ** Compute cost of electricity **
410 IF kwh <= 846 THEN KwhCost = kwh * KwhLoRate: GOTO 510
420 KwhCost = 846 * KwhLoRate + (kwh - 846) * KwhHiRate

500 REM ** Print costs of gas, electricity, and total cost **
510 PRINT
520 PRINT "Cost of gas:            ";
530 PRINT USING format$; GasCost
540 PRINT "Cost of electricity:  ";
550 PRINT USING format$; KwhCost
560 PRINT "Total utilities cost: ";
570 PRINT USING format$; GasCost + KwhCost
```

| PROGRAM D-9. | Cost of Energy, Gas & Electricity |

| 6.5 | **EXERCISES** |

1. a. 0, 1, 2, 3, 4, 5
   b. .5, 1.5, 2.5
   c. 1, 2

    d. 1, 1.5, 2, 2.5

    e. 100, 110, 120, 130, 140, 150, 160, 170, 180, 190, 200

2. **a.** `FOR t = 0 TO 9 STEP 3`

    b. `FOR down = 10 TO 0 STEP -2`

    c. `FOR frequency = 1000 TO 3000 STEP 1000`

    d. `FOR duration = 3 TO 1 STEP -.5`

3.
```
10 CLS
20 PRINT "Value of n",  "Value of 1.01 ^ n"
30 FOR n = 600 TO 700 STEP 20
40   PRINT n, 1.01 ^ n
50 NEXT n
```

Change line 30 to

```
30 FOR n = 640 TO 660
```

and run the program. The smallest integer value for which 1.01^n is less than or equal to n is 651.

EXERCISES

1. No answers required.
2. See Program D-10, SOUND04 (Sound Effects Experimenter #2).

MASTERY SKILLS CHECK

1.

pi   (PhoneNumber$) (x$) Naym (number$)

2. **a.** The variable *format* is a numeric variable. You cannot assign a string to a numeric variable. Use a string variable, such as *format$*.

    b. *Naym$* is a string variable. To assign a string to a string variable, enclose the string in quotation marks.

```
1 REM ** Sound Effects Experimenter #2 **
2 ' Teach Yourself GW-BASIC, Chapter 6.  Filename: SOUND04.BAS

100 REM ** Set up **
110 CLS

200 REM ** Get parameters for experiment **
210 LOCATE 1, 1: INPUT "Low frequency       "; LoFreq
220 LOCATE 3, 1: INPUT "High frequency      "; HiFreq
230 LOCATE 5, 1: INPUT "Frequency step size"; StepSize
240 LOCATE 7, 1: INPUT "Duration each sound"; duration
260 LOCATE 9, 1: INPUT "Number of times     "; NmbrTimes

300 REM ** Make the sound **
310 FOR k = 1 TO NmbrTimes
315    ' Rising pitch
320    FOR frequency = LoFreq TO HiFreq STEP StepSize
330       SOUND frequency, duration
340    NEXT frequency
345    ' Falling pitch
350    FOR frequency = HiFreq TO LoFreq STEP -StepSize
360       SOUND frequency, duration
370    NEXT frequency
380 NEXT k

400 REM ** Go back for a new set of data **
410 GOTO 110
```

PROGRAM D-10.   Sound Effects Experimenter #2

3. Here are two solutions.

```
PRINT City$ + ", " + State$ + " " + Zipcode$

PRINT City$; ", "; State$; " "; Zipcode$
```

4.
```
10 CLS
20 INPUT "City$   "; City$
30 INPUT "State$ "; State$
40 INPUT "Zipcode"; Zipcode$
50 PRINT
60 PRINT City$ + ", " + State$ + " " + Zipcode$
```

5.
```
30 IF number% MOD 2 = 0 THEN PRINT "even"

40 IF number% MOD 2 = 1 THEN PRINT "odd"
```

6. See Program D-11, LB0Z01 (Add Weights Given in Pounds & Ounces).

7.
```
10 CLS
20 WHILE 1
30    SOUND 262, 9
40    SOUND 440, 9
50    SOUND 523, 9
60 WEND
```

```
1 REM ** Add Weights Given in Pounds and Ounces **
2 ' Teach Yourself GW-BASIC, Chapter 6.  Filename: LB0Z01.BAS

100 REM ** Set up **
110 CLS
120 TotalPounds = 0
130 TotalOunces = 0

200 REM ** Get weight in pounds & ounces, exit if pounds < 0 **
210 INPUT "Pounds"; pounds
220 IF pounds < 0 THEN 410
230 INPUT "Ounces"; ounces

300 REM ** Add to previous totals and go back for more data **
310 TotalPounds = TotalPounds + pounds
320 TotalOunces = TotalOunces + ounces
330 PRINT : GOTO 210

400 REM ** Convert ounces to pounds & ounces, compute totals **
410 TotalPounds = TotalPounds + TotalOunces \ 16
420 TotalOunces = TotalOunces MOD 16

500 REM ** Print totals **
510 PRINT
520 PRINT "Total weight:";
530 PRINT TotalPounds; "pounds, "; TotalOunces; "ounces"
```

PROGRAM D-11.   Add Weights Given in Pounds and Ounces

8. Program 8a:

```
10 CLS
15 k = 1
20 WHILE k <= 5
30    SOUND 262, 9
40    SOUND 440, 9
50    SOUND 523, 9
60    k = k + 1
70 WEND
```

Program 8b:

```
10 CLS
20 FOR k = 1 TO 5
30    SOUND 262, 9
40    SOUND 440, 9
50    SOUND 523, 9
70 NEXT k
```

9. In the following program, lines 20 through 50 display an empty screen (except for the key line) in each background color (0 to 7) for two seconds. Line 60 returns the screen to a black background as the program ends.

```
10 CLS
20 FOR kolor = 0 TO 7
30    COLOR , kolor: CLS
40    start = TIMER: WHILE TIMER < start + 2: WEND
50 NEXT kolor
60 COLOR , 0: CLS
```

10. a. See Program D-12, ZAPPY03A (Zappy Artist Plots Pixels Pixilatedly).

b. See Program D-13, ZAPPY03B (Zappy Artist Plots Pixels Pixilatedly).

7.1 EXERCISES

1. Use a direct PRINT statement to compute the average time.

```
PRINT (51587.06 - 51574.65) / 10000
 1.241016E-03
```

The average time is about 1.24 thousandths of a second, or 1.24 *milliseconds*. Your computer will probably be faster or slower.

```
1 REM ** Zappy Artist Plots Pixels Pixilatedly **
2 ' Teach Yourself GW-BASIC, Chapter 6.  Filename: ZAPPY03A.BAS

100 REM ** Set up **
110 SCREEN 1: CLS
120 RANDOMIZE TIMER
130 COLOR 0, 1

200 REM ** Use a WHILE...WEND loop to plot random pixels **
210 WHILE 1
220   PSET (319 * RND, 199 * RND), 3 * RND
230   SOUND 3000 * RND + 1000, 9
240 WEND
```

PROGRAM D-12.   Zappy Artist Plots Pixels Pixilatedly (*version A*)

2. See Program D-14, MULTTIME (How Long to Multiply Two Numbers?).

```
1 REM ** Zappy Artist Plots Pixels Pixilatedly **
2 ' Teach Yourself GW-BASIC, Chapter 6.  Filename: ZAPPY03B.BAS

100 REM ** Set up **
110 SCREEN 1: CLS
120 RANDOMIZE TIMER
130 COLOR 0, 1

200 REM ** Get number of pixels to plot **
210 INPUT "How many pixels shall I plot"; NmbrPixels

300 REM ** Use a FOR...NEXT loop to plot random pixels **
310 FOR pixel = 1 TO NmbrPixels
320   PSET (319 * RND, 199 * RND), 3 * RND
330   SOUND 3000 * RND + 1000, 9
340 NEXT pixel
```

PROGRAM D-13.   Zappy Artist Plots Pixels Pixilatedly (*version B*)

```
1 REM ** How Long to Multiply Two Numbers? **
2 ' Teach Yourself GW-BASIC, Chapter 7.  MULTTIME.BAS

100 REM ** Set up **
110 CLS
120 Start = TIMER

200 REM ** Do 10000 multiplications **
210 FOR k = 1 TO 1000
220    product = 1.23 * 4.56
230    product = 1.23 * 4.56
240    product = 1.23 * 4.56
250    product = 1.23 * 4.56
260    product = 1.23 * 4.56
270    product = 1.23 * 4.56
280    product = 1.23 * 4.56
290    product = 1.23 * 4.56
300    product = 1.23 * 4.56
310    product = 1.23 * 4.56
320 NEXT k
330 Finish = TIMER

400 REM ** Print times: start, finish, elapsed, average **
410 PRINT "Start:   TIMER ="; Start
420 PRINT "Finish:  TIMER ="; Finish
430 PRINT "Elapsed time:   "; Finish - Start
440 PRINT "Average time:   "; (Finish - Start) / 10000
```

PROGRAM D-14.　　How Long to Multiply Two Numbers?

3.
```
10 CLS
20 WHILE INKEY$ <> " "
30    PRINT "Press the space bar to stop me"
40 WEND
```

7.2 　EXERCISES

1.
```
10 CLS
20 WHILE 1
```

```
30    INPUT "Dividend"; dividend#
40    INPUT "Divisor "; divisor#
50    PRINT
60    PRINT "Integer quotient: "; FIX(dividend# / divisor#)
70    PRINT
80 WEND
```

2.
```
10 CLS
20 WHILE 1
30    INPUT "Dividend"; dividend#
40    INPUT "Divisor "; divisor#
50    quotient# = FIX(dividend# / divisor#)
60    remainder# = dividend# - divisor# * quotient#
65    PRINT
70    PRINT "Integer quotient:  "; quotient#
80    PRINT "Integer remainder: "; remainder#
85    PRINT
90 WEND
```

3. a. The decimal digits: 0, 1, 2, 3, 4, 5, 6, 7, 8, 9
   b. Zero (0)
   c. The integers from 0 to 100, inclusive
   d. −1, 0, 1
   e. 1, 3, 5, 7, 9
   f. 0, .1, .2, .3, .4, .5, .6, .7, .8, .9

4.
```
10 CLS
20 RANDOMIZE TIMER
30 INPUT "How many rolls"; NmbrRolls
40 PRINT
50 FOR roll = 1 TO NmbrRolls
60    die = INT(6 * RND) + 1
70    PRINT die,
80 NEXT roll
```

5.
```
10 CLS
20 RANDOMIZE TIMER
30 INPUT "How many flips"; NmbrFlips
35 PRINT
40 FOR flip = 1 TO NmbrFlips
50    coin = INT(2 * RND)
60    IF coin = 0 THEN PRINT "Head",
70    IF coin = 1 THEN PRINT "Tail",
80 NEXT flip
```

7.3   EXERCISES

1. `40     ThreeKey$ = INPUT$(3)`

2.
```
10 CLS
20 INPUT "Enter a 3-letter word: ", wrd$
30 rvrs$ = MID$(wrd$, 3, 1) + MID$(wrd$, 2, 1) + MID$(wrd$, 1, 1)
40 PRINT "The reverse word is: "; rvrs$
50 PRINT : GOTO 20
```

3. Changes, beginning with line 250, are shown here:
```
250    ' Add vowel, cons, cons, vowel, cons, vowel
260    word$ = word$ + MID$(vowel$, INT(6 * RND) + 1, 1)
270    word$ = word$ + MID$(consonant$, INT(21 * RND) + 1, 1)
280    word$ = word$ + MID$(consonant$, INT(21 * RND) + 1, 1)
290    word$ = word$ + MID$(vowel$, INT(6 * RND) + 1, 1)
300    word$ = word$ + MID$(consonant$, INT(21 * RND) + 1 ,1)
310    word$ = word$ + MID$(vowel$, INT(6 * RND) + 1, 1)

320    ' Print the word
330    PRINT "Your random 'vccvcv' word is: "; word$
340    PRINT

350 WEND
```

7.5   EXERCISES

1.
```
10 CLS
20 WHILE 1
30    INPUT "Length of side a"; a
40    INPUT "Length of side b"; b
50    c = SQR(a ^ 2 + b ^ 2)
60    PRINT: PRINT "Length of hypotenuse:"; c
70    PRINT
80 WEND
```

2.
```
10 CLS
20 WHILE 1
30    INPUT "Number, please "; x
40    Log10 = .4342945 * LOG(x)
50    PRINT "Log base 10 is "; Log10
60    PRINT
70 WEND
```

3.
```
10 CLS
20 WHILE 1
```

```
30    INPUT "Value of time "; t
40    ratio = EXP(-3.5 * t)
50    PRINT "P / P0 ratio is "; ratio
60    PRINT
70 WEND
```

4. First program:

```
10 CLS
20 WHILE 1
30    INPUT "Angle in degrees"; degrees#
40    radians# = 3.141592653589793 * degrees# / 180
50    PRINT "The sine is    "; SIN(radians#)
60    PRINT "The cosine is  "; COS(radians#)
70    PRINT "The tangent is "; TAN(radians#)
80    PRINT
90 WEND
```

Second program:

```
10 CLS
20 pi# = 3.141592653589793#
30 WHILE 1
40    INPUT "Number, please    "; x#
50    PRINT "ATN in radians is "; ATN(x#)
60    PRINT "ATN in degrees is "; ATN(x#) * 180 / pi#
70    PRINT
80 WEND
```

EXERCISES

7.6

1. Change block 200 to

```
200 REM ** Get ASCII code for wiggler$ and amount of delay **
210 INPUT "ASCII code "; ascii
220 INPUT "Delay (sec)"; delay
230 wiggler$ = CHR$(ascii)
```

Then delete line 360, by typing 360 and pressing ⟨ENTER⟩.

2. `325    x = 3.141593 * degrees / 180`

MASTERY SKILLS CHECK

MASTERY
SKILLS
CHECK

1. function: d

argument: e
numeric function: a, d
string function: d, g
ASC: a, d, h
EXP(1): a, d, j
INKEY$: d, f, g
LOG: a, d, i
MID$: c, d, g
RND: a, b, d, f

2.
```
50 hours = INT(minutes / 60)
60 minutes = minutes - 60 * hours
```

3. The program does not work for negative numbers, as you can see from the run shown here:

```
Number, please? -3.14
Rounded to nearest integer: -2

Number, please? -2.718
Rounded to nearest integer: -2

Number, please? -7.5
Rounded to nearest integer: -7
```

Change line 40 to

```
40 rounded = INT(number + .5)
```

The modified program works for all the test numbers except 7.5. The easiest way to solve this problem is to use a function called SGN. Change line 40 to

```
40 rounded = SGN(number) * INT(ABS(number) + .5)
```

The value of SGN(*number*) is –1 if *number* is negative, 0 if *number* is zero, and 1 if *number* is positive. This version of line 40 rounds the absolute value of *number*, and then multiples by SGN(*number*) to give the proper sign.

4.
```
10 RANDOMIZE TIMER: CLS
20 INPUT "How many rolls"; NmbrRolls
30 PRINT
40 FOR roll = 1 TO NmbrRolls
50   die1 = INT(6 * RND)+ 1
60   die2 = INT(6 * RND) + 1
70   PRINT die1 + die2,
80 NEXT roll
```

5.
```
10 RANDOMIZE TIMER: CLS
20 INPUT "How many flips"; NmbrFlips
30 PRINT
40 FOR flip = 1 TO NmbrFlips
50   coins = INT(4 * RND)
60   PRINT MID$("HHHTTHTT", 2 * coins + 1, 2),
70 NEXT flip
80 PRINT: PRINT: GOTO 20
```

6. The modified program draws vertical lines in columns determined by the exponential function (EXP). Near the left edge of the screen, the lines are close together. The lines become progressively farther apart as the value of k goes from 0 to 46.

7. Zappy Artist did it with pizzazz, as shown in Program D-15, ZAPPY09 (Zappy Artist Draws a Sine Wave in SCREEN 1).

```
1 REM ** Zappy Artist Draws a Sine Wave in SCREEN 1 **
2 ' Teach Yourself GW-BASIC, Chapter 7.  ZAPPY09.BAS

100 REM ** Set up **
110 SCREEN 1: CLS : KEY OFF
120 COLOR 0, 1
130 scale = 2 * 3.141593 / 320    '2 pi / width of SCREEN 1

200 REM ** Make one sine wave across entire screen **
210 CLS
220 FOR x = 0 TO 319
230   y = 99 * SIN(scale * x)
240   PSET (x, 100 - y), INT(3 * RND) + 1
250   SOUND 1200 + 10 * y, .25
260 NEXT x

300 REM ** Do it again if ESC not pressed **
310 IF INKEY$ <> CHR$(27) THEN 210     'Press ESC to quit
320 SCREEN 0: WIDTH 80: KEY ON: END    'Return to normal screen
```

PROGRAM D-15.   Zappy Artist Draws a Sine Wave in SCREEN 1

8.1

EXERCISES

1. Answer to 1a and 1b:

```
10 DEF FNdigit = INT(10 * RND)
20 RANDOMIZE TIMER
30 CLS
40 FOR k = 1 TO 20
50   PRINT FNdigit,
60 NEXT k
```

2. Change only block 400 of Program RPGAME01, as follows:

```
400 REM ** Roll 3D6 for each characteristic — print it **
410 PRINT "Strength", FNroll3D6
420 PRINT "Intelligence", FNroll3D6
430 PRINT "Wisdom", FNroll3D6
440 PRINT "Dexterity", FNroll3D6
450 PRINT "Constitution", FNroll3D6
460 PRINT "Charisma", FNroll3D6
```

8.2

EXERCISES

1. `DEF FNLttr$ = CHR$(INT(26 * RND) + 97) 'Lowercase letters`

2. `DEF FNchar$ = CHR$(INT(132 * RND) + 123)`

8.3

EXERCISES

1. **a.** Change lines 30 and 40 to

```
30 a = FNran(12)
40 b = FNran(12)
```

b. Change lines 30 and 40 to

```
30 a = FNran(10) - 1
40 b = FNran(20) - 1
```

2.
```
20 DEF FNpop(p, r, n) = p * (1 + r / 100) ^ n
40 PRINT "The projected population is: "; FNpop(p0, r, n)
```

EXERCISES

1. `DEF FNUpper$(Lower$) = CHR$(ASC(Lower$) - 32)`

2. Answer to 2a, 2b, and 2c:

```
DEF FNmonth$(m)="JanFebMarAprMayJunJulAugSepOctNovDec",3*(m-1)+1,3)
```

EXERCISES

1. Change line 940, as follows:

```
940    character$ = CHR$(ASC(character$) + 32)
```

2.
```
900 REM ** SUBROUTINE: UPCASE **
905 ' Changes letters in strng$ to uppercase
910 FOR kk% = 1 TO LEN(strng$)
920    character$ = MID$(strng$, kk%, 1)
930    IF character$ < "a" OR character$ > "z" THEN 960
940    character$ = CHR$(ASC(character$) - 32)
950    MID$(strng$, kk%, 1) = character$
960 NEXT kk%
970 RETURN
```

EXERCISES

The author does not want to deprive you of the enjoyment of searching dictionaries for answers to these questions. Remember, to some extent your answers will depend on the dictionary you use. This is a good family or classroom activity.

MASTERY SKILLS CHECK

1.
```
10 DEF FNday = INT(365 * RND) + 1
40    PRINT FNday,
```

For a group of 30 people, there is about a 71% chance that two people have their birthdays on the same day of the year.

2. a. The number of hours is contained in the first two characters of TIME$. Define FNhr$ like this:

```
DEF FNhr$ = MID$(TIME$, 1, 2)
```

   b. The number of minutes appears in the fourth and fifth characters of TIME$. Define FNmin$ as follows:

```
DEF FNmin$ = MID$(TIME$, 4, 2)
```

   c. The number of seconds begins at character position 7 in TIME$, and is two characters long. Define FNsec$ as shown here:

```
DEF FNsec$ = MID$(TIME$, 7, 2)
```

3. Answers to 3a through 3d:

```
DEF FNVsphere(r) = 4 * 3.141593 * r ^ 3 / 3

DEF FNVcylinder(r, h) = 3.141593 * r ^ 2 * h

DEF FNnpwrn#(n#) = n# ^ n#

DEF FNd(x1, y1, x2, y2) = SQR((x1 = x2) ^ 2 + (y1 - y2) ^ 2)
```

4.
```
CLS
DEF FNsuit$(n) = CHR$(n + 2)
WHILE 1
  INPUT "Suit number (1 to 4)"; SuitNmbr
  PRINT "Your suit is: "; FNsuit$(SuitNmbr)
  PRINT
WEND
```

5.
```
CLS
DEF FNcard$(n) = MID$(" A 2 3 4 5 6 7 8 9 10 J Q K", 2*(n-1)+1, 2)
WHILE 1
  INPUT "Card number (1 to 13)"; n
  PRINT "Your card is: "; FNcard$(n)
  PRINT
WEND
```

6. Line 30 and the subroutine to roll dice are shown here:

```
30 GOSUB 1010

1000 REM ** SUBROUTINE: Roll NmbrD6 6-sided dice **
1010 DiceTotal = 0
```

```
1030 FOR kk% = 1 TO NmbrD6
1040    die = INT(6 * RND) + 1
1050    DiceTotal = DiceTotal + die
1070 NEXT kk%
1100 RETURN
```

7. **Line 30 and the subroutine to flip coins are shown here:**

```
30 GOSUB 1010

1000 REM ** SUBROUTINE: Price Valiant game coin flipper **
1010 NmbrHeads = 0
1020 NmbrTails = 0
1030 FOR kk% = 1 TO NmbrCoins
1040    ZeroOrOne = INT(2 * RND)    '0 = heads, 1 = tails
1050    IF ZeroOrOne = 0 THEN NmbrHeads = NmbrHeads + 1
1060    IF ZeroOrOne = 1 THEN NmbrTails = NmbrTails + 1
1070 NEXT kk%
1080 PctHeads = 100 * NmbrHeads / NmbrCoins
1090 PctTails = 100 * NmbrTails / NmbrCoins
1100 RETURN
```

EXERCISES ———————————————— $\boxed{9.1}$

1.
```
Stardrake
Laran
April 1
1991
Out of DATA in 30
Ok
—
```

2. **Change only lines 100, 140, 160, 170, and 190.**

```
100 REM ** Read Japanese, English, print English, Japanese **

140    LOCATE 1, 1: PRINT "Press a key for English word or phrase"

160    LOCATE 3, 1: PRINT English$

170    LOCATE 5, 1: PRINT "Press a key for Japanese word or phrase"

190    LOCATE 7, 1: PRINT Japanese$
```

9.2 | EXERCISES

1. See Program D-16, FLSHCD04 (Random Flashcard Program to Show Side A, Then Side B).

2. See Program D-17, FLSHCD05 (Random Flashcard Program with Time Delay).

9.3 | EXERCISES

1. *VoteTally(0)*, *VoteTally(1)*, *VoteTally(2)*, and *VoteTally(3)*

2. The *frequency()* array has 14 elements. Therefore, it requires 56 bytes of memory space. Dimension it like this:

```
DIM frequency(13)
```

3. The *word$()* array has 101 elements. Each element requires a three-byte string pointer, plus three bytes for each three-letter word that has been assigned, for a total of six bytes. Therefore, this array requires 606 bytes of memory space.

9.4 | EXERCISES

1.

Array Variable	Value
nzp$(0)	Empty string ("")
nzp$(1)	Negative
nzp$(2)	Zero
nzp$(3)	Positive

2. You can modify Program STAT01 to obtain the program required for this exercise. One way to do it is shown by Program D-18, STAT02 (High, Low, and Average Temperature for One Week).

```
1 REM ** Random Flashcard Program to Show Side A, Then Side B **
2 ' Teach Yourself GW-BASIC, Chapter 9.  Filename: FLSHCD04.BAS

100 REM ** Set up **
110 RANDOMIZE TIMER
120 CLS

200 REM ** Get random flashcard **
210 RESTORE
220 READ NmbrCards
230 FOR k = 1 TO INT(NmbrCards * RND) + 1
240   READ SideA$, SideB$
250 NEXT k

300 REM ** Print side A, then side B **
310 CLS
320 LOCATE 1, 1: PRINT "Press a key for side A"
330 akey$ = INPUT$(1)
340 LOCATE 3, 1: PRINT SideA$

350 LOCATE 5, 1: PRINT "Press a key for side B"
360 akey$ = INPUT$(1)
370 LOCATE 7, 1: PRINT SideB$

400 REM ** Continue practice or quit **
410 LOCATE 9, 1: PRINT "Press a key to continue, or ESC to quit"
420 akey$ = INPUT$(1)
430 IF akey$ <> CHR$(27) THEN 210 ELSE END

10000 REM ** Data: SideA$, SideB$ **
10005 DATA 7
10010 DATA Nihon'go, Japanese language
10020 DATA Ohayo gozaimasu, Good morning
10030 DATA Kon'nichi wa, Hello or Good day
10040 DATA Kon'ban wa, Good evening
10050 DATA Oyasumi nasai, Good night
10060 DATA "Jaa, mata ashita", "Well, I'll see you again tomorrow"
10070 DATA Sayonara, Goodbye
```

PROGRAM D-16. Random Flashcard Program to Show Side A, Then Side B

```
1 REM ** Random Flashcard Program with Time Delay **
2 ' Teach Yourself GW-BASIC, Chapter 9.  Filename: FLSHCD05.BAS

100 REM ** Set up **
110 RANDOMIZE TIMER
120 CLS

200 REM ** Get random flashcard **
210 RESTORE
220 READ NmbrCards
230 FOR k = 1 TO INT(NmbrCards * RND) + 1
240   READ SideA$, SideB$
250 NEXT k

300 REM ** Show side A, delay, then show side B **
310 CLS
320 LOCATE 1, 1: PRINT SideA$     'Show side A
330 delay = 5: GOSUB 510          'Use time delay subroutine
340 LOCATE 3, 1: PRINT SideB$     'Show side B

400 REM ** Continue practice or quit **
410 LOCATE 5, 1: PRINT "Press a key to continue, or ESC to quit"
420 akey$ = INPUT$(1)
430 IF akey$ <> CHR$(27) THEN 210 ELSE END

500 REM ** SUBROUTINE: Variable time delay **
510 start = TIMER: WHILE TIMER < start + delay: WEND: RETURN

10000 REM ** Data: SideA$, SideB$ **
10005 DATA 7
10010 DATA Nihon'go, Japanese language
10020 DATA Ohayo gozaimasu, Good morning
10030 DATA Kon'nichi wa, Hello or Good day
10040 DATA Kon'ban wa, Good evening
10050 DATA Oyasumi nasai, Good night
10060 DATA "Jaa, mata ashita", "Well, I'll see you again tomorrow"
10070 DATA Sayonara, Goodbye
```

PROGRAM D-17. Random Flashcard Program with Time Delay

```
1 REM ** High, Low, and Average Temperature for One Week **
2 ' Teach Yourself GW-BASIC, Chapter 9.  Filename: STAT02.BAS

100 REM ** Set up **
110 DIM temperature(7)          'Dimension array
120 CLS

200 REM ** Acquire data entered from keyboard **
210 FOR day = 1 TO 7
220    READ DayOfWeek$
230    PRINT DayOfWeek$; TAB(10); : INPUT temperature(day)
240 NEXT day
250 DATA Sunday, Monday, Tuesday, Wednesday
260 DATA Thursday, Friday, Saturday

300 REM ** Find high temperature **
310 High = temperature(1)
320 FOR day = 2 TO 7
330    IF temperature(day) > High THEN High = temperature(day)
340 NEXT day

400 REM ** Find low temperature **
410 Low = temperature(1)
420 FOR day = 2 TO 7
430    IF temperature(day) < Low THEN Low = temperature(day)
440 NEXT day

500 REM ** Compute average temperature **
510 Total = 0
520 FOR day = 1 TO 7
530    Total = Total + temperature(day)
540 NEXT day
550 Average = Total / 7

700 REM ** Print high, low, and average temperatures **
710 PRINT
720 PRINT "High:", High
730 PRINT "Low:", Low
740 PRINT "Average:", Average
```

PROGRAM D-18.   High, Low, and Average Temperatures for One Week

9.5 EXERCISES

1. See Program D-19, POLL02A (The People's Poll #2, Modified). The data shown in line 1010 produces the following summaries:

```
Total 'Yes' answers:         4
Total 'No' answers:          3
Total 'Sometimes' answers:  2
Total invalid answers:      2
```

2.
```
10 RANDOMIZE TIMER: CLS
20 DIM Tally(12)
30 INPUT "How many rolls of 2D6"; NmbrRolls
40 FOR roll = 1 TO NmbrRolls
50    dice = INT(6 * RND) + INT(6 * RND) + 2
60    Tally(dice) = Tally(dice) + 1
70 NEXT roll
80 PRINT : PRINT "Outcome", "Number of times"
100 FOR outcome = 2 TO 12
110    PRINT outcome, Tally(outcome)
120 NEXT outcome
```

9.6 EXERCISES

1. Here is a new block 500. It computes the row and column totals.

```
500 REM ** Compute row and column totals **
510 FOR row = 1 TO 3
520    Tally(row, 0)= Tally(row, 1) + Tally(row, 2)
530 NEXT row
540 FOR col = 0 TO 2
550    Tally(0, col) = Tally(1, col) + Tally(2, col) + Tally(3, col)
560 NEXT col
```

Block 600 then prints the final tallies, including the row and column totals computed by block 500.

```
600 REM ** Print the final tallies **
610 PRINT
620 PRINT "Answer", "18 or under", "Over 18", "Row totals"
630 PRINT
640 PRINT "Yes", Tally(1, 1), Tally(1, 2), Tally(1, 0)
650 PRINT "No", Tally(2, 1), Tally(2, 2), Tally(2, 0)
660 PRINT "Sometimes", Tally(3, 1), Tally(3, 2), Tally(3, 0)
670 PRINT "Column totals", Tally(0, 1), Tally(0, 2), Tally(0, 0)
```

```
1 REM ** The People's Poll #2, Modified **
2 ' Teach Yourself GW-BASIC, Chapter 9.  Filename: POLL02A.BAS

100 REM ** Set up **
110 DIM Tally(4)
120 CLS

200 REM ** Set tallies to zero **
210 Tally(1) = 0                    'Tally for 'Yes' answers
220 Tally(2) = 0                    'Tally for 'No' answers
230 Tally(3) = 0                    'Tally for 'Sometimes' answers
240 Tally(4) = 0                    'Tally for invalid answers

400 REM ** Get answers and count them **
410 WHILE 1
420   READ answer
450   IF answer = 0 THEN 510        'If zero, go print tallies

455   ' If not a valid answer, count it & go for another
460   IF answer <> FIX(answer) THEN Tally(4) = Tally(4) + 1: GOTO 420
470   IF answer < 0 THEN Tally(4) = Tally(4) + 1: GOTO 420
475   IF answer > 3 THEN Tally(4) = Tally(4) + 1: GOTO 420

480   Tally(answer) = Tally(answer) + 1     'Count the answer
490 WEND

500 REM ** Print the final tallies **
510 PRINT
520 PRINT "Total 'Yes' answers:       "; Tally(1)
530 PRINT "Total 'No' answers:        "; Tally(2)
540 PRINT "Total 'Sometimes' answers:"; Tally(3)
550 PRINT "Total invalid answers:     "; Tally(4)

1000 REM ** Data: valid answer is 1, 2, 3, or 0 to quit **
1010 DATA 1, 2, -1, 2, 1, 2, 1.3, 1, 1, 3, 3, 0
```

PROGRAM D-19. The People's Poll #2, Modified

2. Program D-20, POLL05 (The People's Poll #5) is a modification of Program POLL03. Look for changes in lines 1, 2, 110, 220, 520, 540, 550, 560, and in block 1000, the data block. Here is a sample run.

Answer	18 or under	19 to 29	30 or over
Yes	10	5	1
No	4	6	2
Sometimes	2	1	1

```
1 REM ** The People's Poll #5 **
2 ' Teach Yourself GW-BASIC, Chapter 9.  Filename: POLL05.BAS

100 REM ** Set up **
110 DIM Tally(3, 3)                      'Two-dimensional array
120 CLS

200 REM ** Set tallies to zero **
210 FOR row = 0 TO 3
220    FOR col = 0 TO 3
230       Tally(row, col) = 0
240    NEXT col
250 NEXT row

400 REM ** Get answers and count them **
410 WHILE 1
420    READ ans1, ans2
450    IF ans1 = 0 THEN 510                'Exit if zero
480    Tally(ans1, ans2) = Tally(ans1, ans2) + 1  'Count the  answer
490 WEND

500 REM ** Print the final tallies **
510 PRINT
520 PRINT "Answer", "18 or under", "19 to 29", "30 or over"
530 PRINT
540 PRINT "Yes", Tally(1, 1), Tally(1, 2), Tally(1, 3)
550 PRINT "No", Tally(2, 1), Tally(2, 2), Tally(2, 3)
560 PRINT "Sometimes", Tally(3, 1), Tally(3, 2), Tally(3, 3)

1000 REM ** Data: answer to question 1, answer to question 2 **
1010 DATA 1,2, 2,1, 3,2, 1,1, 2,2, 2,2, 1,1, 2,1, 1,2, 2,3
1020 DATA 2,2, 3,1, 2,2, 1,1, 1,1, 2,2, 1,2, 3,3, 2,3, 2,1
1030 DATA 1,1, 1,1, 1,1, 1,2, 1,1, 1,2, 2,1, 1,3, 2,2, 1,1
1040 DATA 3,1, 1,1, 0,0
```

PROGRAM D-20. The People's Poll #5

MASTERY SKILLS CHECK

1. **a.** There should be no comma immediately following the keyword DATA.

   b. There should be no comma following the last data item.

   c. Data items should be separated by commas, not semicolons.

2. No answers are shown for 2a, 2b, and 2c. The answer to 2d is Program D-21, STAT03 (Number, Sum, and Average of Numbers in DATA Statements). You can modify this program to obtain any of the others.

3. See Program D-22, LBOZ02 (Add Pounds and Ounces in DATA Statements).

```
1 REM ** Number, Sum, and Average of Numbers in DATA Statements  **
2 ' Teach Yourself GW-BASIC, Chapter 9.  Filename: STAT03.BAS

100 REM ** Set up **
110 CLS
120 sum = 0                    'Set sum of numbers to zero
130 n = 0                      'Set number of numbers to zero

200 REM ** Read numbers, count them, and compute sum **
210 READ number
220 IF number = 1E+38 THEN 310
230 sum = sum + number
240 n = n + 1
250 GOTO 210

300 REM ** Print the answers **
310 PRINT "Number of numbers:  "; n
320 PRINT "Sum of numbers:     "; sum
330 PRINT "Average of numbers: "; sum / n

900 REM ** Data: 1E38 is end of data flag **
910 DATA 68, 67, 70, 72, 75, 80, 77, 1E38
```

PROGRAM D-21. Number, Sum, and Average of Numbers in DATA Statements

```
1 REM ** Add Pounds and Ounces in DATA Statements **
2 ' Teach Yourself GW-BASIC, Chapter 9.  Filename: LBOZO2.BAS

100 REM ** Set up **
110 CLS
120 TotalPounds = 0
130 TotalOunces = 0
140 PRINT "Pounds", "Ounces"

200 REM ** Get weight in pounds & ounces, exit if pounds < 0 **
210 READ pounds, ounces
220 IF pounds < 0 THEN 410
230 PRINT pounds, ounces

300 REM ** Add to previous totals and go back for more data **
310 TotalPounds = TotalPounds + pounds
320 TotalOunces = TotalOunces + ounces
330 GOTO 210

400 REM ** Convert ounces to pounds & ounces, compute totals **
410 TotalPounds = TotalPounds + TotalOunces \ 16
420 TotalOunces = TotalOunces MOD 16

500 REM ** Print totals **
510 PRINT "----", "----"
520 PRINT TotalPounds, TotalOunces

900 REM ** Data: pounds, ounces -- end of data flag is -1, -1 **
910 DATA 7,12, 0,6, 5,0, 3,13, 10,8, -1,-1
```

PROGRAM D-22.   Add Pounds and Ounces in DATA Statements

4. See Program D-23, GUESSWRD (Guess My Word Game).

5. Here is a very compact program. Note that lines 20 and 40 contain complete FOR...NEXT loops.

```
10 DIM score(5)
20 FOR k = 1 TO 5: READ score(k): NEXT k
30 Total = 0
40 FOR k = 1 TO 5: sum = sum + score(k): NEXT k
```

```
50 avg = sum / 5
60 CLS : PRINT "Score", "Deviation"
70 FOR k = 1 TO 5:
80   PRINT score(k), : PRINT USING "###.#"; score(k) - avg
90 NEXT item
100 DATA 77, 83, 68, 73, 95
```

```
1 REM ** Guess My Word Game **
2 ' Teach Yourself GW-BASIC, Chapter 9.  Filename: GUESSWRD.BAS

100 REM ** Set up **
110 DIM word$(100)
120 RANDOMIZE TIMER

200 REM ** Read and count words -- exit on zzz **
210 NmbrWords = 0
220 index = 1
230 READ word$(index)
240 IF word$(index) = "zzz" THEN 310
250 NmbrWords = NmbrWords + 1: index = index + 1: GOTO 230

300 REM ** Tell how to play **
310 CLS
320 PRINT "I'll think of a 3-letter word.  You try to guess my word."
330 PRINT "If you miss, I'll give you a hint like the ones below:"
340 PRINT
350 PRINT "   'Higher' means higher in the alphabet, towards z"
360 PRINT
370 PRINT "   'Lower' means lower in the alphabet, towards a"
380 PRINT
390 PRINT "Ok, I've got a secret word.  Good luck!"

400 REM ** Pick a random secret word, Secret$ **
410 RanIndx = INT(NmbrWords * RND) + 1
420 Secret$ = word$(RanIndx)
```

PROGRAM D-23.   Guess My Word Game

```
500 REM ** Get a guess and tell about it ****
510 PRINT : INPUT "What is your guess"; Guess$
520 IF Guess$ = Secret$ THEN 610
530 IF Guess$ > Secret$ THEN PRINT "Try a lower word"
540 IF Guess$ < Secret$ THEN PRINT "Try a higher word"
550 GOTO 510

600 REM ** Player has guessed the word **
610 FOR k = 1 TO 7                         'Sound effects
620    FOR f = 1000 TO 3000 STEP 100
630       SOUND f, .25
640    NEXT f
650 NEXT k
660 PRINT : PRINT "That's it!!!  My secret word is: "; Secret$
670 PRINT "Press ESC to quit, or another key to play again."
680 akey$ = INPUT$(1)
690 IF akey$ <> CHR$(27) THEN 310 ELSE END

900 REM ** Data: 3-letter word -- end of data flag is zzz **
DATA aha, auk, baa, boy, cat, cry, dog, duo, elf, erg
DATA fez, fun, gee, gnu, hex, hum, icy, ivy, jib, joy
DATA key, kid, lei, leu, mew, mom, nay, nub, obi, owl
DATA pal, pry, rho, rue, sea, sty, toy, try, ugh, use
DATA vex, via, wan, win, yak, yew, zen, zoo, zzz
```

PROGRAM D-23.	Guess My Word Game (*continued*)

6. See Program D-24, STAT04 (Compute Averages for Five Students, Three Quizzes).

7. See Program D-25, STAT05 (Multiple Guess Quiz Analysis).

```
1 REM ** Compute Averages for Five Students, Three Quizzes **
2 ' Teach Yourself GW-BASIC, Chapter 9.  Filename: STAT04.BAS

100 REM ** Set up **
110 DIM Score(5, 3), Savg(5), Qavg(3)      '5 students, 3 quizzes

200 REM ** Read data into Score() array **
210 FOR student = 1 TO 5
220   FOR quiz = 1 TO 3: READ Score(student, quiz): NEXT quiz
230 NEXT student

300 REM ** Compute averages for students, Savg() **
310 FOR student = 1 TO 5
320   SumScores = 0
330   FOR quiz = 1 TO 3
340     SumScores = SumScores + Score(student, quiz)
350   NEXT quiz
360   Savg(student) = SumScores / 3        'Average of 3 quizzes
370 NEXT student

400 REM ** Compute averages for quizzes, Qavg() **
410 FOR quiz = 1 TO 3
420   SumQuizzes = 0
430   FOR student = 1 TO 5
440     SumQuizzes = SumQuizzes + Score(student, quiz)
450   NEXT student
460   Qavg(quiz) = SumQuizzes / 5            'Average of 5 students
470 NEXT quiz

500 REM ** Print report
510 CLS
520 PRINT "Student", "Quiz 1", "Quiz 2", "Quiz 3", "Average"
530 FOR student = 1 TO 5
540   PRINT student,
550   FOR quiz = 1 TO 3: PRINT Score(student, quiz), : NEXT quiz
560   PRINT Savg(student)
570 NEXT student
580 PRINT : PRINT "Quiz avg:",
590 FOR quiz = 1 TO 3: PRINT Qavg(quiz), : NEXT quiz
600 PRINT : END
```

PROGRAM D-24.   Compute Averages for Five Students, Three Quizzes

```
900 REM ** Data: Each DATA holds 3 scores for 1 student **
910 DATA 65, 57, 71
920 DATA 81, 90, 91
930 DATA 45, 38, 44
940 DATA 70, 68, 83
950 DATA 98, 92, 100
```

PROGRAM D-24.	Compute Averages for Five Students, Three Quizzes (*continued*)

```
1 REM ** Multiple Guess Quiz Analysis **
2 ' Teach Yourself GW-BASIC, Chapter 9.  Filename: STAT05.BAS

100 REM ** Set up **
110 DIM Tally(10, 4)                    '10 questions, 4 choices

200 REM ** Initialize Tally() array to zero **
210 FOR row = 1 TO 10
220   FOR col = 1 TO 4: Tally(row, col) = 0: NEXT col
230 NEXT row

300 REM ** Read & count students' answers **
310 READ NmbrStudents
320 FOR student = 1 TO NmbrStudents
330   FOR question = 1 TO 10
340     READ answer
350     Tally(question, answer) = Tally(question, answer) + 1
360   NEXT question
370 NEXT student
```

PROGRAM D-25.	Multiple Guess Quiz Analysis

```
400 REM ** Print quiz analysis report **
410 CLS
420 PRINT "Question", "Answer 1", "Answer 2", "Answer 3", "Answer 4"
430 FOR question = 1 TO 10
440   PRINT question,
450   FOR answer = 1 TO 4
460     PRINT Tally(question, answer),
470   NEXT answer
480 NEXT question
490 END

900 REM ** Data: Number of students followed by their answers **
910 DATA 7
920 DATA 2, 3, 1, 1, 1, 2, 4, 3, 4, 1
930 DATA 2, 3, 2, 4, 1, 2, 4, 2, 1, 3
940 DATA 2, 3, 3, 1, 1, 4, 3, 3, 4, 1
950 DATA 3, 2, 4, 1, 1, 2, 3, 3, 4, 2
960 DATA 2, 3, 4, 1, 1, 3, 4, 3, 4, 1
970 DATA 2, 1, 2, 3, 1, 2, 4, 3, 4, 1
980 DATA 3, 4, 1, 1, 1, 4, 3, 1, 4, 2
```

PROGRAM D-25. Multiple Guess Quiz Analysis (*continued*)

►Index◄

The manuscript for this book was prepared and
submitted to Osborne/McGraw-Hill in electronic form.
The acquisitions editor for this project was Elizabeth Fisher,
and the technical reviewer was Paul Sevigny.

Text design by Marcela Hancik, using
Palatino for text body and display.

Typesetting, screen dumps, and technical illustrations
by Peter Hancik - EuroDesign.

Cover art by Bay Graphics Design, Inc.
Color separation and cover supplier,
Phoenix Color Corporation.
Screens produced with InSet, from
InSet Systems, Inc. Book printed and bound
by R.R. Donnelley & Sons Company,
Crawfordsville, Indiana.